SHOOTING THE TRUTH

SHOOTING THE TRUTH

THE RISE OF AMERICAN POLITICAL DOCUMENTARIES

James McEnteer

Westport, Connecticut
London

Library of Congress Cataloging-in-Publication Data

McEnteer, James, 1945–
    Shooting the truth : the rise of American political documentaries / James McEnteer.
        p.   cm.
    Includes bibliographical references and index.
    ISBN 0-275-98760-4 (alk. paper)
  1. Documentary films—United States—History and criticism. 2. United
States—Politics and government—2001–   I. Title.
    PN1995.9.D6M38   2006
    070.1'8—dc22   2005019270

British Library Cataloguing in Publication Data is available.

Library of Congress Catalog Card Number: 2005019270
ISBN: 0-275-98760-4

First published in 2006

Praeger Publishers, 88 Post Road West, Westport, CT 06881
An imprint of Greenwood Publishing Group, Inc.
www.praeger.com

The paper used in this book complies with the
Permanent Paper Standard issued by the National
Information Standards Organization (Z39.48-1984).

10 9 8 7 6 5 4 3 2 1

Copyright Acknowledgments

Excerpts from "Little Gidding" in *Four Quartets*, copyright 1942 by T.S. Eliot
and renewed 1970 by Esme Valerie Eliot, reprinted by permission of Harcourt, Inc.

Excerpts from "Little Gidding" in *Four Quartets*, copyright 1942 by T.S. Eliot
and renewed 1970 by Esme Valerie Eliot, reprinted by permission of Faber and Faber Ltd.

to
my three favorite people
Cristina, Nicolas, Joaquin

CONTENTS

ACKNOWLEDGMENTS

This book owes a great deal to the generosity of David Tetzlaff. David graciously shared his superior knowledge of film history with me. He suggested many films I would never otherwise have seen and provided me with copies, significantly enlarging my understanding of the political documentary tradition. His students—among whom I count myself—are fortunate to have his guidance. David cannot be blamed for my interpretations of individual films, or for my more general conclusions. I look forward to reading his own, more sophisticated work on these and other film topics. Thank you, David. I am extremely grateful for your help.

Gary Handman, of the University of California at Berkeley, also shared some of his great understanding of the documentary tradition with me. His insights and suggestions improved my book. He also facilitated my use of Berkeley's Media Resource Center, where Ann Moen made my time both profitable and pleasurable. My thanks to Professor Handman and to Ms. Moen for their help.

Glenn Jacobs read the first third of the manuscript with a critical eye and offered many useful suggestions for clarifying my ideas. I very much appreciate the effort and acumen he brought to bear. It was good to have you in the neighborhood, Glenn.

My wife, Cristina Cielo, offered valuable editorial advice and thoughtful insights, as always, which greatly improved my text, proving that clarity begins at home. You're the best, mi amor. Te amo tanto.

For assistance in obtaining materials I am grateful to Emily Kunstler of Off-Center Films, Richard Rowley of Big Noise Films, Tricia Wilk of The Global Department Store, and Craig Hymson of Cabin Creek Films. Many thanks.

INTRODUCTION

Consciously or not, even those of us old enough to know better still regard the movies as a mirror.

—A.O. Scott

George W. Bush is addressing a well-dressed crowd at a formal dinner party: "It's a pleasure to be here among the haves and the have-mores . . ." he says to appreciative chuckles. "Some call you the elite. I call you my base . . ." as the laughter ripples. That's from Michael Moore's *Fahrenheit 9/11.*

Cut to angry "citizens" crowding a Miami-Dade courthouse to demand the end of the vote recount in Florida's 2000 presidential election. The frame freezes and the faces are isolated and identified as staffers from the offices of Congressman Tom DeLay and other Republicans, flown down from Washington as part of a concerted effort to disrupt the vote-counting process. That's from Richard Ray Perez and Joan Sekler's *Unprecedented.*

Cut to the voice of a small child on a telephone: "Are you going to come in and kill me?" Jim Cavanaugh, U.S. government negotiator, replies: "No, honey, nobody's coming in . . ." as the Branch Davidian Community Center blazes and smokes, a fire in which eighty-six men, women, and children died near Waco, Texas, on April 19, 1993. That's from William Gazecki's *Waco: The Rules of Engagement.*

Cut to chaos in the streets of Seattle during the World Trade Organization meeting in 1999, where police battled thousands of demonstrators and the Big Noise film collective handed out more than one hundred video cameras to film the protest from the ground up in *This Is What Democracy Looks Like*.

Documentary films—long considered marginally profitable or even noncommercial enterprises, confined to the ghettos of public television or educational institutions—have made a recent, dramatic popular surge. Fifteen million viewers paid to see Michael Moore's *Fahrenheit 9/11* in its first month of release. The anti-Bush film grossed nearly $120 million domestically, outstripping the previous top earner, Moore's 2002 *Bowling for Columbine*, which made $21.5 million. Eight of the ten top-grossing documentaries of all time were released since 2002.

Why the sudden prominence of nonfiction films? There exists in America a great hunger to understand what's really going on. These films help feed that need. Much of that hunger has to do with the concentrated ownership of news media, the corporatization and trivialization of the news, and the decreasing spectrum of information. Instead of innovation and investigation, we get repetition and imitation.

In the twenty-four-hour news cycle, staged and scripted pseudo-events, concocted by government press offices and public relations firms, bombard the airwaves and print media. Journalists rewrite and repeat press handouts without corroborating their "facts." Reporters lift stories from one another instead of digging up their own. In the high-profit, high-stakes news profession, there is no time or money for protracted, expensive investigative news stories.

Much of what now passes for "news" includes massive doses of celebrity gossip, leaving many more important events unreported. Mass media shy away from stories of complexity, as reflected by the speed of news delivery, in rapid-fire sound bites; the shortening lengths of stories; and the glitzing up and dumbing down of news reports to hold the viewers' attention. Reporters tend to accept government versions of events. And any stories that might offend the corporate owners of media, their clients, or their friends—all of whom together represent a significant portion of American economic power—have also become off limits.

As news morphs into infotainment, an increasing number of Americans feel unable to make sense of the world by means of mass media news. We know we are missing essential pieces of the reality puzzle. Americans who truly wish to be informed about current events have begun to turn elsewhere for their information, including to nonfiction films. Of course, having credible information on which to base one's decisions is the very foundation of a healthy democracy. If we take the current form and content of media news as our measure, our democracy is in serious trouble.

Progressive documentary makers assume that the news media have failed. Some of them—Robert Greenwald, in *Outfoxed*; Robert Kane Pappas, in *Orwell Rolls in His Grave*; and Danny Schechter, in *WMD: Weapons of Mass Deception*—have made that problem the subject of their films. Conservatives propagate the myth of a "liberal" media to justify strident talk radio programs and the slant of the Fox TV Network, which *Outfoxed* depicts as Rupert Murdoch's right-wing, Bush administration mouthpiece. Progressives have tried to answer in kind, with the Air America radio network. But liberals apparently find it hard to match the Right, shout for shout. They are much more comfortable using documentary films to propound their views. But as we shall see, in recent years, conservatives too have produced polemical films.

Philosopher Louis Menand believes documentaries are a natural "medium of progressivism" because "progressives . . . feel good about expressing their activism in an artistic medium that requires hardship and teamwork" and because "the documentary has a built-in bias against officialdom." A critical stance suggests dissatisfaction with the status quo and an implicit—or explicit—call for change. In some cases, conservative documentaries have been produced to counter charges made by progressive films. Four full-length movies were made specifically to rebut Michael Moore's *Fahrenheit 9/11*.

This book is not a history of documentary films. Several good histories already exist. Rather, we shall explore the political evolution of American nonfiction films over the past half-century. Documentaries offer us a valuable alternative history, a patchwork political narrative that is often at odds with the official version of events. As we look back from the political documentaries of the early twenty-first century, including those meant to influence the 2004 election, we want to identify their progenitors and learn how the voices of contemporary filmmakers developed. Only if we understand where we came from can we know where we are.

Of the terms in this book's subtitle—the rise of American political documentaries—only *rise* requires no explanation or debate. By almost any definition, from popular success to technical expertise, the best nonfiction films ever made are those of recent vintage. Of course, earlier eras produced great documentary movies too, and we shall look at some of them. But generally speaking, we are living in the golden age of documentary film production right now.

The term *American* (meaning "from the United States") is a bit more problematic. This book concentrates on American films and American filmmakers, but now, more than ever, few artists live or work in isolation from the global artistic community. American movies influence those of other countries and vice versa. For instance, it is difficult to discuss recent films critical of mass media, such as *Outfoxed, Orwell Rolls in His Grave*, or *Ammo for the Info Warrior*, without acknowledging *Manufacturing Consent: Noam Chomsky and the Media*, made by Canadians Mark Achbar and Peter Wintonick in 1992. Without that innovative Chomsky movie, the later films might not have been made as they were, or at all. Some films cross national boundaries in their creative process or their subject matter, making them harder to define as purely American products.

Were the September 11 terrorist attacks on the World Trade Center an American event? Some of the most sensitive cinematic renditions of that horror were produced by non-Americans—British, French, and Mexican—but seemed to demand inclusion here. The issue of modern American identity is complicated by a U.S. solipsism that tends to discount other countries, and the fears of many outside the United States that *globalization* is merely a grandiose term for the American corporate destruction of traditional cultures.

The term *political* is even more slippery. Every film, whatever its subject, has political implications. Ethnographies could be construed as political, for example. Or what about Morgan Spurlock's *Supersize Me* (2004)? This funny, disturbing film strikes at the larded heart of our consumer culture, probing behind the happy face of misleading fast food advertising to dramatize the health risks for the billions and billions who are poorly served. Loaded as it is with political implications, Spurlock's film lacks the explicit political content to be included here, though his conversation with Eric Schlosser, author of *Fast Food Nation*, appended to the DVD version, does address the political implications of his culinary/medical experiment.

Even the universe of overtly "political" films is too large for a single book to explore in any meaningful way. We concentrate here on films that examine the American political process or challenge official government narratives and offer competing alternative narratives of their own. Within this framework we touch only incidentally on other political genres, such as environmental films and films about gender, whether traditionally constructed or with a gay or lesbian focus, or films about race and ethnicity, portraying African Americans, Mexican Americans, Muslim Americans, or others. All these subjects deserve separate investigation and explication.

Films about political dissidents also constitute a genre of their own, from Emile de Antonio's *Underground* (1968), in which he interviews members of the SDS Weatherman faction, to *Berkeley in the Sixties* (1990), Helen Garvey's *Rebels with a Cause* (2000), *The Weather Underground* (2002), and *Guerrilla: The Taking of Patty Hearst* (2004), among others. The recent release of many of these films testifies to our ongoing interest in deciphering the meaning of the social and political upheavals of the 1960s. But political dissidents, or fetishized versions of their countercultural lifestyles, are of less moment than the issues they—and progressive filmmakers—stood for and protested against, especially the Vietnam War.

Documentary is the most difficult term to describe with precision, partly because the form continues to evolve. British film pioneer John Grierson defined it as "the creative treatment of reality." Documentary makers use actual people, settings, and situations, rather than inventing their own. But as Erik Barnouw points out, any claim to objectivity by nonfiction filmmakers is "meaningless" because of the "endless choices" they have to make—from the topic, to the individual shots, to the final order of edited sequences. The "creative treatment" of real subjects includes various forms and levels of manipulation. For Nanook of the North (1922), about the disappearing Eskimo way of life, Robert Flaherty directed the Inuit families he was shooting to perform and repeat various activities. A number of iconic historical moments, like the Marines raising the American flag over Iwo Jima in World War II, have been restaged for cameras. Of course, the very act of filming an event, however unobtrusively, may distort it, as anyone who has ever tried to take candid shots at a party well knows.

Every nonfiction film is a form of propaganda, trying to persuade us of something, even if only that what we are seeing "actually happened." Critics who denigrate *Fahrenheit 9/11* as propaganda are those who oppose its point of view. For today's cynical moviegoer, *propaganda* is a lie you dislike, *honesty* is a lie in service to a greater truth, and documentary truth is certainly not *the* truth, if such exists. Meaning is in the eye of the beholder. The chance video of White Los Angeles police officers beating African American motorist Rodney King appeared to indict the police for excessive use of force. Police defense lawyers played that tape for the jury over and over, supplying a narrative of Black aggression and police vigilance, and thus altering its truth and enabling the jury to acquit their clients.

The modern documentary revolution began in the early 1960s, when technical advances and more portable equipment allowed filmmakers greater freedom of motion and access than they had ever known. These expanded abilities endowed nonfiction films with new levels of intimacy and power. Certain mediated images—widely broadcast and repeated by the newly dominant medium of television—achieved iconic significance beyond their own contexts, creating a community across the United States and beyond, bound together and defined by images such as those of John F. Kennedy alive and dead, fighting in Vietnam, or riots in urban America. Television had already disavowed the 1950s documentary news style of Edward R. Murrow. Television's corporate bosses deemed Murrow's approach too contentious for a medium that did not want to alienate any potential customers.

The power of television rivaled that of politicians, who fiercely attacked the medium. President Lyndon Johnson blamed television for his decision not to run for reelection in 1968. Some in the Pentagon blamed media for the U.S. defeat in Vietnam. Nixon and his vice president, Spiro Agnew, declared war on the "unelected media elite" who opposed their policies. Fittingly, the televised Watergate hearings forced Nixon to resign in 1974. Ronald Reagan's media handlers largely scripted TV news in the 1980s, beginning the ongoing shift from opposing the media news agenda to co-opting it.

Corporate and political pressures on television content forced documentary filmmakers to tailor their work for the media marketplace or else forgo media support. In that sense, television has had a profound influence on the latest generations of documentary films, helping to create independent films of uncompromising vision, while limiting their audiences. As documentaries have become less available via mass media, their messages have become more urgent.

Films recording and criticizing American political campaign and election processes began in 1960 and have become more prevalent, climaxing with the disputed election of 2000. Films challenging official government versions of political and military events in Vietnam began in the mid-1960s, shifting their emphasis in the 1970s and 1980s to chronicle unpredicted effects and victims of the war. Vietnam—an unnecessary war—continues to haunt American filmmakers and the American mind. Errol Morris's *The Fog of War*—debriefing Vietnam War architect Robert McNamara in 2002—shows us, as William Faulkner said, that the past isn't dead, it isn't even past. Objections to the Vietnam War presaged a more general condemnation of U.S. militarism that continues today. Anti–Vietnam War films led directly to anti–Iraq invasion films, as the Iraq war—another discretionary conflict—revived political sentiments dormant since Vietnam.

In the first three chapters we look at how nonfiction films engaged American electoral processes and the Vietnam War, on television and—mostly—off. Television pioneer Edward R. Murrow tried to pursue the public interest in news documentaries about issues and personalities. Corporate media shut Murrow down, narrowing the range of discourse in order to cultivate the largest possible audiences. The fight for ratings and advertising dollars drove thoughtful, controversial documentaries off the air. Murrow's story is significant, foreshadowing the ongoing trivialization of TV news content and defining the need for an independent film movement outside the mass media.

Though the "credibility gap" between what the U.S. government reported and the reality that journalists could see for themselves largely disappeared on television after Vietnam, independent filmmakers continued to expose the lies told by successive U.S. regimes: the Reagan administration during Iran-Contra, the first Bush administration during and after invasions of Panama and Iraq (1991), and the Clinton administration after the massacre of American religious dissidents in Waco, Texas.

Vietnam taught the Pentagon the need to manage conflict coverage. Officials experimented until they got it right. They barred the press from the U.S. invasions of Grenada and Panama. They limited and directed news media during the 1991 Gulf War. Then, for the 2003 Iraq invasion, the military co-opted media, embedding correspondents with field units and top officials at TV network studios. Danny Schechter's *WMD: Weapons of Mass Deception* (2004) analyses the result of these manipulations.

Independent filmmakers must work harder than ever to get beyond the government's stonewalls and scripted camouflage. But the tradition of doubt and critical independent investigation engendered by Vietnam—and largely absent from American television—prepared filmmakers to expose the lies of the George W. Bush administration about the 2000 election, the terrorist attacks on the United States, the Patriot Act, the War on Terror, and the 2003 invasion of Iraq.

Among the many talented documentarians working now, a few names stand out. In four separate chapters, we focus on individuals whose careers and bodies of work deserve detailed attention for different, but compelling reasons: Barbara Kopple, Michael Moore, Errol Morris, and Robert Greenwald. Their prolific, influential work has done much to shape our understanding of contemporary reality and the role films can play in communicating and even creating it. All of them challenge official narratives by offering more complex narratives of their own, from radically different perspectives.

Barbara Kopple won two Academy Awards for documentaries about labor disputes at a Kentucky coal mine and a Minnesota meat packing plant. In her wide-ranging career, Kopple has probed feminist issues, the rise and fall of boxer Mike Tyson, the JFK murder conspiracy, and—in a television miniseries—the culture of the wealthy. Kopple explored the Woodstock legacy in rockumentaries, showed an *American Standoff* between the Teamsters union and James Hoffa, Jr., and produced an emotional film about children with AIDS, titled *Friends for Life,* among other projects.

Fearless, with an uncanny ability to be on the scene when difficult and pivotal events are unfolding on the streets or behind closed doors, Barbara Kopple has enlarged the scope of documentary discourse by reporting on social upheavals and cultural trends in ways that clearly delineate the relationship of individual trajectories/lives/narratives to a larger political and economic context. Kopple uses personal stories to undermine the feel-good economic fables that corporate culture deploys to mask oppressive behaviors. Recently she was one of three producers of *Bearing Witness* (2005), about female war reporters in Iraq, and served as executive producer for Denny Schechter's *Weapons of Mass Deception* (2004), detailing media complicity in Bush administration lies.

Concern for unionism and the plight of the wage slave came naturally to Michael Moore, whose father and grandfather were both General Motors employees and active union members. Moore started a weekly paper in Flint, Michigan, that took a critical stance toward GM's treatment of its workers and its hometown. He achieved instant national fame with his 1989 documentary *Roger & Me*, depicting his efforts to confront General Motors CEO Roger Smith about the mass firings of GM employees. The film introduced Moore's unique blend of comedy and pathos, powered by his own performance as a shambling, slovenly— if bright and relentless—Everyman, confronting the heartless Corporate Beast. His iconoclastic television series, full of daring, satirical anticorporate gambits, ran for two years.

Moore's 2002 exploration of the U.S. culture of guns and violence, *Bowling for Columbine*, grossed more than $20 million and won an Oscar. Its treatment of the national gun obsession, the National Rifle Association, the militia mentality, and the 1999 shootings at Columbine High School in Colorado stirred passionate controversy. His 2004 anti–Bush administration film, *Fahrenheit 9/11*, won the Palme d'Or award at Cannes and shattered all records for documentary films. One measure of its potency is the backlash it inspired of critical books and Web sites and four full-length films.

Errol Morris won the 2003 Academy Award for Best Documentary for *The Fog of War*, an intensive interview with Robert McNamara, former Secretary of Defense under Presidents Kennedy and Johnson and a principal architect of the Vietnam War. Morris and McNamara toured college campuses, with McNamara refusing to criticize the current U.S. involvement in Iraq. But viewers of the film cannot help but compare how every generation rationalizes the case for war. Unlike Kopple, who uses a "fly on the wall" technique to capture history that seems to be happening without awareness of the camera, Morris prefers "to be as obtrusive as possible." His subjects play to the camera and even perform for it. But unlike Moore, he does not play provocative on-camera tricks to tease responses from his subjects. He just lets them talk.

Morris makes nonfiction films resembling no others. From his first film, *Gates of Heaven* (1978), about two California pet cemeteries, Morris has kept his focus on individuals more than issues, an instinctive affirmation of Ralph Waldo Emerson's belief that "properly speaking, there is no history, only biography." Morris's 1988 film, *The Thin Blue Line*, tells the true story of a man on death row in Texas, falsely accused of murdering a Dallas police officer. The film became famous for causing the release of the man from prison after twelve years and identifying the real murderer. Morris has also made oddly engaging films of British physicist Stephen Hawking's *Brief History of Time* and *Mr. Death*, about the bizarre career of a Holocaust denier.

Robert Greenwald's extensive filmography dates from the mid-1970s, but most of his films are fictional features. Greenwald recently turned his career into a high-gear assault upon the Bush administration. He produced *Unprecedented: The 2000 Presidential Election* (2002), which explains in precise, graphic detail how the Republican party stole the presidential election in Florida. Greenwald formed Public Interest Pictures and then produced and directed *Uncovered: The Whole Truth about the Iraq War* (2003). The film uses stock footage of Bush administration officials interspersed with career insider experts from the CIA and the Pentagon to refute the Bush claims point-by-point, identifying the lies and misconceptions.

Uncovered was sponsored by MoveOn and the Center for American Progress, which also funded Greenwald's next producing and directing effort, *Outfoxed: Rupert Murdoch's War on Journalism* (2004). Utilizing MoveOn's two-million-member network, both films were introduced at house parties and sold over the Internet on DVD before being released to theaters, bypassing the traditional, time-consuming screening processes of theatrical distributors and buyers for the ever-larger theater chains. Backed by the American Civil Liberties Union, Greenwald produced a third "Un" film, *Unconstitutional* (2004), about how the Bush administration cynically used the events of 9/11 to erode civil rights and to quash dissent with the Patriot Act.

Besides the work of Moore and Greenwald, an unprecedented number of documentary films were produced specifically to influence the 2004 election. These films look back on events but also forward, to that election and beyond. They not only want to inform audiences, but also to activate them. Vietnam was a major campaign theme in 2004. Both candidates were of the Vietnam generation and played different roles during that war. Partisan filmmakers on both sides of the presidential election made films defending, even glorifying, their candidates. Two films recount the military service of John Kerry as the commander of a Swift boat in the Mekong Delta of Vietnam in 1969: *Brothers in Arms* and *Going Upriver: The Long War of John Kerry*.

Bush partisans countered with *George W. Bush: Faith in the White House*, a reverential presentation of Bush as a devout Christian, guided by a deep faith. This pro-Bush film was released the same day *Fahrenheit 9/11* came out on DVD. While Swift Boat Veterans for Truth attacked Kerry on TV from the right, liberals took on the man they saw as the evil genius behind the president. *Bush's Brain*, based on a book by two Texas political reporters, chronicles Karl Rove's wildly successful "junkyard dog approach to politics." Did these cinematic efforts change any hearts or minds? Or were the election-year filmmakers merely preaching to their own choirs?

The final chapter of the book evaluates trends in documentary films that are taking us into new aesthetic and epistemological territory, including the globalization of techniques and outlooks, the empowerment of nontraditional filmmakers, and the increasingly blurred borders between fact and fiction.

Some film producers circumvent media spin control by distributing cheap, portable video cameras to a large number of people, who provide multiple perspectives of events or situations, and whose perspectives are later combined to create a different order of reality. Big Noise films and the Seattle Independent Media Center used this method to cover the 1999 World Trade Organization (WTO) protests in Seattle for *This Is What Democracy Looks Like*. Directors of *Voices of Iraq* gave cameras to hundreds of ordinary citizens in order to convey a more accurate, composite picture of Iraq than what the vested interests on either side of occupation politics present. These experiments in populist cinema, beyond the structural control of traditional film producers or directors, and apart from ideologues, show "us" to "each other" in new and exciting ways, liberated from stereotypes and political clichés.

In our age of digital imaging, computer-generated graphics, and slick image manipulation, can we trust what we see? Our difficulty will only increase as technology becomes more sophisticated. Not only must viewers weigh the more or less overt bias of filmmakers, but we must also judge reality based on the "blurred boundaries" of films, which combine factual and fictional elements in various ways. Do fact-based advocacy films help viewers understand reality, or do they merely confuse it with new agendas and illusions? We will investigate the implications of breaking through the "illusion barrier" in film.

The lessons our government took from Vietnam were not moral, but tactical. Bureaucrats are more skilled now in concealing and shaping events for popular consumption. With American mass media in corporate hands, media have become de facto government mouthpieces. How long will political documentaries continue their crusade? Shortly after Michael Moore's incredible success with *Fahrenheit 9/11,* the Carlyle Group, powerful political insiders who usually invest in weapons systems and arms makers, bought the Loews chain of 400 movie theaters. They seem to be getting the message—and are perhaps acquiring the means to contain it.

Chapter 1

LENSES WITH ATTITUDE

"Anyone who believes that every individual film must present a 'balanced' picture, knows nothing about either balance or pictures."
—Edward R. Murrow

The raw, rainy Wisconsin spring landscape looks bleaker in black and white. Bare trees and houses flash by beyond the flicking windshield wipers. Senator Hubert Humphrey explains to the driver how snow brings nitrogen to the soil. In a school gym, he tells farmers that no one in the East Coast power establishment cares about them. Only he understands their concerns. A dozen kids play "Davy Crockett" on their accordions, and the refrain is sung as "Hubert, Hubert Humphrey." Later, Humphrey accosts passersby on the nearly empty streets of a small Wisconsin town, pressing his business cards into the hands of children and adults, smiling and chatting compulsively, running for president.

Senator John Kennedy and his glamorous wife stand on stage in a packed auditorium, looking a bit stranded as the crowd strikes up a squeaky rendition of "High Hopes," with Kennedy campaign lyrics. Behind her back, Jackie nervously kneads her white-gloved hands. Then she speaks a few words in Polish to the delighted audience. Kennedy makes a tough speech about military preparedness: "We can see the enemy's campfires burning on the distant hills." He wades into the crowd. His intense charisma enchants some people and makes others turn away. He signs autographs for excited children like a rock star.

Primary (1960) renders a world remote from our own. The film is poignant today, not just because we know that Kennedy will finally win this election and then be assassinated, but also because the America on display here is long gone, its innocence shattered forever by a series of national traumas and media overkill: the racial violence of the 1960s, political murders, Vietnam, Watergate, Iran-Contra, the 9/11 attacks, and more.

Primary proved influential, part of the early 1960s revolution in documentary filmmaking sparked by new technology that opened more of the world to the filmmaker's gaze. At the same time, television began to shun controversy, so as not to alienate mass audiences or anger government officials. Amid these conflicting trends, the Vietnam War exploded the faith of many Americans in their own government and set off a fierce struggle to control the images and narratives of that conflict and succeeding ones.

The sight of John Kennedy standing alone at a factory gate to shake workers' hands seems exotic, almost surreal. He is not yet the mythical martyred icon of Camelot, just a politician seeking votes. The novelty of the shot in 1960 was that no one had ever filmed this grassroots political exercise before. The novelty today is that Kennedy stands by himself, without handlers or security guards or the hordes of reporters with cameras and microphones that now dog candidates every step of the way.

"Nobody knew what we were doing," says filmmaker Robert Drew in the 1999 DVD voiceover. "That was our advantage." With *Primary*, Drew wanted to create "a new kind of reporting, a new form of history." He admonished his crew to shoot stories "without imposing ourselves." He did not conduct interviews or ask anyone he was filming to repeat a line or an action or to do anything at all.

Unlike Humphrey and Kennedy in 1960, later presidential candidates were always "on" and "on message," too self-aware and media savvy. Suspense lay elsewhere. As cinematographer Richard Leacock admits in the *Primary* DVD narration, "we created the problem" of media overkill. On election night in Wisconsin, Leacock filmed John Kennedy, with his advisors and family members, awaiting the results in his hotel room. The scene has an intimacy and spontaneity absent from subsequent campaign films. Two of those responsible for killing that spontaneity were in that room: Leacock himself, holding the camera, and Theodore H. White, who wrote *The Making of the President, 1960.*

White's book spun the grueling grind of state primaries as a dramatic democratic ritual. By the time White was covering his fourth election, in 1972, crowded with the journalists he and Drew had attracted to the campaign trail, Timothy Crouse found as much drama—and comedy—reporting on the media as on the candidates in his classic, *The Boys on the*

Bus. But then, most of the important stories that media cover ultimately turn into stories about the coverage itself.

At the 1972 political party conventions, as covered by a pioneering group of alternative television filmmakers, network journalists played cranky supporting roles. "Top Value Television, better known as TVTV, was the best-known and most controversial guerrilla television group of the decade." For their video report, *Four More Years,* nineteen TVTV reporters infiltrated the Republican National Convention in Miami Beach, mostly ignoring podium events in order to interview delegates and journalists. In blurry black and white, using small hand-held cameras, they move from the scruffy, shaggy Vietnam veteran war protestors in Flamingo Park, to the plaid, pleated, buttoned-down Republicans, who were observing those demonstrators from afar with fear and loathing.

TVTV interviewers Maureen Orth and Skip Blumberg catch network stars like NBC's Cassie Mackin admitting that the convention is plastic, packaged, and dull. Mike Wallace of CBS complains that he's on the floor where little is happening while Dan Rather gets to cover the VIP section. "I'd rather be watching this at home," says Wallace. CBS convention chief Walter Cronkite presides from on high, in a glass booth above the convention floor, where some delegates complain he stayed seated during the playing of the National Anthem. "How does feedback affect you?" TVTV asks him. Cronkite says he hopes it doesn't, but admits he can't really know. He despairs that too many people depend only on television for their news.

TVTV reveals the television networks to be dinosaurs, stuck inside their own clichés, tethered to the podium and to the Republican script by their massive equipment, scheduling imperatives, and vanilla objectivity. Traveling light, the TVTV crews chronicle the coached "spontaneity" of Young Republicans and the synthetic charm of the hostess "Nixonettes." They ride a delegate bus, where a petition to prosecute antiwar actress Jane Fonda "to the fullest extent of the law" passes up and down the aisle.

Appalled by the demonstrators, a few delegates claim that "some of them aren't really veterans at all." One man, who identifies himself as a veteran of an earlier war, says that "*these* guys were hopped up and the guys *next* to 'em died. That's why *they're* alive." The TVTV interviewer asks him, "Were *you* hopped up?" Delegates call for the National Guard to hold back the protesting vets. TVTV makes a deft transition from the ragtag veterans behind a barbed wire fence playing the National Anthem on kazoos to the immaculate orchestral rendition inside the convention hall. And they cut from a mechanical smiling Nixon, accepting the nomination, to veterans in wheelchairs screaming "Stop the bombing! Stop the killing!" and subsumed by screams of "Four More Years! Four More Years!" still ringing as the camera pans an empty convention center.

When TVTV asks Mike Wallace his opinion of advocacy reporting, Wallace replies, "I'm not a big fan of it." Nor are the TV networks. Independent documentaries were never staples of commercial television. Opinionated voices espousing unpopular or minority views are unwelcome intruders in television's corporate mass marketplace. But in the medium's earliest days—now called its "Golden Age"—when TV was still experimental and finding its way, some edgy documentaries did appear.

Primary took no political stance, but rather cast an ethnographic gaze at rituals of the American political subculture. Filmmakers who worked with Drew on *Primary*—Albert Maysles, Donn Alan Pennebaker, and Richard Leacock—later made seminal films about the rock and roll subculture, including *Don't Look Back* (1965), *Monterey Pop* (1968), and *Gimme Shelter* (1970). Pennebaker and his wife, Chris Hegedus, made another presidential campaign film, *The War Room*, about 1992, with a focus, not on the candidates, but on Clinton strategists James Carville and George Stephanopoulos.

The Road to the Presidency, released in 2004, attempts a more comprehensive, if Clinton-centered, view of the 1992 race. At two and a half hours, it feels like a campaign recap by the Borges character "Funes, the Memorious," whose total recall requires 24 hours to remember a 24-hour day. The film lacks wit and economy. Poet Barbara Bang compares primaries to the Miss America contest, convention manager John Hart madly orchestrates events behind the scenes, and post-debate spinmeisters talk trash. But these great moments are buried in an indiscriminate flood of trivia. Alexandra Pelosi's *Journeys with George*, about Bush's 2000 campaign, turns *Primary* upside down. Instead of ignoring the camera, Bush plays to it. He charms the lens and turns it back on Pelosi, subverting her status as an observer and appropriating her "documentary" for his own self-promotion. He is less an actor in her production than she is a prop in his.

The year of *Primary*, 1960, marked a significant transition in American media. Edward R. Murrow left broadcasting. With his partner, Fred Friendly, Murrow largely invented the television public affairs documentary. Learning as they went, Murrow and Friendly used "television's intrinsic characteristics of intimacy and immediacy" to move beyond formulaic "hard news" stories. Their video essays on people and issues often invited conclusions from their viewers and sometimes supplied them.

Murrow's thoughtful, innovative work on the CBS News program *See It Now,* brought great prestige to the fledgling television network, but also great controversy. By the late 1950s, with TV ownership growing nationwide and three networks dominating the airwaves, the television business had become lucrative beyond the wildest dreams of its founders. Controversial subjects or viewpoints risked alienating viewers and advertisers, jeopardizing the huge network profits. The controversial Murrow had to go.

NOW YOU SEE IT, NOW YOU DON'T

World War II made Edward R. Murrow a star. Murrow reported and personified the steadfast British resistance to fascist aggression. His wartime radio broadcasts from London during German bombardments of the city made him a symbol of grace under fire. He returned to the United States as the preeminent radio journalist of the postwar years.

When fighting broke out in Korea in 1950, Murrow covered the U.S. involvement there and came home with strong doubts. "The question now arises whether serious mistakes have been made," Murrow wrote, for his August 14, 1950, broadcast. The U.S. officials had promised an early end to the fighting. "To paraphrase the GIs in Korea," said Murrow, "that ain't the way it looks from here. So far as this reporter is concerned, he doesn't see where or when this conflict will end." When CBS news editors read the transcript of Murrow's radio broadcast, they refused to allow it on the air. Ultimately, Murrow's independent voice would clash too often with the corporate priorities of his employer to sustain his career.

Murrow and his partner, Fred Friendly, first broadcast *See It Now* on CBS television in November 1951. "This is an old team, trying to learn a new trade," Murrow said, to open his first TV program. Pronouncing himself impressed by the power of television, Murrow pledged, "We shall hope to use it and not to abuse it." Having no precedent to go by, Murrow and Friendly married their radio journalism skills to the format of the movie newsreels.

They covered the biggest news of the day: the Korean War, the Supreme Court order to desegregate American schools, and Senator Joseph McCarthy's Red Scare witch hunts. Murrow's personal integrity and sense of fairness compelled him not simply to report these stories but to characterize their significance. CBS newscaster Charles Kuralt thought, "Murrow was a bit of an evangelist. He wanted to change the world for the better." Murrow reported—and largely concocted—the ten-year anniversary of the first successful "controlled release of nuclear energy" at the University of Chicago, which led to the atomic bomb. He noted that immigrant scientists such as Leo Szilard and Enrico Fermi, whose contributions were central to the project, would probably be denied entrance to the United States under the McCarran Immigration Act. He quoted Hitler as saying that "the great strength of a totalitarian regime will force those who fear it to imitate it." This was not objective journalism, but it was incisive social commentary.

"Christmas in Korea" showed American soldiers in 1952 missing their families as Korean children sang carols. Instead of battle reports or body counts, Murrow concentrated on the personal stories of men and women coping with war's costs. "There is no conclusion to this report about Korea because there is no end to this war," said Murrow. CBS silently endured the racist critics of Murrow's stories on Louis Armstrong's European concerts or Marian Anderson's U.S. Information Agency tour of Asia. Less comfortable for the network were Murrow's reports from southern high schools—Black and White—reacting to federally mandated desegregation, which spotlighted unregenerate institutional racism and annoyed local affiliate stations. But Murrow took great personal and professional risks to attack Joseph McCarthy.

Murrow collected McCarthy material for over a year before using it. It is easy now to second-guess Murrow's hesitation but difficult to conjure the fear that McCarthy and his friends exploited for their own ends. McCarthy's accusations of communism or communist "sympathies" against individuals in government, academia, or broadcasting—uncorroborated by any evidence—were often enough to end their careers. McCarthy's victims included several Murrow colleagues. Murrow understood his responsibility. His broadcast was the first to challenge McCarthy's methods.

Murrow led up to his direct attack by first reporting on the case of an Air Force officer asked to resign after fourteen years because his father and sister had been charged with reading "subversive" newspapers. Lt. Milo Radulovich refused to resign, forcing a hearing on the charges. Radulovich was articulate in his defense and appalled that his accusers were never identified, nor were their exact charges. He refused to break off relations with his father and sister, as ordered. His lawyer prepared witnesses and testimony, none of which the Air Force allowed. *See It Now* interviewed Radulovich's father, a Yugoslavian emigrant, retired auto-worker, and World War I veteran who read Serbo-Croatian newspapers, and his sister, who said what she read was nobody's business. "It seems to us—that is, to Fred Friendly and myself—that this subject should be argued about endlessly," said Murrow, to conclude the show. In the end, the Air Force backed down and reinstated Radulovich, a small but exceptional victory.

On March 9, 1954, *See It Now* concentrated on Joseph McCarthy. Film clips of McCarthy speeches ran interspersed with commentary from Murrow, correcting and refuting him. Murrow concluded by saying that "the line between investigation and persecution is a fine one and the junior senator from Wisconsin has stepped over it repeatedly. . . . We must not confuse dissent with disloyalty. . . . We will not walk in fear, one of another. We will not be driven by fear into an age of unreason . . . we cannot defend freedom abroad by deserting it at home."

Murrow offered to let McCarthy respond on *See It Now*. McCarthy wanted time to prepare. So the next program considered the case of Annie Lee Moss, a cafeteria worker accused by a McCarthy informant of being a communist with access to secret government codes. Moments after Moss, an elderly African American woman, was sworn in before McCarthy's committee, McCarthy excused himself from the proceedings. Moss's near-illiteracy amused some committee members, since the charges against her involved her detailed knowledge of secret codes. Moss's White "Communist Party contact" proved to be a non-communist Black man with the same name. McCarthy's charges and tactics appeared slipshod and nasty.

On April 6, McCarthy appeared on *See It Now*, calling Murrow "the leader and the cleverest of the jackal pack which is always found at the throat of anyone who dares to expose individual Communists and traitors." McCarthy accused Murrow of membership in the International Workers of the World, "a terrorist organization," and of sponsoring a communist school in Moscow in the 1930s for the Institute of International Education. Murrow couldn't claim "youth or ignorance," said McCarthy, since he had "for the past six months followed the communist line." McCarthy quoted *The Daily Worker*'s praise for *See It Now*, and concluded that "if . . . Mr. Murrow is giving aid and comfort to our enemies, he ought not to be invited into the homes of millions of Americans by the Columbia Broadcasting System." The following week Murrow refuted McCarthy's charges point by point.

Murrow seemed to win the confrontation. McCarthy's power and popularity declined that spring, during thirty-six days of televised Army–McCarthy hearings. Then the Senate voted to censure him. *See It Now*—the most honored series on television—earned more honors and awards. But no public accolades could equal the advertising dollars that more popular programming—like the new, high-stakes quiz shows—brought the network. In 1955, CBS reduced *See It Now*'s weekly broadcasts to eight or ten yearly specials. "Wags began calling it *See It Now and Then.*"

Murrow appeared on the cover of *Time* on September 30, 1957. Pronouncing him television's outstanding journalist, who made "serious matters" appeal to large audiences, *Time* applauded Murrow's "social conscience." Less than six months later, CBS canceled *See It Now*, the program that *Time* called "the only continuing issue-oriented series" on the network, officially because it cost too much to produce. CBS chairman William Paley told Murrow and Friendly he didn't want the stomachaches every time they did a controversial broadcast. Said Murrow, "It comes with the job."

By October 1958, *See It Now* was gone and the scandal over rigged quiz shows had begun to play out in the press. Murrow told the Radio and Television News Directors Association that "television in the main is being used to distract, delude, amuse and insulate us. . . . If we go on as we are then history will take its revenge. . . . There is a great and perhaps decisive battle to be fought against ignorance, intolerance and indifference. This weapon of television could be useful."

Public outcry against the crooked quiz shows, culminating in a congressional inquiry, pressured CBS president Frank Stanton to pledge a renewed emphasis on public affairs. Stanton designed *CBS Reports* to be a company show, unconnected to Murrow, but with "the same intensive approach to critical issues" as *See It Now* and produced by Murrow's former partner, Fred Friendly. Murrow introduced and narrated the first *CBS Reports* program, "Biography of a Missile," but his input and appearances on the new program were, by design, occasional.

Murrow's valedictory broadcast was his 1960 narration of "Harvest of Shame," about the miserable conditions of migrant farm laborers in Florida. His closing comments appealed for action to remedy the situation. Then Murrow accepted President Kennedy's appointment to head the United States Information Agency. One of his first acts as director was to try to stop the British Broadcasting Corporation from showing "Harvest of Shame." His attempt failed, but word of it leaked to the press, embarrassing the novice bureaucrat. Murrow, the government propaganda chief, had tried to censor Murrow, the muckraking journalist.

THEN IT'S ONE, TWO, THREE, WHAT ARE WE FIGHTING FOR?

The cultural and political upheaval of the 1960s called forth a surge of documentary films about long-marginalized issues and groups. The struggles of racial minorities, women, organized labor, political radicals, and a youthful, antimaterialist counterculture demanded recognition from a society reluctant to admit their existence. Above all, the Vietnam War, and the exclusion of any but the mildest critical responses to the war from mainstream media, fueled an oppositional impulse among documentary (and some feature) filmmakers that continues in the twenty-first century, targeting American electoral politics and the war in Iraq, decades after the Americans left Vietnam.

Murrow's *See It Now* had been the only primetime program to discuss Vietnam on a regular basis, starting in 1954. When Vice President Nixon said he favored sending U.S. troops to Indochina to help the French, Murrow found his call for intervention "premature and even unrealistic." French journalist Jean-Jacques Servan-Schreiber told Murrow's viewers that U.S. support for France in Indochina was "tragically wrong." But after joining the Kennedy administration in 1961, Murrow swallowed his doubts and adopted the hard-line cold war view that Vietnam must not be allowed to "fall."

The escalating catastrophe in Vietnam attracted documentary filmmakers from outside the United States, but the first Vietnam film many Americans saw was *Why Vietnam?* (1965). A pro-war production of the Department of Defense, "the film was used to indoctrinate Vietnam-bound draftees, and was also loaned to schools." *Why Vietnam?* begins with Hitler and Chamberlain in Munich in 1938, "a meeting that opens the door to dictatorship." Ignoring communist aggression in Vietnam is like appeasing the Nazis, according to the film. United States President Lyndon Johnson explains that "retreat does not bring safety, weakness does not bring peace."

When Vietnamese forces defeated the French colonial army at Dien Bien Phu, in 1954, Vietnam was divided, north and south, until free elections could be held. But "behind Ho Chi Minh's smile is a mind plotting a reign of terror," says the narrator, as if Ho were Ming the Merciless. North Vietnam terrorized South Vietnam, making free elections impossible and waging "politically camouflaged aggression" disguised as a "so-called war of liberation." In reality, the United States forestalled Vietnamese elections in the 1950s because they knew the Marxist populist, Ho Chi Minh, would win overwhelmingly.

Secretary of State Dean Rusk says, "Hanoi has rebuffed all attempts at peace negotiations . . . has refused to come to the United Nations." Lyndon Johnson says, "We will not bully or flaunt our power, but we will not surrender, we will not retreat." The narrator concludes, "if freedom is to survive in American hometowns, it must be preserved in places like South Vietnam. And so, the war goes on. Clearly it is the communists who have made that choice" The film's misleading politics and false rationalizations for war were not apparent to most Americans, who only knew about Vietnam from watching the TV news.

The Vietnam War temporarily alienated media from government, opening a "credibility gap" based on Johnson administration claims of an impending American victory in Southeast Asia and the very different reality reporters could witness for themselves. Journalists pointed to these contradictions, even on television, causing some conservatives to blame media for the U.S. defeat in Vietnam. The living room war changed drastically when North Vietnam launched the Tet offensive, early in 1968, invading dozens of South Vietnamese cities and attacking the U.S. embassy in Saigon. Startled American TV viewers saw that the enemy was neither weak nor waning, as official U.S. propaganda had claimed for several years. CBS news anchor Walter Cronkite visited Vietnam and returned to express his doubt on the air about a U.S. victory in Vietnam, similar to reservations Edward R. Murrow had about Korea eighteen years earlier, but without network censorship. A month after Cronkite publicly predicted "stalemate" in Vietnam, Lyndon Johnson told a national TV audience he would not run for reelection. The day after his speech, Johnson addressed the National Association of Broadcasters, blaming them for his defeat.

Radical filmmaker Emile de Antonio was "angry about Vietnam and wanted to do something." Television coverage of the war appalled him. "Every day we saw the war. Every day we saw dead Americans, dead Vietnamese, bombings . . . but never one program on why; never one program on the history of it . . . attempting to place it in context." De Antonio obtained some films and outtakes from American television networks. He used his left-ist connections to obtain rare archival footage, much of it from Eastern Europe, to piece together a colonial history of Indochina since World War II.

Vietnam: In the Year of the Pig (1968) condemned the American war in Vietnam as a continuation of corrupt French colonialism—antithetical to the cause of freedom it pretended to uphold. De Antonio did not claim to take a dispassionate approach. Instead he denounced as dishonest the pretense of objectivity among documentary producers. "There is no film made without pointing a camera and the pointing of that camera is already . . . a definitive gesture of prejudice." De Antonio—an avowed Marxist— admitted that "my prejudice is under and in everything I do."

His first film, *Point of Order* (1963), distilled the televised Army–McCarthy hearings of 1954. De Antonio edited 188 hours of the recorded sessions into "a taut 97-minute drama of political theater." *Point of Order* broke new ground as "the first full-length political documentary without one line of narration," in de Antonio's words. He considered narration "inherently fascist and condescending in the sense that you are telling other people what it is they are looking at while they are looking at it."

CBS had covered the hearings with a few fixed cameras. The raw, ill-defined images of the black-and-white kinescopes render government officials as media phantoms performing an arcane political Kabuki. De Antonio made a virtue of these cinematic limitations, crafting a drama of words and personalities with no distractions. McCarthy, and the political paranoia he exploited, defined the 1950s for De Antonio, and exposed the corrupt American system. There were no heroes, only degrees of complicity in the travesty. *Point of Order* appeared at the first New York International Film Festival, in 1963, and later at Cannes, and it enjoyed a successful theater run. Susan Sontag called the film "the real *comédie noire* of the season, as well as the best political drama."

In the Year of the Pig mixes archival footage with contemporary interviews to make the case for Vietnamese independence and against American intervention. De Antonio gets Republican Senator Thruston Morton to admit that, "whether we like him or not," Ho Chi Minh is "the George Washington of his country for millions of Vietnamese." *Year of the Pig* gives us Ho's life story, a saga of exile, determination, sacrifice, and betrayal by the West. Ho lives simply—peasant style—unencumbered by the trappings and pretensions of high office. Ho and his generals are also brilliant military tacticians, fired by an intense desire for self-determination.

De Antonio likens the Vietnamese struggle to the American Revolution. His opening montage includes Lafayette's words, engraved on his statue in New York's Union Square: "As soon as I heard of American independence my heart was enlisted." We then see "Make Love, Not War" painted on a GI helmet, followed by a Buddhist monk on fire to protest the violence against his people.

The film outlines the terms of the 1954 partition of Vietnam in Geneva after the French military defeat, movingly portrayed by an oriental lute playing "La Marseillaise" as a dirge over shots of jungle graves and airlifted corpses. The Unites States violated the Geneva provisions against the introduction of foreign troops and the creation of foreign bases in Vietnam. The treaty also called for free elections. But as Senator Wayne Morse says, "We knew Ho would be elected in 1956 so we refused to hold those elections." Lyndon Johnson says, "I didn't get you into Vietnam. You've been in Vietnam for ten years." To the great discredit of U.S. media, most of this was news to most Americans.

De Antonio exploits some officials for their shock value, such as General Curtis LeMay, who says, "We must use our air power in the most humane way possible to end the war." LeMay then defines what he means by "humane": "We must be willing to continue our bombing to destroy every work of man in North Vietnam if that's what it takes to win." LeMay's command destroyed many Japanese cities during World War II, and included the atomic attacks on Hiroshima and Nagasaki.

During the Cuban missile crisis, with the United States and the Soviet Union on the brink of nuclear war, LeMay advocated massive air strikes against Cuba to reduce the island to rubble. Stanley Kubrick's 1964 dark comedy, *Dr. Strangelove*, satirized LeMay as the lunatic General Jack D. Ripper. He may have been a cartoonish cold war grotesque, but Curtis LeMay's ethic guided U.S. military operations for decades and still persists in the highest reaches of the Pentagon, though never so bluntly expressed.

LeMay also posits the racist view that "Orientals hold life less dearly" than we do. General Mark Clark says, "I wouldn't trade one dead American for fifty dead Chinamen," conflating the Vietnamese with their traditional enemy, with whom we were not at war. General William Westmoreland echoes LeMay's sentiments in the 1974 Peter Davis film *Hearts and Minds*. Davis covers much of the same ground as *Year of the Pig*, though with less emphasis on historical context and more detail about the war's effect on the Americans. Released six years later, as the war was winding down, and after other important Vietnam films, *Hearts and Minds* was a different order of document, provoking a different kind of cultural and emotional response, than de Antonio's film.

In the Year of the Pig exhibits the ugly racist violence practiced by American soldiers trained to believe, as one Army deserter says, "The only good gook is a dead gook." Westmoreland tells us that U.S. prisoners are not being mistreated, as de Antonio shows us GIs beating and kicking bound captives. We see grinning U.S. soldiers burning down villages and destroying food supplies as villagers—mostly old women and children— shiver and cry. Films like *Interviews with My Lai Veterans* (1970) and *Winter Soldier* (1972) confirm and elaborate in sickening detail how the Vietnam War—like all war—brutalizes those who fight it, desensitizing and dehumanizing them. De Antonio's film was the first to show this brutalization of "our boys" in Asia. It invited denunciation and denial from the sort of people who think the abuse of Iraqis by U.S. soldiers at Baghdad's Abu Ghraib prison was the aberrant work of a few bad apples.

In one of *Year of the Pig*'s better known scenes, Colonel George S. Patton III flashes a huge grin as he describes his men: "They're a bloody good bunch of killers." The scene is famous partly because Davis also uses it in *Hearts and Minds*. Patton's attitude, like LeMay's, is hardly unusual. Describing his military exploits in Afghanistan and Iraq, Marine Lt. Gen. James N. Mattis—"Mad Dog" Mattis to his troops—told a San Diego audience in 2005: "Actually, it's a lot of fun to fight, you know. It's a hell of a hoot. It's fun to shoot some people. I'll be right up front with you. I like brawling."

The darkest heart of de Antonio's film is different now than when it came out. In 1968, the fighting in Vietnam, based on lies, was fierce and ongoing. That was the tragedy. These days, U.S. military forces are engaged elsewhere, fighting for other lies. And rather than bemoan the history we cannot change in *Year of the Pig*, we are more likely to focus on the words of the exhausted-looking Senator Thruston Morton, who has already acknowledged the extent of U.S. folly in Southeast Asia. Morton reminds us that U.S. "military expenditures exceed $50 billion a year" *not including* the cost of the Vietnam War. Morton warns that "the great danger, because so much of our economy is military, is that the military-industrial complex is in danger of dictating policy."

Eugene Jarecki's film *Why We Fight* (2005) explores precisely this issue: To what extent do military industries not simply profit from war, but compel us to wage it? Is militarism the dominant political characteristic of American culture now, as most of us avert our eyes? Emile de Antonio's *In the Year of the Pig* retains its capacity to shock, now more than ever, as we don't seem to have learned very much in the past forty years.

THE BANALITY OF EVIL

Before he made *Hearts and Minds*, Peter Davis produced documentaries for CBS. As film scholar William Rothman notes, "By the end of the sixties, the hard-hitting network investigative documentary of the kind CBS pioneered in the fifties had already become an endangered species, with one of the last being *The Selling of the Pentagon* (1971, Peter Davis), made for CBS." *The Selling of the Pentagon* opens with bombs bursting and jets strafing a meadow. This is not Vietnam but North Carolina, narrator Roger Mudd explains, as the camera pulls back to show us an audience in bleachers watching the battle, being briefed by an officer on what they are seeing. Such displays help the Pentagon spread "the gospel of militarism" to the American public. The CBS program looks at various ways in which the Pentagon uses its huge public relations budget of $190 million—more than the combined budgets of the three network news divisions—to market itself and promote the war, with a special appeal to children.

The Army Exhibit Unit spends nearly a million dollars every year with displays of weaponry, claiming that they go only where they're invited. CBS then talks to a mall manager who says the Army approached him to set up their equipment in the mall. A team of traveling Pentagon colonels rehearses the domino theory to an audience in Peoria, Illinois, promoting the U.S. presence in Vietnam. Every night in the United States six to ten Pentagon speakers address American audiences. Marine General Lewis Walt proclaims that without the protests this war would already be over. Green Berets demonstrate hand-to-hand combat, as children try to emulate their moves.

The Pentagon was spending $12 million a year making propaganda films. Some are hosted by movies stars like Jack Webb, Robert Stack, and John Wayne. Others are narrated by journalists like Chet Huntley and Walter Cronkite. The sample clips we see are didactic and melodramatic. Over Castro's bearded face superimposed on a map of Cuba, Cronkite intones, "Whiskers do not hide the naked face of dictatorship." Mudd—at that time still a potential Cronkite successor for the CBS news anchor spot—tells us that the "roles of journalist and government spokesman are incompatible."

It's easy for the Department of Defense to stonewall the press at will. The Pentagon is simply too vast and labyrinthine for the press to cover. Most media don't even try. "More newsmen cover the pennant race than the arms race," Mudd tells us. *Washington Post* military affairs reporter George Wilson says that "weapons often dictate policies," but he is not asked to elaborate on that ominous theme. A former Army information officer explains how easily he was able to mislead reporters who came to Vietnam to cover the war. He admits that the Army's propaganda effort is "so pervasive it convinced the U.S. public to support Vietnam, and could lead us to another Vietnam."

The official response to *The Selling of the Pentagon* was swift and furious. Vice President Spiro Agnew accused CBS of "propagandist manipulation" and one Congressman called the program "the most un-American thing I've ever seen on the tube." A House subcommittee investigated the documentary, but the hearings turned into a tussle over the subpoena powers of the government versus the freedom of the press. None of the program's allegations were challenged, only the network's editing policies. CBS repeated the program, giving rebuttal time to critics, and replied to them in turn. After standing up to Congress and receiving awards for *The Selling of the Pentagon*, CBS President Frank Stanton discontinued *CBS Reports* as a regular series, reducing its appearances to an occasional "special," a retreat reminiscent of the Murrow era.

As the dark side of the Vietnam War surfaced in U.S. media, Joseph Strick won a 1970 Academy Award for his short documentary, *Interviews with My Lai Veterans*. Strick spoke with five young men who were present on March 16, 1968, at the Vietnamese village of My Lai, where U.S. soldiers murdered hundreds of unarmed civilians, one of the most infamous massacres to reach public view. Strick talks with the men individually in casual settings. One is filmed in a moving car, another on the front steps of a house, the others in apartments. They speak quietly, matter-of-factly, without affect, showing no emotion.

What was it like? "It was a free-for-all. We were told to shoot anything you want, any living thing." "Our mission was to search and destroy. This is something we were told to do and we did it." "We encountered no return fire." "I killed 18–20 people, including two children."

"Guys looked like they were having a good time." "The Vietnamese didn't seem to care if they lived or died."

Why kill the little children? "Nobody knew . . . they were there, that's all." "There was no resistance at all." "The babies, when they grow up, they'll be V.C., so you might as well kill them now." The soldiers mutilated the bodies. Some scalped their victims, others cut off ears. "We were about just shooting gooks. . . ." "We did head counts later."

What did you think? "It just didn't faze me." Were there rapes? "Yes." Why? "I don't know." "They were expected to do what they did, but not to get caught doing it." "We didn't think it was such a publicity stunt. It happened a lot of places." "Everybody else was doing it so I figured I'd get some target practice." "I guess you'd say it was senseless." "I didn't figure it was any big deal. It had happened many times before." Can anything be done to prevent this kind of thing? "Get out of Vietnam."

Here are average American boys turned remorseless killers—spiritual heirs to Nazi extermination manager Adolf Eichmann—who were "only following orders," as Eichmann claimed in his trial defense. Trained to obey, they did so without thinking or feeling anything. The five men in this film are clearly still numb, hard, and untouchable, more astonished by the public revulsion to the massacre than by the acts they saw or committed. Yet they look no different than anyone we might pass in the street. They wear no bells or scarlet letters. Strick's chilling interviews contrast sharply with the testimonies of Vietnam veterans at the Winter Soldier hearings of 1972.

Winter Soldier documents the confessions of returning soldiers struggling to regain the humanity they lost in Vietnam. Early in the film, a young John Kerry debriefs other vets and remarks that the war has "hurt a whole generation of Americans and Vietnamese." George Butler included clips from *Winter Soldier* in his Kerry campaign film, *Going Upriver*, as we shall see in Chapter 8.

Winter Soldier is a massive group therapy session for stunned Vietnam veterans, horrified at what they have done and what they have become. They are trying to reclaim their souls by means of this public scourging—recounting atrocities they have witnessed or committed in order to disillusion any of their fellow citizens who might think the war is some kind of noble cause. This film is about the suffering of those who inflict suffering. These men are trying to inoculate their society from the brutality of conquest, to warn their compatriots that whether or not we win the war we lose ourselves by waging it. McCarthyism raised the cold war question, How repressive must we be to combat repression? The Winter Soldier veterans are asking how depraved we must become to fight depravity. Must we become the monster we despise in order to fight that monster? The question is biblical: What does it profit a man—or a nation—to gain the whole world but lose his own soul? America's soul was severely wounded in Vietnam.

Winter Soldier presents another level of horror than *My Lai Veterans*. These young men are more thoughtful, more sensitive, and fully aware of the enormity of their crimes. If such men can lose their humanity, none of us is immune. Simply hearing about the atrocities is numbing. This film, like the veterans themselves, is an act of witness. It is also an admission that the post-Holocaust imperative, "Never again!" has already been violated. As long as wars are waged and race hatred is used to motivate the troops, we cannot hope to evolve beyond the most primitive possibilities of ourselves.

"On my first day in Vietnam," one vet says to the microphone, "I was in truck with a group of soldiers. Some kids waved to us. The truck stopped and the soldiers shot those five or six kids dead. Then the truck started up again. That was my first day there." A helicopter pilot says, "You were instructed to count your prisoners when you unload them, not when you load them, since you might have fewer when you landed than when you took off." One lieutenant awarded himself a bronze star for pushing people out of airplanes during interrogations. There were killing competitions between men, platoons, and battalions. "We used civilians to inflate the body counts. We killed children out of boredom." How do you know they're Viet Cong? "They're dead."

The recitation of horrors goes on and on, with graphic details that vouch for their authenticity. These casual, gratuitous cruelties bespeak a rage and self-loathing turned outward in Vietnam and redirected back home against the government that sanctioned these practices and against each veteran's own unspeakable self. *Winter Soldier* reminds us that wars do not end when the shooting stops. They enter new, no less deadly, phases.

For film historian Richard Barsam, "The best single film about Vietnam is Peter Davis's *Hearts and Minds* (1974)." Hollywood agreed, awarding it the Oscar for best documentary. Davis wanted the film to address three questions: Why did we go to Vietnam? What did we do there? What did that do to us? He uses some stock battle footage and some of the same clips as in *Year of the Pig*. Also like de Antonio, Davis does not use a narrator. But *Hearts and Minds* is far more polished and better produced. Its color photography endows the explosive tropical war with another dimension of beauty and terror and renders the American scenes more accessible.

In the 2001 DVD director's commentary, Davis said he grew up thinking that "anti-communism was like a religion, an ideology in America which strangled thought." Perhaps not surprisingly he found "Murrow a hero." Davis uses clips from propaganda films with Ronald Reagan alerting us to the "international communist conspiracy," J. Edgar Hoover telling Congress there is one communist for every 1800 Americans, and McCarthy warning that the United States will be an island in a communist sea.

These are the false, hysterical claims behind the domino theory and the Vietnam War. The Gulf of Tonkin incident, Lyndon Johnson's pretext for massive escalation in Vietnam "is a lie," says J. William Fulbright. But it was Fulbright who guided the Tonkin Gulf Resolution through Congress, giving Johnson immense war powers in Asia. When Davis asks Vietnam War architect Walt Rostow why the U.S. was needed in Vietnam, Rostow snarls that the "goddamn silly question" is "sophomoric."

Davis interviews U.S. officials and veterans, but also Vietnamese civilians, who relate their personal costs of the war. A veteran pilot in Oklahoma talks about the "incredible excitement" of bombing runs, which he found "thrilling . . . deeply satisfying." Davis cuts to the rubble of a bombed village, where a man says he has lost his livelihood. Two old women talk about the death of their 78-year-old sister from the bombs, the destruction of their home, and their own wounds. The film impresses upon us the immense suffering and the utterly pointless loss of life on both sides of the conflict.

Throughout the film, Davis cuts to the New Jersey homecoming of Lt. George Coker, treated as a hero after seven years as a prisoner of war. He speaks to a class of young school children, who ask why we went to Vietnam. Coker says, "The reason we went there was to win this war." What does Vietnam look like? "If it wasn't for the people, it was very pretty," Coker replies. "They just make a mess out of everything."

After Westmoreland tells Davis that "the Oriental doesn't put the same high price on life as we do," we see the funeral of a Vietnamese soldier, mourned by his wife and son, who are clearly devastated. Davis says he was criticized for this juxtaposition but adds that he tried putting

Westmoreland's statement elsewhere in the film and found that it "detonates" any footage around it. "People told me it was unfair to quote his remark out of context," said Davis. "But tell me, in what context would it be accurate?"

Emile de Antonio said he found *Hearts and Minds* "both heartless and mindless. . . . Its greatest weakness is its snideness." He thought the film condescended to Lt. Coker, the P.O.W. pilot. He also found scenes of two soldiers in a Saigon brothel "just cheap. It's the old network mentality to manipulate people rather than film." Davis used the brothel scene to show the "use and abuse of one human being by another." De Antonio also objected to a sequence about an American high school football game Davis used as an analogy to war, with a minister saying God is on our side and the coach demanding sacrifice. De Antonio thought Davis deceived the coach and players, who "thought they were going to be used in a film about high school football."

De Antonio may have been annoyed by the much greater acclaim and financial success of *Hearts and Minds* compared with his own earlier, pioneering effort. When Davis and producer Bert Schneider accepted the Academy Award, Davis said, "it was ironic to get an award for a war movie while suffering continues in Vietnam." Schneider read a telegram from the Viet Cong delegation at the Paris Peace Talks.

These remarks caused Academy Award presenter Frank Sinatra to announce, "I've been asked by the Academy to make the following statement regarding a statement made by a winner." Clutching a note written by an irate Bob Hope backstage, Sinatra read, "The Academy is saying we are not responsible for any political references made on the program and we are sorry they had to take place this evening." Years later Davis said, "I was surprised that a singer and a comedian would bring themselves to condemn [a telegram] that was essentially an offer of friendship as a long war drew to a close."

Hearts and Minds was re-released to theaters in 2004 during the United States's occupation of Iraq. *The New Yorker*'s Anthony Lane thought "the strategic parallels with Iraq are too creaky to be of much use." He faulted the film for its "minimal effort" to "provide a chronology of the conflict," which he thought might leave younger viewers "repelled and underinformed." For Lane, Davis's cutting from a football game to the Tet offensive prefigures Michael Moore's "notion of the documentary as blunderbuss."

Strategic parallels between Vietnam and Iraq may be "creaky," but the moral and political parallels are abundantly clear. Attacking the conduct of the Vietnam War and the lies used to justify it, documentary filmmakers had only begun to explore the cost of a conflict from which America has not yet recovered. Hiding the truth honors no one. The chronology of Vietnam should be taught in U.S. high schools, perhaps using selected documentary films, to adolescents who will soon be asked by recruiters to consider military careers. For many who never reached full adulthood, those lessons came too late.

Emboldened by the Vietnam credibility gap, documentary filmmakers of the 1960s and 1970s produced narratives contradicting the official stories about the war. Through control of broadcasting licenses and legislation, government pressured the television networks to limit criticism and ban more radical attacks on its versions of events. By the 1980s, as filmmakers explored the lingering physical, emotional, moral, and political damage from Vietnam, the Reagan and Bush administrations limited media appraisals of their policies by stonewalling, restricting access, and scripting photo opportunities and stories of the day. As media became less critical, independent films became an important means of circumventing the veils of fantasy and disinformation.

Chapter 2

REEL HISTORY AND THE POLITICS OF DECEPTION

Democracy is a great conversation, a community defined by the scope and substance of its discourse.

—James David Barber

On January 23, 1982, *CBS Reports* aired a 90-minute documentary, *The Uncounted Enemy: A Vietnam Deception*, alleging "conspiracy at the highest levels of American military intelligence." In his clipped, prosecutorial style, Mike Wallace promised new, damning information about the ended, but still raw, Vietnam War, "the only war America has ever lost." In 1967, leading up to the pivotal Tet offensive, General William C. Westmoreland ordered his military intelligence officers "to suppress and alter critical intelligence on the enemy," to mislead the American people, the congress, and the president about the size and strength of the enemy forces in Vietnam.

In "a war in which statistics reigned supreme," such an underestimate gave the false impression that the United States was "winning the war of attrition" in Vietnam, when in fact we were losing it. Wallace confronted Westmoreland on the broadcast. The former Vietnam commander looked trapped. He kept licking his lips. President Johnson "wanted bad news—like a hole in the head," he admitted. Several other former intelligence officers agreed that falsification of the facts was "dishonorable" and "shoddy," but said they manipulated enemy troop estimates because they were ordered to do so for "political" reasons. A *New York Times* editorial the next day said the CBS program "showed that Lyndon Johnson was victimized by mendacious intelligence." "More than a matter of history," the show was a cautionary tale for the current Reagan administration, mired in its own military misadventures in Central America.

Shades of Ed Murrow, or so it seemed. CBS investigative reporters had unearthed and explained a complex scandal that changed our understanding of Vietnam. A hard-hitting television documentary could still make a difference. No wonder U.S. forces were unprepared for Tet. Our troops were facing a much larger enemy than we thought. Were these calculated lies—by our own military commanders—the reason we lost the war? General Westmoreland held a press conference after the program to deny the CBS charges. He produced military intelligence officers, including several CBS had declined to interview, to back him up. Media coverage of the briefing was skeptical.

Four months later, a *TV Guide* article, "Anatomy of a Smear," attacked the documentary not for its arguments, but for its breaches of journalistic integrity. *TV Guide* charged that the CBS allegations were old news, based on a 1975 *Harper's* article by a former CIA official, Sam Adams. Without saying so, CBS had paid Adams $25,000 and rehearsed his on-camera interview, but had not corroborated his evidence. After the broadcast, Adams himself disavowed the program's thesis, that Westmoreland had conspired to suppress the true size of the enemy. CBS had ignored crucial witnesses, coached others, spliced interview tapes to match certain answers to different questions, and deleted phrases or lifted them out of context to help support the show's thesis.

The *TV Guide* accusations prompted CBS News to initiate its own internal investigation of *The Uncounted Enemy*, which largely concurred with *TV Guide*'s analysis. In September 1982, Westmoreland filed a libel suit against CBS, asking $120 million in compensatory and punitive damages. Westmoreland said, "The issue here is not money, not vengeance . . . not whether the war in Vietnam was right or wrong. . . . The only question is whether CBS had an obligation to be accurate in is facts before it attempted to destroy a man's character, the work of his lifetime."

In April 1983, 15 months after the original program, media critic Hodding Carter devoted his PBS program, *Inside Story*, to an analysis of *The Uncounted Enemy*, a rare critique of TV by TV. Carter interviewed officials CBS had never consulted, several others CBS had interviewed but did not include in the program, and some who objected to how CBS had presented them. Carter concluded that "CBS is entitled to its opinion, but we are entitled to a more balanced presentation. Even if you are sure of guilt, there is a vast difference between a fair trail and a lynching. It's a distinction that was badly blurred when CBS made *The Uncounted Enemy: A Vietnam Deception*."

Most media accounts of the *Westmoreland v. CBS* trial sympathized with the network producers. But Renata Adler, covering the case for *The New Yorker*, found the program's thesis "preposterous. . . . What motive would a general have to *underestimate* to his commanders the size and strength of the enemy when his every interest and inclination would fall more naturally on the other side; to overestimate, in order to make whatever victories there were heroic and whatever defeats explicable and to sustain a demand for more troops of his own?" Only the trial process—by deposing witnesses and making tapes and documents public—revealed the full extent of the biased, deceptive production practices CBS employed to create this dishonest program.

Westmoreland withdrew his suit in February 1985 in the middle of the legal proceedings, leading many in the media to conclude that CBS had won the case. But CBS suffered from the public exposure of its highly dubious documentary production methods, many of which violated the network's own standards of journalistic practice. The program's producer, George Crile, was suspended and ultimately fired. More significantly, the expense and the notoriety of the Westmoreland trial helped diminish further the network's dwindling appetite for producing and showing public affairs documentaries. Then the FCC administered the coup de grâce.

"In 1984, the Federal Communications Commission's guidelines on programming, which had been outlined in 1960, were formally abandoned. The public service element in American commercial broadcasting was significantly diluted. Gone was any requirement for public affairs programming and, within a few years, the networks' documentary departments were consigned to history." The networks' retreat from Edward R. Murrow and *See It Now* was complete. PBS was left to pick up the slack.

Originally intended as an alternative to commercial television, the Public Broadcasting System was meant to provide cultural enrichment and public education that included presenting documentaries about public issues from diverse points of view. Government funding was supposed to free PBS from market pressures and allow the network greater freedom of expression for a range of voices, to foster controversy and encourage public debate. But that ideal proved difficult to implement.

President Lyndon Johnson signed the Public Broadcasting Act into law two months before leaving office, in 1967. An indeterminate percentage of the funding for PBS was to come from the federal government. In 1969, while PBS financing was still being set up, New York's educational station, NET (later WNET), decided to broadcast "a series of documentaries critical of the U.S. role in Vietnam, beginning with 'Inside North Vietnam.'" Thirty-three congressmen demanded the show's cancellation. But NET continued to broadcast programs critical of U.S. foreign policy as President Richard Nixon secretly invaded Laos and Cambodia in 1970.

In 1972, Nixon vetoed the federal appropriation for public broadcasting. A more modest funding bill eventually passed, but Nixon succeeded in decentralizing PBS, taking power away from New York and Washington and giving it to local stations that "tended to be more conservative." Nixon White House aide Patrick Buchanan told the audience of ABC's *Dick Cavett Show* in 1973 that some PBS programs—such as *Bill Moyers' Journal* and *Washington Week in Review*—were "unbalanced against us." In 1981, the Reagan administration tried to strip public broadcasting of all public money. And in 1994, House Speaker Newt Gingrich joined Christian conservatives who wanted to abolish the Corporation for Public Broadcasting.

In her book *Public Television: Politics and the Battle over Documentary Film*, B. J. Bullert recounts the difficulties independent documentary filmmakers experienced in the 1980s and 1990s trying to get PBS to show any material considered "controversial." For example, *Dark Circle*, a documentary critical of nuclear safety, won film festival prizes and laudatory reviews in national media in 1982. But PBS judged the movie too biased against the nuclear industry. Not until 1989—after it had already aired on TBS and Bravo, and problems had surfaced at the Rocky Flats nuclear plant that vindicated the filmmakers' concerns—did PBS finally broadcast *Dark Circle*.

Afraid of conservative reaction, PBS programmers often block sensitive subjects or unusual treatments from broadcast to avoid political and financial reprisals. PBS did show several exceptional documentaries, such as the 13-part series *Vietnam* (1983) and Henry Hampton's magisterial civil rights series, *Eyes on the Prize* (1987). But, like the elegiac Ken Burns epic *The Civil War* (1990), these films were historical when they aired, not views of current events. Bullert details the tortuous process documentaries must endure to achieve broadcast on PBS programs such as *Frontline* or *P.O.V.* She sees *Frontline*, "the only long-format current affairs documentary series on American national television," excluding cable, as the heir to former network programs such as *CBS Reports*.

Others are not as effusive about the series. As filmmaker Barbara Trent opines, "*Frontline* appears to be controversial, but it often produces no more than an inoffensive whitewash of an issue, thereby posing no threat to PBS's corporate sponsors or the U.S. government, its primary sponsor." These circumscribed, self-censored versions of investigative journalism define the limits of debate and eliminate more powerful explorations of a topic from the video marketplace. The PBS imprimatur is prestigious and authoritative in the minds of most American liberals. When PBS refuses to air a documentary, that film may be relegated to the fringes of the conspiracy culture. Television can exalt or kill an independent film.

PBS continues to experience financial problems and political pressures, which limit the range of its documentary options. Republicans decry PBS as "elitist and liberal," while liberal critics say the network has "become too much like 'the culture of the Beltway.'" In February 2005, PBS chairman Alberto Ibargüen described the network's dilemma in a "world of increased cable competition, less and less government funding, and cutbacks in corporate image advertising. . . . The risk is, the tighter your budgets get, the less you can afford to fail. If you can't afford to fail, you can't afford to take risks."

While some independent documentaries do show up on HBO, Bravo, Sundance, or the Independent Film channel, most cable movies are fictional features. Sheila Nevins, head of documentary programming for HBO, says, "The truth is that documentaries are not the bread and butter of HBO. They are more like the dessert or appetizer but . . . not the main course." The sad fact is that television, the dominant medium of our culture, has largely failed to provide a platform for critical, independent, or minority voices, greatly diminishing the scope and substance of our democratic discourse.

Entrenched corporate and government powers resist an openness that may challenge their preeminence. They use their political and financial clout to restrict the content of American television. Murrow's 1958 admonition that television should be enlisted in the "great and perhaps decisive battle to be fought against ignorance, intolerance, and indifference" seems wildly idealistic today, as television apparently exists to trumpet majoritarian values, kill time, and hawk material wares. It's not a marketplace of ideas, just a marketplace. New technologies have made television more seductive, but not more substantive.

The increasingly formulaic, politically limited content of television from the 1980s to the present emphasizes the increasing importance of independent documentary film production. Despite the financial and cultural odds, American filmmakers in recent decades have created some of the most innovative, thoughtful, and courageous nonfiction films ever made. Their outsider status, in terms of television norms, allows them to develop uncompromising visions and voices. Cheaper, more portable, more sophisticated equipment gives filmmakers unprecedented access to venues well off the physical and political maps of mainstream media, opening up more of the real world to our gaze.

BRINGING THE WAR HOME

The United States withdrew from Vietnam in 1975. Millions of American and Vietnamese lives had been destroyed or disrupted. A hellish, man-made tsunami, the war caused waves of misery to engulf many who were far from the carnage in space and time. American filmmakers shifted from battle coverage to more complex, but no less dramatic, stories of the war's great personal and social consequences. Perhaps the most heart-rending film about the war is *Dear America: Letters Home from Vietnam* (1988). Told entirely in the words of the young men who fought, the film depicts America's loss of innocence one person at a time, using photos and home movies of the letter writers. The cost of that war to our country has never been so graphically portrayed.

There are no reenactments in the film, but the director, Bill Couturiè, sometimes shows us photos or clips of the young men whose letters we are hearing, like 19-year-old Private Raymond Griffiths, who wrote his girl-friend, "I doubt if I'll come out of this war alive. In my original squad I'm the only one left unharmed. . . . It seems every day another young guy 18 and 19 years old like myself is killed in action. . . . All of us are scared 'cause we know a lot of us won't make it." Griffiths was killed on July 4, 1966.

Couturiè began working with a 1986 anthology of letters home from U.S. soldiers in Vietnam, whose title HBO used for its program. "Then he [viewed] the entire archive of TV news footage shot by NBC-TV from 1967 to 1969—2 million feet of film, totaling 926 hours. He also gained access to footage from the Defense Department, including previously classified film." For his soundtrack, Couturiè uses pop music of the period, including the Beach Boys and Alice Cooper, emphasizing the youth of the U.S. troops. But, as one soldier informs his parents, "You'd be amazed at how much a man can age on one patrol." The letters are read as voiceovers by well-known actors, but the distraction of trying to identify the readers soon gives way to hearing what they say.

One soldier writes to his father about his dead friend: "He was a good man. . . . He could not understand this conflict that killed him. . . . This war is all wrong, Dad." The elegiac, prematurely weary tone of these letters bears a striking resemblance to the letters soldiers sent from the front as quoted in the Ken Burns series *The Civil War*. Some things don't change. Young men are sent to fight and die in wars whose purpose they may not comprehend. One man reports home from Vietnam that "morale is high, despite the fact that most men here believe the war is being run incorrectly . . . the staggering fact is that most men don't think we're going to win."

The epilog to the film, as to the book, is a letter written by the mother of a 21-year-old soldier killed in Vietnam. We see the Vietnam Memorial and hear Bruce Springsteen's "Born in the USA." "Dear Bill, today is February 13, 1984. I came to this black wall again to see and touch your name, and as I do, I stop to wonder if anyone ever stops to realize that next to your name, on this black wall, is your mother's heart. A heart broken 15 years ago today, when you lost your life in Vietnam.

"They tell me the letters I write to you and leave here at this memorial are waking others up to the fact that there is still much pain left, after all these years, from the Vietnam War. But this I know. I would rather to have had you for 21 years, and all the pain that goes with losing you, than never to have had you at all. Mom."

Navy Lieutenant Richard Strandberg wrote to his wife, "Maybe the war will end soon. Wishful thinking? Yes. The Vietnam War will never end."

Director Bill Couturiè, who won an Emmy for *Dear America*, was much faster off the mark with his Iraq version. Instead of waiting until thirteen years after the war ended, Couturiè's *Last Letters Home: Voices of American Troops from the Battlefields of Iraq*, premiered on HBO in November of 2004, nineteen months after the U.S. invasion, in the midst of the violent occupation of Iraq. If the U.S. government failed to learn important lessons from the earlier war, the filmmaker learned several.

Last Letters spends an hour on the correspondence of ten U.S. servicemen and servicewomen in Iraq, all of whom were killed. Instead of using actors, Couturiè has the families of the dead soldiers read the letters and describe "the moment when they learned when a loved one would never come home." Broadcast just after a bitter presidential election that focused more on Vietnam than on Iraq, *Last Letters Home* was produced by HBO and the *New York Times*, which gave it a long review. The *Times* reviewer thought some might see the film as "inherently political" or even "exploitative—reality TV at its most maudlin." But for her, *Last Letters* "feels like someone's heart-breaking home movie. . . . Rarely has grief been presented so purely."

Some of the most dreaded letters military families receive are sent by the Department of Defense and begin with the words, "We regret to inform." Barbara Sonneborn's *Regret to Inform* (1998) opens with her words: "On my 24th birthday I got the news that my husband, Jeff, had been killed in Vietnam." Twenty years later, in 1988, Sonneborn decided she "had to go to Vietnam" to get closure on Jeff's death. She only knew one other widow of a Vietnam veteran. Support groups existed for veterans but not for their widows, so Sonneborn formed a production team and sent out several thousand letters, soliciting stories from women whose husbands were killed in Vietnam. Sonneborn and her staff spoke to more than 200 widows during preproduction.

In 1992, Sonneborn traveled to Vietnam. *Regret to Inform* chronicles her journey to Que Son, where her husband was killed. Her translator was a Vietnamese woman whose husband had died fighting for South Vietnam. They met and interviewed many Vietnamese women, who fought and/or lost family members on both sides. Sonneborn interjects interviews with American widows into her journey through the lush, tropical Vietnamese landscape, scene of so much violence and heartbreak. The war accomplished nothing but horror and loss, and the waste of lives—including three million Vietnamese.

"He wanted to be patriotic. He wanted to help," says the widow of a Native American soldier. "But once he saw all the killing . . . the Vietnamese looking just like him, the same skin color, the same height. That really made him think, what is he doing here?" Another widow shrugs, trying to cope: "Is your husband a hero or a murderer?" One woman received a letter from her husband after she had been notified of his death. "And I thought maybe, well, he's not dead! Oh, they made a mistake and this is proof and then I read the date on it and I realized. . . ."

The suffering of the Vietnamese women Sonneborn meets is profound. They were caught up directly in the barbarities of war. They endured the deaths and sufferings of family members and sometimes torture inflicted on them by U.S. or South Vietnamese troops. "The cruelty that we experienced was longer than a river, higher than a mountain, deeper than an ocean," says one woman, who was hung upside down while her tormentors shot electricity through her fingers and nipples. And still, thanks to the U.S. spraying of Agent Orange, the war continues: "We have many health problems. I have terrible arthritis and strange skin problems. Many people here have died young of cancer—sick suddenly, then dead. We have lots of deformed babies. Lots."

After Sonneborn's film won several festival awards in 1999, and received an Academy Award nomination, it was broadcast on the PBS series *P.O.V.* in 2000. Her film is available to schools with a teaching guide, to show students that our real enemy is war itself. She wants her healing journey to inoculate the future against the past. Her film is a candle in the darkness.

Another American woman who went to Vietnam hoping to make peace with her past ended up compounding her emotional confusion, not resolving it. Gail Dolgin's and Vicente Franco's *Daughter from Danang* (2002) chronicles the journey of Heidi, a.k.a. Mai Thi Hiep, to meet her birth mother. Born in Danang in 1968 to a Vietnamese woman and an American serviceman, Heidi was flown at age seven to the United States in Operation Babylift, which removed mixed-race children from Vietnam, supposedly for their own safety. Raised by an emotionally distant single mother in Pulaski, Tennessee, home of the original Ku Klux Klan, Heidi managed to "pass" racially among her peers, partly by adopting white southern values. She married a career military man.

Her return to Vietnam after 22 years provokes intense, conflicting emotions for Heidi, her birth mother, and her Vietnamese family. The reunion is joyful, painful, and complex. We soon learn that Heidi was no love child. Her mother's husband went off to fight against the Americans, leaving Heidi's mother without resources, and she did what she had to do to survive. Her husband is back with her now, and Heidi meets several half-brothers and half-sisters. At first intoxicated with emotion, Heidi is quickly appalled by the squalor she confronts and her mother's naked request for financial help. Expecting a warm embrace, Heidi recoils from the harsh reality of needs that challenge her own needs and from her harsh desire to get away as soon as possible. Dolgin and Franco do not flinch from the cultural and emotional complications of this story, rendered in the painful, intimate encounters of individuals whose lives incarnate unexpected variations of the war's ongoing damage.

Several Vietnam films measure the war in terms of its political effects on the United States. *The War at Home* (1979) shows how the war transformed campus life at the University of Wisconsin in the 1960s and 1970s. It's a fascinating account of a university, and the larger community, becoming politicized as growing resistance to the war provokes increasingly intemperate official reaction. In 1963, "an unprecedented boom year," Madison, Wisconsin, was "voted the best place to live in America," we are told, as a marching band plays the familiar football anthem, "On, Wisconsin."

But changes were already in the air. Civil rights issues had begun to engage Blacks and White campus liberals. The first tiny, barely noticed, anti–Vietnam War protest took place in October 1963. Lyndon Johnson won the presidency in 1964 promising not to widen the war in Asia, a promise he soon broke. In 1965, activists held hearings on Vietnam in Madison because "none were being held in Washington." The following spring, students and professors held a "teach-in" at the administration building. Ted Kennedy, opposed to unilateral U.S. withdrawal from Vietnam, found himself hooted down by antiwar protesters on a campus he had considered friendly territory.

Events accelerated. In 1967, Betty Boardman sailed to North Vietnam with a group of Quakers and ten thousand dollars' worth of medical supplies. Campus recruiters for Dow Chemical Company, producers of napalm, were met with protests large enough for the campus police to call for help. City police waded into the student crowd swinging clubs and tossing tear gas. In the words of Paul Soglin, a student who later became mayor of Madison, "A lot of politicization took place in those fifteen to twenty minutes." Officials claimed that "the protestors were being led by professionals from outside the city and the police were fighting for their lives."

By 1968, the student movement spread to the larger community, which supported Minnesota Senator Eugene McCarthy's run for president on an antiwar platform. During the violent 1968 Democratic National Convention in Chicago, the Wisconsin delegation proposed adjourning for two weeks to relocate the convention. Nixon promised not to "invade North Vietnam or other countries in the area." In 1969, the National Guard was called to the university during the Black student strike. A hippie block party, busted by the police, turned into a riot. And the antiwar protest was becoming ever more militant. We see a huge banner on campus: "To be against the war and to do nothing is indefensible."

Protest lit up the country, reaching a fever pitch. At the November 15 National Moratorium in Washington, a veteran told the crowd that William Calley and the My Lai atrocities "are no aberrations." Over the Christmas holidays, somebody bombed the ROTC building on the Wisconsin campus. When Nixon's invasion of Cambodia came to light in the spring of 1970, Wisconsin joined the hundreds of universities that shut down. On May 4, four students at Kent State were shot dead by the Ohio National Guard. Huge demonstrations on the Madison campus turned into ten days of chaos. On May 15, two more students were killed at Jackson State in Mississippi. Then a bomb blew up the Army Math Research Center at Wisconsin, killing a graduate student. A couple of local boys were indicted for the crime.

The idea of filmmakers Glenn Silber and Barry Alexander Brown to use Madison as a microcosm of America during the Vietnam War was shrewd. Though more radical than many American college towns, especially in the heartland, Madison was not on the leading edge of antiwar protest like Columbia or Berkeley. Escalation of the war caused a protest movement to mushroom, provoking a severe police reaction. Excesses were everywhere: in the prosecution of the war, the reaction against it, and the effort to quell the protest. After the peace accords were signed in 1973, the protest movement faded.

Twenty years after the Kent State shootings, filmmaker Jim Klein visited that Ohio campus to look for echoes of the massacre and assess the social consciousness of the current students. Kent State is "an average Midwestern university" of 23,000 students. Only that violent historical event, the killing of four students by the National Guard, sets the school apart. A student tour guide tells a group visiting the campus, "May 4, 1970, is something we do remember, but we're trying to move on." Narrating his film, *Letter to the Next Generation* (1990), Klein tells us "I was 21" when it happened, "it hit me hard." Only one of the four murdered students was an antiwar protestor. One was in ROTC and the other two were simply in the wrong place at the wrong time.

Students Klein approaches to discuss "the event" are sick of hearing about it. "It's overdone," they tell him. Some say they doubt whether the students who got shot were really "innocent." Klein tells us, because of his age, that he identifies more with the professors than the students now. He does not tell us that, in fact, he *is* a professor. Tom Loft, a Kent State professor since 1967, tells Klein "students aren't asking many questions these days." Loft says he's made himself "comfortable within a rotten system." Klein finds students interested in making money, drinking, and other trivial pursuits. Klein says to a student, "I hear a bad rap that you're materialistic. You don't care about issues." "That's true," replies the student, "but it's not bad." "Why did you choose Kent State for school?" Klein asks. "It's got a lower drinking age than where I'm from."

Klein's superficial survey of social values seems facile. He acknowledges that college kids have always liked to party, even during the 1960s and 1970s. NAACP leader Julian Bond's campus speech alienates some students who find him too liberal. Klein has already shown us that racism remains a large—largely unacknowledged—campus problem. "Students aren't apathetic," one of them tells Klein, "they're just not concerned with the same things." What about social change? "It amounted to nothing, so we'd be walking in the footsteps of failure." Klein wonders, "Were we to blame because we raised expectations and then sold out?"

The corporate values Wisconsin students demonstrated against in 1968 are attractive to Kent State students in 1990. Higher college costs have raised the stakes for kids who want to succeed financially. They want good grades in order to get good jobs. They have little curiosity about life beyond their own career track. They are "on the American conveyor belt," as Klein says. As he quizzes several students about their aspirations, one says, "I never really thought about helping my fellow man."

Klein's film begins to approach more fundamental generational differences when he touches on the students' use of TV. Few read books. Many watch TV in every spare moment. These young adults have spent more time with television than in school. Every student Klein asks knows the theme song to *The Brady Bunch* by heart. Some of the most spirited moments in this film are when the kids sing that song alone or in groups. The "Brady Bunch" theme song is as much a touchstone for this generation as the Kent State shootings were for Klein's. "My sympathies were with the people in the streets," Klein tells us of his student days. But the current crop of students doesn't know about the streets. They aren't really citizens of the world. They grew up in TV-land.

They suffer from a kind of corporate provincialism, having consumed only carefully preselected images their whole lives. They are isolated, not liberated, by media. They feel a kind of agoraphobia about "the rest of the world" beyond their own country. They are living proof that Murrow's fears were no exaggeration. Media have cut them off, not clued them in.

Klein wants to send a letter, not to the college students he interviews, but to the *next* generation, today's small children, whom he might still be able to reach, perhaps.

The Trials of Henry Kissinger (2002) belongs among films relevant to Vietnam. Based on a book by Christopher Hitchens that indicts Kissinger as a war criminal, the movie strengthens the case that Kissinger richly merits legal prosecution. Using stock footage and previously classified, heavily redacted documents obtained through the Freedom of Information Act, *Trials* shows Kissinger as the principal architect of the secret bombing of Cambodia in 1970, the removal of the democratically elected president of Chile in 1973, and the approval of genocide in East Timor in 1975. Critics charge the film—and the book—with a one-sided view, with only token defense of Kissinger from the likes of former Kissinger errand boy Alexander Haig. But the point of the movie is to challenge a man who wielded immense power for many years with abusing that power, often for his own aggrandizement. In the DVD commentary, filmmakers Eugene Jarecki and Alex Gibney say they had to finance their film outside the United States. Kissinger's influence—which he sells at high rates—remains formidable.

To attain his positions of power, Kissinger affixed himself to powerful patrons, ditching them for their rivals when it furthered his own cause. He jumped from the staff of Republican presidential hopeful Nelson Rockefeller to the peace delegation of President Lyndon Johnson. While at the Paris peace talks with Vietnam in 1968, Kissinger fed inside information to the Nixon campaign. He planned to have a high position in the next U.S. administration, whoever won. When Kissinger "warned" Nixon that a peace agreement was near, Nixon pressured South Vietnamese President Thieu not to sign it, promising better terms once he became president. Thieu scuttled the agreement, Nixon was elected, Kissinger became national security advisor and secretary of state, and the Vietnam War continued for seven more years. To call Kissinger Machiavellian is to degrade Machiavelli.

When Kissinger finally crafted a peace accord with North Vietnam, the terms were almost identical to those offered by Johnson in 1968. As Hitchens points out in the film, almost half the names on the Vietnam Memorial died on dates after January 1969. Former Kissinger colleague Roger Morris, who resigned over Cambodia, found the awarding of the 1973 Nobel Peace Prize to Kissinger appalling. "He was a war maker, not a peace maker," says Morris. North Vietnamese negotiator Le Duc Tho, jointly awarded the prize, refused it on the sensible grounds that there was no peace in Vietnam. Fighting continued there until 1975. Though Nixon and most of his staff succumbed to Watergate, Kissinger himself survived into the Ford administration, when he blessed Suharto's genocide in East Timor, executed with American weapons.

In 1999, Kissinger said, "We couldn't do anything" to stop Indonesia. But David Newsom, a diplomat who attended the meeting with Kissinger and Suharto, tells the filmmakers he heard Kissinger give the invasion his okay. The film makes a strong case that a public trial would reveal the truth about several shameful, highly lethal episodes and might serve to warn others in high positions of public trust that they could be held accountable for their abuses. Of course, it is more likely that this film—and the Hitchens book it is based on—is the only trial Henry Kissinger will ever have to endure.

REFRAMING HISTORY

Independent filmmakers exposed government lies about Vietnam and explored some of the war's unforeseen social and psychic consequences. Armed with doubt and distrust engendered by official duplicity and illegal acts of top U.S. officials, American filmmakers in the 1970s, 1980s, and 1990s revisited other relatively recent events with their newly acquired skepticism. Liberated from blind acceptance of historical "truth" by their own antiestablishment rebellion, filmmakers endeavored to cast a new light on groups and events condemned or marginalized by official America. The Nixon administration and the FBI portrayed the war protestors as "communist-inspired radicals" to discourage support for their cause within the "silent majority." They spied on dissidents, harassed them, and put some of them on trial. Post–Vietnam era filmmakers wondered what the U.S. government had done to others who had dared to challenge mainstream orthodoxy.

Jim Klein and Julia Reichert found three women to guide them through the 1930s labor movement in *Union Maids* (1976). That same year, Barbara Kopple released her Academy Award–winning look at a contemporary labor dispute, *Harlan County, USA,* which we'll look at more closely in Chapter 4. Labor unions had received scant media treatment before the 1970s, except to be condemned for their violence and corruption. Corporate sponsors of television programs had little interest in unionism—their nemesis—as a popular subject.

With period music and archival footage, *Union Maids* plunges us into the streets and the factories as we hear the personal stories of Stella, Kate, and Sylvia, struggling for survival and dignity in Depression Chicago. Tough, smart, militant, and courageous, the women explain the class warfare that pitted police against workers. The women are all contented souls, knowing their cause was just. Still feisty, they think unions now are too conservative. White-collar workers ought to organize and demand a long list of reforms.

Reichert and Klein went further in 1983 with *Seeing Red*, stories of present and former members of the communist party. "From the 1930s to the 1950s, more than one million Americans passed through the communist party," Reichert tells us. She appears on camera as an active interviewer, inviting these perennial outsiders into the frame with her, and into the "normal" world of viewers, for whom the word *communist* may still set off a screaming red alert. As Reichert's interviews proceed, we see these former mill workers, longshoremen, and teachers not as foaming crazies but as gentle, thoughtful individuals, trying to gauge their responsibilities to society and to history.

One unrepentant party member, Sylvia Woods, like most of the other working-class party members, is full of idealism and a sense of righteous opposition to the inequities facing women, minorities, and the poor. Communists stood up and marched against inequality and injustice in the 1920s and 1930s, despite violent police suppression of their activities. The party earned the admiration of American workers, who believed in their goal of a classless society, devoid of racism and sexism, and the glorious experiment of the Soviet Union. The spunky, petite Dorothy Healy, who joined the party at age fourteen and led a strike of cotton pickers in southern California in 1937, says, "There was no we and they, only 'us.'" Her young eyes twinkle in her old face as she tells Reichert: "You think *you* had a counterculture. But *we* had a counterculture." When *Seeing Red* came out, Healy still hosted a program of "Marxist commentary" on a San Francisco radio station.

"We were part of the heart of humanity in our youth," says one former party member. But they all became Cold War casualties. The United States outlawed the Communist Party in 1954. Leftist unions were crushed. We see a street demonstration with a huge placard: "The only

good communist is a dead communist." In 1956, Khrushchev acknowledged the crimes of Joseph Stalin, the mass purges and murders. Many
American party members were disillusioned. Reichert asks, "How could
so many people who questioned capitalism be so uncritical of Stalin and
Soviet oppression?"

The old leftist radicals wanted to believe that somewhere things were
just, and did so, until the evidence became too overwhelming to deny.
Power and paranoia wrecked the Soviet experiment. "Don't call me a
former communist, call me a former party member," said one old radical,
who wants it known he kept his principles intact. Folk singer Pete Seeger,
who defied Congress and endured blacklisting says, wistfully, "It's better
to have struggled and lost than never to have struggled at all." African
American college professor Howard "Stretch" Johnson, with the last,
defiant word, quotes Langston Hughes: "America has never been America
to me." *Seeing Red* shows us that most American communists, far from
threatening the United States, really just wanted the country to live up to
its stated founding principles, of liberty and justice for all.

In 1936, some 3200 American leftist idealists formed the Abraham
Lincoln Brigade to fight fascist aggression in Spain. Narrated by Studs
Terkel, *The Good Fight* (1984, directed by Mary Dore, Noel Buckner, and
Sam Sills) documents the stories of the volunteers, using interviews with
surviving veterans and seldom-seen period footage. After King Alfonso
abdicated the Spanish throne in 1931, Spain declared itself a Republic and
held national elections. But when the Spanish people voted in an antifascist
Popular Front government, the army, led by General Francisco Franco on
behalf of the oligarchs, rose against it.

Eager to test their weapons and their troops, Hitler and Mussolini sent
arms and 100,000 soldiers to help Franco subdue his own people. Spain
appealed for help, but Europe and America would not intervene. For the
first time in its history, the United States refused to sell arms to a democratically elected government. Some forty thousand volunteers from 52
countries came to fight for the Spanish Republic. The Abraham Lincoln
Brigade was a gallant bunch of politically conscious civilians, untrained
and unprepared, lacking food and weapons or anything much besides
heart. More than 70 % of them lost their lives, and the survivors never got
over the fall of free Spain.

The Good Fight illuminates an episode largely forgotten in American
history. Most valuably, it introduces us to a remarkable breed of American,

men and women willing to fight and die for the idea of freedom, like Milt Wolff, Ruth Davidow, Bill Bailey, Salaria Kea O'Reilly, and Ed Balchowsky, who lost an arm in Spain but can still bang out the songs on his piano that roused the volunteer army to its cause. Their moral clarity burns brightly in them, despite their many years. They're the kind of people I'm proud to call my countrymen and -women. Just knowing they exist is a comfort.

Abraham Lincoln Brigade alumnus Abe Osheroff tells Ivy Meeropol that "City College in the 1930s makes Berkeley in the 1960s look pale." Meeropol is interviewing old leftist radicals, trying to find out the truth about her grandparents in her film *Heir to an Execution* (2004). Her grandparents, Ethel and Julius Rosenberg, were executed in 1953 for giving atomic secrets to the Soviets. Miriam Moskowitz, an inmate with Ethel in a house of detention, tells Meeropol,"You had to be dead from the neck up *not* to be radical" in the 1930s, with mass unemployment and hunger and evictions.

How radical were Julius and Ethel Rosenberg? Meeropol talks with their co-defendant, Morton Sobell, still looking stunned after his nineteen years in prison. She drives past the house of her uncle, David Greenglass, Ethel's brother, who admitted to Bob Simon on *60 Minutes* that he had lied about his sister to save himself. He spent ten years in prison. "I don't care how I'm remembered," he says. Meeropol can't bear to confront Greenglass, whom she thinks of as "evil incarnate." Her main informant is her father, Michael, the older of the Rosenbergs' two sons. We see archival footage of him at 8 and his brother, Robert, 6, visiting their parents at Sing Sing prison, which they did for two years. These clips are heartbreaking, as are Ethel's death row letters to her boys.

Meeropol grew up believing her grandparents were innocent. But FBI files released in 1995 suggest a certain ambiguity. Abe Osheroff says, of Julius: "What he was convicted for he couldn't have done. But he *was* guilty of illegal activities." The dapper 103-year-old Harry Steingart tells Meeropol his name was one of twenty-five on a list the FBI showed the Rosenbergs on death row. The FBI told the couple if they testified against anyone on the list their sentences would be commuted. But the Rosenbergs refused. "They saved my life," the old man says, tears in his eyes. The United States apparently arrested Ethel to pressure Julius to confess his crimes, or to get Ethel to testify against him. But neither broke and both were electrocuted, victims of cold war hysteria. "What did they die for?" Meeropol wonders. "What do I tell *my* kids?"

Reconsidering the legacy of leftist politics, post–Vietnam era American documentary filmmakers also looked back at government propaganda pertaining to the weapon that dominated cold war thinking and for which the Rosenbergs were killed—the Bomb. *The Day after Trinity* (1980) profiles Manhattan Project director J. Robert Oppenheimer, the self-styled "philosopher-king" who supervised the creation of the atomic bomb. Oppenheimer was given unlimited funding and access to the best physicists and mathematicians in the country, in order to provide America with the ultimate weapon, a true Faustian bargain, as physicist Freeman Dyson recognizes.

The Manhattan Project scientists wanted to save the world from the Nazis, but when Germany surrendered, they kept right on building the bomb. The phrase *shock and awe* fails to convey the reaction of all who saw the first atomic detonation at New Mexico's Trinity site. Oppenheimer and other scientists said they thought such a weapon should never be used. So why—less than a month after the Trinity test—was the bomb dropped on human beings in Hiroshima? "Because the bureaucratic apparatus existed to do it," in Freeman Dyson's words, and "nobody had the courage to say no." That "bureaucratic apparatus" has continued to drive American policy in Vietnam, in Central America, and up to the present moment in Afghanistan and Iraq. The spread of "freedom" is how politicians justify their aggressive actions to the American people, who are only too happy to accept that flimsy rhetorical cover as absolution for murder.

Shortly before his death in 1967, Oppenheimer was asked about imposing strict controls on nuclear weapons. "It's twenty years too late," he says. "It should have been done the day after Trinity." Oppenheimer was a genuine genius. But it didn't take one to know that the atomic genie, once released, could never be returned to the lamp. He knew that the time to have stopped the Bomb was *before* Trinity. But as Freeman Dyson says in the film, Oppenheimer succumbed to the "technical arrogance that overcomes people when they see what they can do with their minds." It's a pity Oppenheimer didn't live long enough to sit down with Errol Morris, as did Robert McNamara. Our last view of him, in the film, shows him staring like a deer caught in the headlights of history, quoting the *Bhagavad Gita*: "Now I am become Death, the destroyer of worlds."

The Trinity test footage opens *The Atomic Café* (1982), a witty compilation of Bomb-related newsreels and government propaganda film clips, chock full of misinformation. Kevin Rafferty, Pierce Rafferty, and Jayne

Loader assembled a nostalgic pastiche of mistaken notions and blatant falsehoods about the atomic bomb, comic and surreal. After announcing that the bomb was dropped on the Japanese, President Harry Truman invokes God's help: "We pray that He may guide us to use it in His ways and for His purposes." What the divine use of an atomic bomb might be is truly mysterious. Newsreel announcer Ed Herlihy asks rhetorically, "Is the atom bomb the answer to the Chinese hordes?" Two congressmen— including Lloyd Bentsen—tell us they believe it is.

We hear country songs about the Bomb, see snatches of an Army training film, and glimpse those icons of paranoia, Whittaker Chambers and Richard Nixon. The Rosenbergs flash past. Reporter Bob Considine describes Ethel's execution in detail. Discussing the hydrogen bomb, President Dwight Eisenhower reminds us that "we have advanced scientifically far more than emotionally or intellectually, hence our concern." Watching this film, we may laugh as the children we once were "duck and cover" in case of nuclear attack, knowing they all would have been vaporized. But looking back on this current era half a century hence will reveal similar grotesqueries. Sadly, there is no one of Eisenhower's stature today who entertains the slightest emotional or intellectual—or moral—doubts. That certitude may prove as fatal to us as any weapon in our arsenal.

We witness the irresponsible exposure of troops and civilians to radiation poisoning from atomic testing with relentlessly upbeat, erroneous assurances from Those in a Position to Know. A uniformed Hugh Beaumont, the wise Ward Cleaver father figure on TV's *Leave It to Beaver* (a low-key *Brady Bunch*; its theme song lacked words), offers calm advice for dealing with atomic fallout. Many new homes in the 1950s came equipped with their own fallout shelters. A priest tells us to defend our shelters against interlopers. And we are advised to stash plenty of tranquilizers. As Dad tells Mom and the kids down in the hole after the Big Blast, "There's nothing to do now but wait for orders from the authorities and relax"— sounds like George W. Bush's advice to "take your family down to Disney World in Florida" during a Code Orange Alert. Pay the Piper, Praise the Lord, and Pass the Percodan.

A third atomic revisionist film, Robert Stone's *Radio Bikini* (1987), concentrates on the United States's atomic tests in the South Pacific after the Japanese surrender. With amazing arrogance, U.S. authorities decided the obscure Bikini Atoll would be a perfect bomb target, even though it was inhabited. No matter. The people who had lived on the island for many generations were relocated to a place they did not know. We see a U.S. military officer under the palm trees at Bikini, addressing the sarong-clad villagers through a translator, explaining about the Bomb and why they have to leave: "Tell them the United States wants to turn this great destructive force into something good for mankind." The translator should have been paid overtime.

John Smitherman was among the thousands of U.S. troops assigned to witness the blast and its aftermath. "Being from the country, I'd never seen anything like it in my lifetime. They said do as you're told and no harm will come to you." No one mentioned anything about radiation. The U.S. sailors swam and washed their clothes in the sea near Ground Zero. Smitherman received a medical discharge from the service in 1947. His legs became swollen and eventually had to be amputated. His left hand was swollen and disfigured. He died in 1983, a slow death from the Bikini tests of the 1940s. The Bikini Islanders have never been able to return home.

Much of the film and many of the still photos of the Bikini test were shot by the U.S. government. They planted some 750 cameras near Ground Zero and shot miles of film, but never used it. Stone found it stuck away in the National Archives. The atomic age quickly claimed many victims. But the fearsome consequences—many unforeseen—and even Oppenheimer's hesitance, did not slow production of the far deadlier hydrogen bomb or of the many other weapons systems we continue to develop at huge expense. International terrorism has replaced international communism as the operative Pentagon boogeyman to maintain a paranoid populace. Though the threat may seem at times incommensurate with the costs, the bureaucratic apparatus that exists to make—and to profit from—sophisticated killing machines, has its own imperatives and momentum. Just do as you're told and no harm will come to you.

Chapter 3

SLOUCHING TOWARD ARMAGEDDON

"We, the people" don't run this government anymore. They do, and they tell all the lies they want.

—Kathy Schroeder, Branch Davidian survivor

The violent post-Reagan era featured U.S. attacks on Panama and Iraq, a government massacre of religious dissidents in Texas, terrorism attacks against the United States, invasions of Afghanistan and Iraq, and the deadly and ongoing occupations of those countries. Documentary films sharply contradicted official explanations of these events. Intrepid filmmakers juxtaposed the self-serving rhetoric of politicians next to searing images of destruction and suffering that belied their spin. Though these films had little effect on policy, they impacted the hearts and minds of audiences, revealing a metastasizing post–cold war arrogance of power among U.S. leaders, whose imperial swagger appeared unfettered by integrity or any sense of shame.

Barbara Trent's 1993 Oscar-winning documentary, *The Panama Deception*, challenged President George H. W. Bush's reasons for the U.S. invasion of Panama in December 1989. Bush claimed that he sent 26,000 U.S. troops—in the largest combat operation since Vietnam—to bring Manuel Noriega to trial in the United States on drug charges and to liberate Panama from his dictatorship. Mainstream American media broadcast the Bush claims without comment. Nor did they contest the official U.S. figures of 250 deaths. A press pool sent to cover the invasion was confined to a base behind the lines and prevented from witnessing any military action for hours.

Trent revealed a very different reality in Panama. Her film showed the terrible physical destruction in Panama's working class neighborhoods. She discovered that the dead actually numbered between 2,500 and 4,000, along with 18,000 residents forced into detention centers and another 7,000 arrested without charges. She showed some of the secret mass graves where U.S. forces dumped thousands of bodies and interviewed detainees still warehoused in Panama years after the invasion. What Bush called a "liberation," she exposed as a gratuitous massacre.

Trent also uncovered the real reason for the invasion: to destroy the Panama Defense Forces (PDF), thus stopping the gradual turnover of the Panama Canal to the Panamanians, scheduled to begin ten days after the invasion. By the terms of the treaty, signed by President Carter in 1978, the United States would cede sovereignty of the canal to Panama, unless Panama were incapable of defending it. Having destroyed the PDF, the United States passed a law in 1991 to ensure continued U.S. presence in the Canal Zone on the grounds that Panama could not defend it. Trent also learned that U.S. forces used the invasion to test new, unheard-of weapons on the Panamanian people, a kind of dress rehearsal for the Persian Gulf War the following year.

Noriega had been well paid by George H. W. Bush's CIA, starting in the 1970s, even though his drug trafficking was well known. He proved helpful as Reagan expanded his secret war against Nicaragua's Sandinista government in the 1980s, keeping a smooth flow through Panama of arms to the Contras and cocaine to the United States to help finance that illegal conflict. But Bush needed a villain in Panama, in order to attack it. As president, Bush encouraged Panamanian officers to oust Noriega. But when insurgent troops took Noriega prisoner, U.S. forces failed to help. Bush wanted the coup to fail, as his excuse to invade. The United Nations condemned the U.S. massacre as a flagrant violation of international law. Former U.S. Attorney General Ramsey Clark decried "the excessive use of force, beyond any possible justification." In the words of Admiral Eugene Carroll, "Bush wanted a big victory—a denial of 'the wimp factor' in spades."

When Trent accepted the Academy Award, she used the opportunity to attack PBS censorship. She lashed out against "the deceptive practices and tactics of our government, with the complicity of the major media." PBS had rejected *The Panama Deception* for broadcast, as it had earlier rejected her 1988 film, *Cover-Up: Behind the Iran-Contra Affair*. Individual stations in a few major cities did air her films, but Trent thought the network avoided them because "our films debunk the purity of the news coverage of public television," revealing a darker, messier reality.

A major theme in both Trent films is the failure of American media to get at the truth behind the official versions of events—media's acceptance and repetition of government falsehoods. "I always tell audiences that the U.S. does have perhaps the freest press in the world, but it is free to the highest bidder," says Trent. "The issue for me is not a free press, but, instead, an independent and courageous one . . . our lack of them is one of the most serious threats to . . . a participatory democracy."

Panama Deception is a true horror film, not just for its graphic proof of the inexcusable devastation wrought upon thousands of innocent people in Panama by self-serving U.S. policies in the Kissinger mode, but for revealing the invasion as a blueprint for weapons testing and media management in upcoming Middle East incursions by Bush the father and Bush the son. Panama was not about democracy. "We went down to restore American power," affirms Admiral Carroll. Nor was it about fighting the drug trade. The General Accounting Office found that cocaine traffic from Panama into the United States doubled in the two years after Noriega's arrest. But the true nature of this cynical, murderous U.S. operation eluded the U.S. media. Only Trent's film—three years after the deadly debacle—offered the Panamanian victims a chance to tell their story.

Drug trafficking in Central America plays a major role in Trent's previous film, *Cover-Up: Behind the Iran-Contra Affair* (1988). Congress failed to conduct a serious investigation into Iran-Contra, partly to prevent public revelations about U.S. government drug smuggling. *Cover-Up* probes beneath Reagan administration falsehoods and the limited congressional hearings that amounted to a whitewash, to reveal the sleazy, complex tale of treason and duplicity in the White House. Trent follows the trails of money, weapons, and drugs, unraveling the connections among a group of self-styled insider super-patriots who considered themselves above the law they were sworn to uphold. *Cover-Up* indicts Vice President George H. W. Bush, Reagan campaign staff, and the CIA—as well as Oliver North, John Poindexter, and Richard Secord, among others—for extralegal machinations that lawmakers chose not to expose.

Four months after Ronald Reagan denied trading weapons to Iran for hostages, he had to admit it was true. Trent shows us those shameful performances back-to-back, as Reagan attempts to deny what he is admitting. It is hard to know—as it was then, perhaps even for Ronald Reagan—how much Reagan knew. The press preferred not to look beyond his affable demeanor at his administration's disdain for democracy or law.

Trent interviews the wife of an American hostage held in Lebanon who says Reagan *needed* hostages as his excuse, in case his arms diversions to Iran were discovered. Ayatollah Ruhollah Khomeini—though he over-threw America's puppet dictator, the Shah Mohammad Reza Pahlavi—was a Reagan-Bush ally, thwarting a Soviet invasion of Iran. According to Reagan campaign insider Barbara Honegger, Khomeini made a deal with the Reagan campaign to delay the release of hostages taken in 1979 until after Reagan was elected, in return for massive arms shipments from the United States and Israel. Reagan supplied weapons to Iran (as well as to its enemy, Iraq) through operatives, in and out of government, who made huge profits from U.S. taxpayers.

Typical of media reaction to *Cover-Up* was the *Washington Post's* Hal Hinson, who found the film's allegations "intriguing" but "unsubstantiated" and therefore "reckless." Honegger's allegations were echoed by former National Security Council official Gary Sick and Iranian ex-president Abolhasan Bani-Sadr, among others. But media, like Congress, largely ignored the evidence of corruption against two U.S. presidents so soon after Watergate. Bush stonewalled the special prosecutor, then pardoned former defense secretary Caspar Weinberger and five other Iran-Contra defendants twelve days before their trial was set to begin, a month before he left office.

About thirteen months after his invasion of Panama, in January 1991, George H. W. Bush ordered the bombing of Iraq. For forty-five days, the United States dropped more tons of bombs on Iraq than on Germany dur-ing all of World War II. As in Panama, Bush vilified Saddam Hussein, a former U.S. asset gone wrong. Why didn't the United States discourage Saddam's planned Kuwaiti invasion? Why did the United States tell the Saudis that satellite photos showed an Iraqi buildup at their border when there was none? Why did the U.S. president reject negotiations and snub all peace initiatives? Because, as in Panama, Bush wanted a pretext for American military intervention in the region.

Enlarging upon this theme is *Hidden Wars of Desert Storm* (2001), an exploration of the Persian Gulf War and U.S.-Iraqi relations by Audrey Brophy and Gerard Ungerman. Like Noriega, Saddam was one of our boys. He came to power in a 1968 coup, supported by the CIA. In 1972, he nationalized Iraqi oil, antagonizing the West. Soon after the Shah of Iran was deposed in 1979, Iran and Iraq went to war. The United States was among 29 countries that supplied arms to both sides.

Unfortunately, it took this intrepid documentary team ten years to rectify the failures of U.S. media at the time to provide any context for

Desert Storm or to challenge the Bush administration's rush to war. As the dependable Henry Kissinger explains in the film, "Oil is too important to be left to the Arabs." The U.S. forces quickly drove Iraq out of Kuwait in 1991, meeting little resistance. As in Panama, Bush urged the Iraqi people to oust their leader. But the Kurds and Shiites, who rose against Saddam, expecting U.S. help, were cut down. On TV on February 27, having spurned diplomacy and belittled the war damage, as in Panama, Bush declared victory.

Fallout from this short war proved more devastating than the actual combat. Sanctions the United States imposed on Iraq took a horrendous toll on ordinary Iraqis, while helping Saddam keep control. Maintaining Saddam in power was the U.S. policy, to justify a military presence in the region, incessant bombardment, and huge U.S. arms sales. The oil-for-food program was a humanitarian failure. Hundreds of thousands of Iraqis, mostly small children, died of starvation and malnutrition. Of the 696,628 U.S. troops who served in the Gulf, 183,629 filed for disability pay. As of September 2000, 9,592 Gulf War veterans had died. The United States used high-toxicity depleted uranium weapons in Iraq, about which American military personnel were never informed.

Problems also surfaced in Iraq's civilian population. In the Basra hospital in 1988, 34 patients died of cancer. By 1998, that number had jumped to 428. Brophy and Ungerman locate the Pentagon's moral and fiscal denial and duplicity regarding the use of depleted uranium in the Gulf War squarely in the tradition of the Bikini test fallout and the use of Agent Orange (which contained dioxin) in Vietnam. Our own soldiers continue as guinea pigs in a series of wartime experiments in the mode of the Nazi "scientist" Josef Mengele.

The United States began bombing Iraq on January 19, 1991. On February 2, Ramsey Clark and video journalist Jon Alpert drove from Jordan to Baghdad to assess the effects of the American bombing campaign on the Iraqi people. *Nowhere to Hide* (1991) documents their perilous, week-long, 2000-mile journey to find the truth on the ground. Clark and Alpert bear witness to a reality much different from CNN's Pentagon-managed images of smart bombs recorded by airborne computers and distant precision strikes like mediagenic fireworks displays over Iraqi cities.

They find Baghdad without telephones, water, or electricity. They tour bombed residential areas, where bodies of civilians still lie in the rubble. Many women and children have been crushed and burned to death. A factory where baby milk was produced lies in ruins. Some Iraqis burn tires near buildings to give American pilots the impression they've already been hit. "Is this precision bombing?" Clark wonders. "It's not the kind of surgery you want performed near where *you* live." Surprisingly, most Iraqis are not hostile to Clark, and many speak at least a few words of English.

In Basra, in southern Iraq—where Clark says there is no legal basis for bombing—they find many more residential areas destroyed. Terrified residents are thinking of blowing up bridges themselves, so the Americans won't keep trying and failing and hitting nearby neighborhoods. A children's hospital, a mosque, and a high school have all been hit, along with a Pepsi plant in operation since the 1950s. "The U.S. military doesn't know as much as they pretend to, and then they lie," says an angry Clark, who apologizes to some Iraqis. Doctors are frustrated, in despair. They have no medicines to treat people, and no water or electricity. The Red Cross estimates a civilian death toll by February 6 of 15,000. America rains death and destruction on a defenseless population.

Nowhere to Hide was a courageous attempt to counter official falsehoods with a timely accurate witness, ultimately frustrated by corporate news entities with huge investments in other agendas. Media ignored this harrowing film. All the networks declined to air it, and NBC ended its long affiliation with Alpert, a seven-time Emmy award winner. Alpert and Clark suffered the naïve hope of true journalists, that the world deserved to know the truth, not some version crafted to comfort us—the bombers—with fairy tale assurances that our weapons punish only the unjust. Dismissing the slaughter of innocents as "collateral damage" fools no one, except perhaps us. If we cannot identify our common humanity with the people of Iraq—or Vietnam or Rwanda—we invite our own moral destruction, or rather, we concede that it has already occurred.

By the Reagan-Bush era, the "credibility gap" was history. Today, media continue to accept the most flagrant falsehoods without comment or investigation, as long as they issue from the president or his surrogates. Dissonant messages or images that contradict the official line are suppressed and ignored. The lack of public accountability encourages ever more outrageous behaviors from officials who expect to be quoted but not observed. Their capacity for shame appears to have atrophied and died.

Not everything can be sanitized or swept under the rug. Occasional public events shine a light in the bureaucratic darkness where the free press fears to tread, revealing the true nature of the authorities whom "we the people" allow to run things while we watch TV. The revelations can be ugly, but damage control is no sweat for the shameless, with only the odd author or independent filmmaker to catch them in the act.

FRIENDS AND ENEMIES OF BILL

The Oscar-nominated *Waco: The Rules of Engagement* (1997) forcefully undermines the official version of what happened in Waco, Texas, in 1993 when the Branch Davidian compound burned to the ground, killing 82 men, women, and children, in the largest domestic assault by law enforcement in U.S. history. Excerpts of the congressional hearings show lawmakers more eager to score political points than to find the truth about the murderous events in Waco. The sessions frequently descend to partisan, self-serving display. Especially egregious is the performance of Charles Schumer, sarcastically sniping at anyone who tries to affirm the humanity of the victims.

The Bureau of Alcohol, Tobacco, and Firearms (ATF), seeking publicity in advance of a budget appropriation for their agency, decided to make a splashy arrest of David Koresh and other members of his religious group, ostensibly on charges of stockpiling illegal weapons. The ATF was never asked to justify why it did not simply serve a search warrant in a peaceful way. Instead, 76 agents staged a "dynamic entry" at the religious group's community center with guns drawn on February 28. But the people inside resisted. A gun battle started. Each side later accused the other of firing first.

Four ATF agents were killed and twenty injured before the ATF ran out of ammunition and slunk away. Federal agents surrounded the house, where 130 men, women, and children resided. During fitful negotiations over the next fifty-one days, several dozen people—mostly children—left the building. On April 19, tired and still angry about the deaths of the ATF agents, the FBI smashed the buildings with tanks and shot in hundreds of canisters of deadly CS gas. The FBI denied starting the fire—claiming the people inside had a suicide wish—but the drafty wooden building quickly ignited and burned, killing eighty-two people, including eighteen children who were ten years old or younger.

Film Director William Gazecki makes powerful use of several cinematic resources, including a video taped by the Branch Davidians during the siege. The FBI sent in the video camera and tapes to find out about the condition of the many children inside, since child abuse had been alleged. The Davidians sent the tape out but the FBI suppressed it—afraid it might gain public sympathy for the group—perhaps the one thing the FBI was right about. It is eerie and sickening to see women, young and old; small children; and whole families as they address the camera, behind graphics revealing that they died in the fire on April 19. They never had a chance to be heard, until this movie.

Gazecki also uses film taken of the Branch Davidian community center by a forward-looking infrared camera (FLIR), a heat-sensitive device that reveals tank movements and gunfire hidden from media, whom the FBI kept at a distance. The FLIR tape shows that law enforcement officers beyond the media gaze machine-gunned anyone who tried to escape the fire. Though that tape was played and the gunfire plainly seen by the congressional committee investigating Waco, it was never mentioned. Instead, Charles Schumer declares, "The FBI did not fire a single shot. Therefore, bodies with bullets are Davidians who killed themselves or each other."

Schumer, other legislators, and FBI officials lie with the ferocity of those who know their lies are transparent. They just don't care. Attorney General Janet Reno looks terrible, saying that the Bradley tanks, which destroyed cars and buildings, were "like a good rent-a-car" and that she has "no doubt at all that the cult members set the fire." Gazecki's film makes clear that neither liberals nor conservatives can be counted on to represent the public interest. In fact, categories like liberal and conservative are irrelevant and misleading. The real division is between those who protect and serve the bureaucratic apparatus that perpetrates crimes against humanity—like career politicians Orrin Hatch and Joe Biden, and FBI thugs Jeff Jamar and Larry Potts—and those like journalist Dick Reavis and Davidian lawyer Dick De Guerin, who seek accountability from individuals and institutions nested within the faceless machinery of death.

The Waco hearings were simply an exercise to shift the blame for government mass murder from the state to the victims. In the end, the moral reversal was complete. Eleven Davidian survivors were put on trial. Nine were convicted and some remain in jail to this day—guilty of defending themselves from armed government attack. The Waco carnage shows that the U.S. government is prepared to turn its firepower not only on citizens of other countries—Panama, Iraq, Wherever—but also on its own people, as long as they can be marginalized as deviants, unworthy of legal protections or human rights.

Immediately after the Waco massacre, President Clinton told the press that "some religious fanatics murdered themselves" down there. But in 2000, ineligible for reelection, Clinton acknowledged, "I made a terrible mistake." Clinton has always been more attractive on the stump or giving public speeches than he was in the White House. His oratorical gifts, his quick mind, and his profound emotional intelligence inspire and embrace his listeners. As president he was distracted and besieged by "a vast right-wing conspiracy" (as Hillary Clinton knew and was ridiculed for saying) that was resentful of Clinton's intrusion into an office they have—since Roosevelt—considered rightfully theirs.

In a DVD extra on *The Hunting of the President* (2004), Clinton appears onstage after a showing of the film, ruminating about the attacks upon him in a larger historical context. His brilliant, offhand performance is beyond the reach of any other U.S. politician, let alone any president (since Jefferson hated public speaking). But, like every wonderful Clinton speech, it leaves a bitter aftertaste, reminding us how far short he fell of his own potential greatness during his eight years in office. *The Hunting of the President*, produced and directed by Harry Thomason and Nickolas Perry and based on the book by Joe Conason and Gene Lyons, looks at the ten-year campaign to destroy Bill and Hillary Clinton.

Some conspirators hated Clinton for ideological reasons. Some envied his success. Others were in it for the money or for their five minutes of notoriety. Though they did manage to precipitate an expensive, protracted, and ultimately fruitless federal investigation and a vote of impeachment in the House of Representatives, the conspirators failed to bring Bill Clinton down. They couldn't find any criminal or political wrongdoing. They had to settle for Paula Jones and Monica Lewinsky.

Richard Mellon-Scaife, chief financial backer of the *American Spectator* magazine, spent $2.4 million on the "Arkansas Project" to discredit Clinton. This man with way too much money found a lot of Arkansas locals with way too much time on their hands, including disgruntled ex-state employee Larry Nichols, fired by then-Governor Clinton for "using a toll-free state phone to solicit funds for the Nicaraguan Contras." Nichols helped bring Gennifer Flowers's alleged 12-year affair with Clinton to the paid attentions of a tabloid newspaper and thus into the 1992 presidential campaign. Nichols also made money as the narrator of the perfect companion film to *Hunting*, *The Clinton Chronicles* (1994), financed by right-wing evangelist Jerry Falwell.

Others eager to bring down Clinton included former Arkansas state troopers who said they drove him to sexual liaisons, a crooked judge who tied Clinton to his own deals to try to save himself, a jealous Arkansas lawyer who met Clinton at Oxford, a Little Rock private eye with a habit of bugging everyone, and many, many more—from lowlife opportunists to the well-groomed, sexually obsessed independent counsel Kenneth Starr. Starr spent five years and $55 million of public money pursuing Clinton. "It was not a career enhancer," said Starr of those years, though he is now dean of the law school at Pepperdine University, an institution heavily endowed by Richard Mellon-Scaife.

To help market *The Clinton Chronicles*, Jerry Falwell made a TV infomercial in which he interviews a man we see only in silhouette, identified as "an investigative reporter." "Could you please tell me and the American people why you think that your life and the lives of others on this video are in danger?" Falwell asks him. The man tells Falwell that two "insiders" he intended to interview were both killed in separate plane crashes an hour before he was to meet them. "Jerry, are these coincidences? I don't think so." Falwell responds, "Be assured, we will be praying for your safety."

But the purported investigative reporter was actually a man named Patrick Matrisciana, head of Citizens for Honest Government, who paid "expert witnesses" to be in the film with Falwell's money. As Matrisciana told *Salon* writer Murray Waas, "Obviously, I'm not an investigative reporter, and I doubt our lives were actually ever in any real danger. That was Jerry's idea to do that. . . . He thought that would be dramatic." Falwell's movie is as honest as his infomercial. The film alleges Clinton's involvement in a major drug-smuggling operation and the murder of White House counsel Vincent Foster, whose death police ruled a suicide. The film names many other individuals close to the Clintons who allegedly died suspicious, untimely deaths. Falwell advertised the *Chronicles* on his *Old-Time Gospel Hour* television program, and the video sold well.

The Clinton Chronicles opens with the titillating promise: Recommended for Mature Audiences. The film's litany of accusations and innuendos against Bill and Hillary Clinton begins with the caveat "What you're about to see, you're not going to believe," even though "all information is true." Cocaine parties, illicit sex, drug running, murder, and cover-ups are all alleged or suggested. As Falwell hoped, his film made waves in the media. "The allegations quickly found their way to talk radio programs and onto the Internet and began moving into the mainstream via articles in the *American Spectator* and the conservative *Washington Times*" and finally, in 1994, to the editorial pages of the *Wall Street Journal*. This is how scurrilous buzz now metamorphoses into legitimate news. Our modern journalism credo: no rumor left behind.

Falwell's enduring presence on the Republican right bespeaks a conservative affinity for a certain kind of religious bigotry. He is one of several well-known hustlers who flaunt their Christianity but teach hate in place of love. Falwell called the Islamic prophet, Mohammed, "a terrorist." Two days after the September 11, 2001, attacks Falwell told a television audience, "The ACLU's got to take a lot of blame for this . . . [along with] "the pagans, and the abortionists, and the feminists and the gays and the lesbians . . . all of them who have tried to secularize America." A documentary entitled *The Eyes of Tammy Faye* (2000) gives us a glimpse of Falwell's spirit. As televangelists Jim and Tammy Faye Bakker endure bad press and financial hardship (largely self-inflicted), they call on "fellow Christian" Jerry Falwell for help. He responds by ripping off their assets, and then blaming the victims at a press conference. Falwell clearly does not comprehend the biblical admonition "Sufficient unto the day is the evil thereof," since he consistently adds to it. If Christ ever does return to earth, Jerry Falwell will be among the first charlatans tossed out of the temple.

Falwell and his soul brother, Pat Robertson, both reside in Virginia, where another measure of malaise came in the form of the 1994 U.S. Senate race, as chronicled in the exquisitely painful film *A Perfect Candidate* (1996) by R. J. Cutler and David Van Taylor. The incumbent Democrat, Charles Robb, had lied about his affair with a teenage girl while governor and about his use of cocaine. Robb's Republican opponent is Oliver North, who admitted lying to Congress about his treasonous Iran-Contra deals.

The film shows North's public confession of perjury during the televised Congressional hearings, and then catches him lying to Virginia schoolchildren during the campaign, denying that he had lied earlier. North continues to insist that he is proud of his role in Iran-Contra. These two morally challenged candidates are virtually tied in the polls. As one Virginia voter puts it, having to choose between Robb and North is like choosing between "the flu or the mumps. The real question is when we'll find a cure for what's wrong with American politics." Robb won, leading

North's campaign manager, Mark Goodin, to conclude that his campaign had not been negative enough.

American electoral politics hit another new low in the 2000 presidential election debacle, as films by Michael Moore (Chapter 5) and Robert Greenwald (Chapter 7) make abundantly clear. Viewed as illegitimate by many Americans, the new Bush administration drifted for months, with only a tax cut on its meager agenda. Then the terrorist attacks of September 11, 2001, changed everything. Television viewers around the world, numbed with despair and disbelief, watched obsessively as a second hijacked passenger jet hit New York's World Trade Center, over and over again. The repetition of the crash served only to sustain our incomprehension. This defining television moment—like Oswald shooting Ruby or the Challenger explosion—was the common vision of a tragedy shared by millions. Several films captured other dimensions.

DISASTER FLICKS FOR REAL

Two French brothers, Jules and Gedeon Naudet, were making a documentary about the training of a rookie New York City fireman in the summer of 2001. Their friend, veteran firefighter James Hanlon, got permission for the brothers to record a young man's probationary period (when he is known as a *proby*) at the firehouse where Hanlon worked, which happened to be the one nearest the World Trade Center. We learn of the superstition that "black clouds" are probies who bring lots of fires, whereas "white clouds" are probies who don't. As Tony Benetatos, the film's proby, nervously waits for his literal trial by fire, he does all the grunt work—polishing the pole, washing the truck, keeping the coffee pot going—in the sweltering city heat. It's a quiet summer, with only a few minor episodes. Knowing what's coming, we are almost as nervous as he is.

Because the World Trade Center dominates the lower Manhattan skyline, the Naudets occasionally flash to the twin towers as a cinematic touchstone. That is why, covering a small fire in the street on the morning of September 11, Jules Naudet pans up to the towers just in time to catch the *first* plane slamming into the north tower. Naudet stays with the crew as they race to the scene and set up a command post in the lobby of the north tower, just before the second plane hits the south tower.

Shaken, but in a clear voice, Naudet tells us he is not going to point his camera at the crushed bodies of those who have jumped from the upper floors to avoid being burned. It's just too terrible. We hear a series of loud thumps, which he tells us are more falling bodies, an unnerving sound for us and for the firemen, who looked dazed and unbelieving but who carry on with plans to evacuate the building. The chiefs huddle, trying to create order out of chaos, as debris and bodies drop from above. Equipment-laden firefighters proceed ever higher up the stairs, as contact with them becomes intermittent. Disoriented civilians wander in and out of the frame. Rumors of a third plane circulate.

Ernest Hemingway defined *guts* as "grace under pressure." And that is what we are privileged to witness here. Nothing has prepared even the oldest, most experienced of the firefighters for an ordeal of this magnitude. Everyone in the department—including the young man filming them—is a "proby" in this hellish new circumstance. We see the elderly fire department chaplain praying for his men. Later, he is carried out of the lobby, dead. Scraping ash and grime from his lens, Naudet follows the firefighters through the frightening smoky darkness and into the ash-covered streets. The workaday world has been transformed into a spooky, malefic wilderness.

We share the joy of the Naudet brothers—who had separated that morning and had feared the worst—when they are reunited at the firehouse. Slowly, more and more of the crews return, to the relief and embraces of their worried comrades, until only one person at the station remains unaccounted for—the new kid, the proby, Tony Benetatos. The Naudets remain with the firefighters in the next difficult days, combing through the wreckage at Ground Zero for bodies. As the horror sinks in, it takes deep reserves of strength and commitment for these exhausted warriors to continue. Most are stunned as the names of their dead or missing friends and colleagues in the department are revealed.

The names keep coming and coming and in the end, we see their faces—young and old, jaunty and serious—posed proudly in their uniforms. They are the heroes of this dark drama, having given their lives to save others. An affectionate portrait of courageous individuals coping with catastrophe, this film is a fitting memorial to their sacrifice. For anyone who wishes to comprehend as fully as possible the events of that terrible day, *9/11*—as this film is titled—provides an incomparable view from the belly of the beast.

Groping for a cinematic response to the terrorist attacks, French producer Alain Brigand commissioned eleven filmmakers from around the world to "commit their subjective conscience" to the event in films exactly 11 minutes, nine seconds long. As might be expected, the resulting feature-length compilation—whose American title is *September 11*—varies radically in quality and range of themes. We shall revisit this film in Chapter 9 because it mixes factual and fictional approaches and events. But two of the fact-based episodes bear discussion here.

Mexican Director Alejandro González Iñárritu, best known for his successful features *Amores Perros* (2000) and *21 Grams* (2003), crafted a stark, eerie portrayal of the tragedy. Much of his segment is total darkness, punctuated by flashes of bodies falling from the World Trade Center— never hitting—just falling. His soundtrack consists of news reports and taped phone calls from the twin towers that morning and from the hijacked airplanes. These are messages of anguish and love, heard over the sounds of the infernal machines, the engines of disaster. Haunting, disturbing, González's film feels like a kinetic memorial sculpture. He has wrested art from this horror by selecting elements of human suffering that news reports tend to deaden with details or repetition. His segment ends with the question, in Arabic and English: "Does God's light guide us or blind us?" Osama bin Laden and George W. Bush think they know the answer. But they are both wrong. As the Japanese director Shohei Imamura affirms at the end of his own segment, "There's no such thing as a holy war."

British director Ken Loach agrees. His short film presents the eloquent emotional testament of a Chilean exile in London, Vladimir Vega. Writing a letter to commiserate with survivors of September 11, 2001, Vega reminds them about September 11, 1973. In the film as George W. Bush says, "On September 11, enemies of freedom committed an act of war against our country," we see footage of the CIA-backed coup against the democratically elected government of Salvador Allende, in Santiago, Chile. Henry Kissinger's scheme murdered Allende and launched a 19-year reign of terror in Chile by right-wing military leaders, causing thirty thousand deaths. We see Kissinger and Pinochet shake hands, two death-skulls grinning atop a pile of corpses.

The Chilean exile sympathizes with the American victims, but can we sympathize with him? Some critics accused Loach of taking a "cheap shot" at the United States at an inappropriate time, by implying that the United States had finally reaped what it had sown in many other countries. But one important function of film is to prod our collective memory. How can we remain ignorant, let alone innocent, of the actions our government performs in our name? Our national products include karma. Our actions have consequences, intended or not. And *our* suffering is not the only suffering. Far from choosing an awkward moment to bring up an old, unpleasant topic, Loach picked perhaps the only time to seek empathy from Americans with any hope that they might understand.

Beyond the horror of September 11 lay the politics. George W. Bush nominated Henry Kissinger to lead an inquiry into the events of that day. But the American people—even Congress—swiftly objected to a probable whitewash by an acknowledged cover-up master. The possibility that he might have to disclose the names of his clients and contacts sent Kissinger scurrying back to his lucrative twilight world, where he peddles his influence to the highest bidders. When the Bush administration could no longer avoid setting up a commission, it delayed handing over requested documents. Why? What were they afraid might be revealed?

Beginning on the first anniversary of the attacks, Guerrilla News Network produced *Aftermath: Unanswered Questions from 9/11* (2003), asking nine individuals eleven provocative questions about that day. University of Ottawa economics professor Michel Chossudovsky claims that al-Qaeda is "not an outside enemy but a creation of U.S. foreign policy and the CIA." Al-Qaeda was a CIA "asset" in Pakistan. General Mahmoud Ahmad, of Pakistani military intelligence, who met with high U.S. intelligence officials in September 2001, is an alleged terrorist moneyman, accused of paying $100 thousand to the leader of the 9/11 hijackers, Mohammed Atta. "Intelligence failure is not the question," says Chossudovsky, "but complicity with the terrorists [is]." Chossudovsky is the most overt conspiracy theorist, but others in this film offer disturbing evidence that enabling the attacks served the current U.S. regime as well as long-term corporate goals. If many people find such a scenario "unthinkable," that may be precisely what Bush and his bosses are counting on.

As one *Aftermath* informant points out, a self-inflicted attack on United States citizens was conceived of long ago, in the early 1960s. In his book *Body of Secrets*, James Bamford reveals the U.S. military plan named *Operation Northwoods*, which Bamford calls "what may be the most corrupt plan ever created by the U.S. government." To fight communism, the joint chiefs of staff "proposed launching a secret and bloody war of terrorism against their own country in order to trick the American public into supporting an ill-conceived war they intended to launch against Cuba." Thus, far from being unthinkable, a staged terrorist attack was planned out in detail forty years ago.

Former Secretary of State Zbigniew Brzezinski's 1997 book *The Grand Chessboard* cites the need for a Western occupation of Central Asia, but admits that without a "Pearl Harbor–like" attack, the U.S. population would never support it. Why occupy Central Asia? "America needs to control the world oil supply," as Berkeley Professor Peter Dale Scott points out. Strategists inside the U.S. government had the means, motive, and opportunity for allowing or abetting 9/11. But did they?

Most *Aftermath* interviewees raise their own questions. Why did the U.S. military not intercept the hijacked planes? Incompetence does not explain the long delay in deploying military aircraft. Why—after all the apparent military and intelligence failures that allowed the attacks to succeed—was the man in charge, General Richard Myers, promoted? Perhaps the most important question the film raises is: How can the public get the truth? Chossudovsky says you must read many different newspapers and "connect the dots. If the press won't connect the dots, the public must." But that is a formidable task in our information age.

The Internet churns out imaginative rumors and possibilities around the clock, based on scanty evidence or none at all. The Bush administration pays journalists to publish propaganda and produces its own phony "news stories" to tout its policy objectives, with no indication that they are anything but "objective reports" from "unbiased news professionals." No wonder many people choose to tune out public affairs entirely, preferring to consume sporting events or soap operas or alcohol, fulfilling the dystopian fantasy of Aldous Huxley's *Island*, elaborated for our media age by Neil Postman in *Amusing Ourselves to Death*.

IRAQ AROUND THE CLOCK

Immediately after the events of September 11, Barbara Trent took a film crew into the streets of Manhattan to gauge the sentiments of those who lived closest to Ground Zero. *Is War the Answer?: New Yorkers Respond to 9/11* (2004) shows a stunned, grieving population, appalled by the capacity of human beings to inflict devastation of such magnitude upon one another. These normally reticent urbanites have been opened up and brought together—however temporarily—by their deep emotions, their common sense of vulnerability, and their own arbitrary survival. Most remarkably, none of the New Yorkers Trent encounters call for vengeance or retaliation.

On the contrary, patrons of a crowded downtown bar, watching as President Bush vows to hunt down and kill the suspected terrorists, boo him and express disappointment at his shallow, predictable response. These New Yorkers want to end violence, not expand it. The huge gulf between the government and its own people—people intimately connected to tragedy of a high order—is clear. The New Yorkers need time to process their grief and take stock of who they want to be.

This monstrous event demands a reassessment of the world we live in and a re-imagining of how that world might be transformed. But Bush—flushed with purpose after months of inaction and drift—girds for a rush to war, a path he will pursue into Afghanistan and Iraq, against the collective will of many millions worldwide, who marched in a hundred cities to protest the Iraq war before it began. The films of Michael Moore and Robert Greenwald expose the lies Bush and company repeated, over and over, to bully Congress, buffalo the U.N., and mislead the American people. Many Americans did not believe the lies, but some still do, even today.

Once the decision was taken to invade Iraq, the official U.S. government propaganda machine turned out *Operation Enduring Freedom: America Fights Back* (2002). Hosted by Secretary of Defense Donald Rumsfeld, the film features Lee Greenwood singing "God Bless the USA." Bush delivers an ultimatum to the Taliban in front of Congress, never indicating that the United States had supported that repressive regime for its anti-Soviet stance. Bush tells the military, "The time is coming when America will act and you will make us proud." Here and throughout the film, we are treated to displays of gleaming weaponry being readied, in the spirit of a Soviet-style May Day parade, when waves of tanks and missiles passed in review before the Kremlin. As apt as Lee Greenwood's music for this film would be Leonard Cohen's line: "I'm guided by the beauty of our weapons." ("First we take Osama, then we take Saddam!")

We get a quick explanation of "why they hate us," including U.S. support for Israel, the Iranian revolution, and the first Gulf War. No mention is made of the 1953 CIA-backed coup that toppled Iranian President Mossadegh and brought the hated Shah to power in Iran, or the 1963 CIA-backed coup that brought the hated Ba'athist party to power in Iraq, or the years of support—in money and arms—that the United States provided to the reviled Saddam Hussein. That famous 1983 photo of Donald Rumsfeld shaking Saddam's hand to seal a massive weapons deal does not appear here, only in the films that oppose the 2003 invasion for which *Enduring Freedom* is preparing us.

"On October 7, Operation Enduring Freedom air strikes began . . . a tragic residual of these bombings are civilian casualties" the narrator tells us, even though the operation was "one of the most intense and accurate bombing attacks in military history." We are given this fact—and others—as Moses was given the stone tablets with divine laws carved upon them. The war happens here in passive voice, a work of abstract art. Thanks to "the full palette of technology and power," the "neutralization of Taliban and al-Qaeda was brought about" and "Hamid Karzai was chosen" to lead Afghanistan.

Occasionally an actual human voice penetrates the jingo jargon, like the Afghani woman who says, "We live in ruins. . . . The sounds of war have begun to shut out the sun." The narrator acknowledges that "a scene of destruction and devastation prevailed as cities of northern Afghanistan began to fall." Medals are awarded, bodies are brought home, and Donald Rumsfeld assures us that "Operation Enduring Freedom is a seminal moment of the American spirit." But it looks like mass murder. How does killing thousands of Afghani civilians compensate America for the lives lost on September 11? "Enduring Freedom" seems barbaric, irrelevant, and just a little insane.

Buried in the Sand: The Deception of America (2004) is a film intended, as its host Mark Taylor says, to counter those who see "our leaders as power-hungry war-mongers" and to rebuke those on "the radical left" (like Michael Moore, among others) who romanticized Muslim life in Saddam's Iraq. *Buried* intends to prove the brutality of Saddam Hussein's regime, to help bolster the rationale for the U.S. invasion. Taylor warns us the film's images of torture and execution are graphic and "not suitable for all viewers." "We will not keep these images—and our heads—buried in the sand. . . . Like the horror of Nazi concentration camps, they demand to be seen so that they cannot be denied . . . by the radical left and much of the media."

Buried in the Sand is true pornography, a hideous collage of unspeakable cruelties methodically inflicted. I confess my inability to watch even half of it and cannot imagine for which viewers this film would be suitable, besides Saddam's son, Uday, whose private collection provided some of the footage. Not only do these displays of inhumanity debase all who see them, the film is worse than pointless. The United States has known of these cruelties for years. We set Saddam up in business in 1979 and turned a blind eye to his brutality for decades, supplying him with weapons to use against anyone he wished: Iranians, Kurds, Shiites, or anyone who annoyed him. After a quarter century of condoning and enabling these horrors, how can we suddenly pretend to moral outrage?

When the lies about Saddam's weapons of mass destruction or his threat to the West became difficult even for Bush, Cheney, Rice, Powell, et al. to sustain, they decried his tyranny—a cynical, hypocritical rationale for war from his longtime sponsors. That photo of Rumsfeld and Saddam shaking hands belongs to the same genre of "grinning skulls" as Kissinger and Pinochet. It's a devil's bargain. We give you the weapons; you kill our enemies. Americans need to ask themselves how they acquired so many enemies and why so many of the grinning skulls in the past half-century belong to their own government officials.

Sinan Antoon fled Iraq in 1991. He returned to Baghdad in July 2003, three months after the fall of Saddam Hussein, to see family and friends and to assess conditions in his old home. Antoon also brought a film crew and produced *About Baghdad* (2004), to "move beyond the sound bites and privilege the complexity of Iraqi voices and perspectives usually marginalized and simplified by mainstream (mis)representations." He finds that most Iraqis feared and hated Saddam, but also resent the Americans. "Yes, the Americans got rid of Saddam, but that was their responsibility, they brought him in," one man tells Antoon. The Iraqis are emotionally exhausted, having endured decades of dictatorship, hurtful economic sanctions, war, and now military occupation.

Saddam was an oppressor and a torturer. No one could speak freely, without fear of retribution. Person after person recounts horrendous personal stories of imprisonment and abuse. Since Saddam has gone, "Even the air has changed." But Iraqis have no health care, no water, no services, and they can't understand why the Americans cannot maintain order or ensure public safety. "It's as if the sanctions are still here," says one man, who explains, "Sanctions did not weaken the regime. They weakened the will of the people to resist." Saddam did not suffer, but as many as half-million Iraqis died. Many Iraqi children starved to death.

Of course the Iraqis are wary of the Americans in Baghdad. After all, in 1917 a British general in Baghdad declared that "we come as liberators, not occupiers," but British forces remained in Iraq for more than thirty years. "Iraqi relief" at Saddam's departure was "hijacked by the U.S. occupation," Antoon tells us. As one Iraqi intellectual puts it, "When I see an American tank in the street, I feel it rolling on my own heart." An angry woman, addressing America through Antoon's camera lens, says, "If you are a liberator, why do you bomb civilians?" Iraqis of Antoon's acquaintance don't believe the Americans care about the Iraqi people, only about their oil. Unlike many Americans, the Iraqis cannot afford any illusions.

Eric Manes, Martin Kunert, and Archie Drury handed out 150 digital video cameras to ordinary Iraqis in the spring of 2004, with the instruction to use them and pass them on. The producers edited 400 hours of these Iraqi videos into *Voices of Iraq* (2004), a vivid, rather different view from the streets than that of the exiled artist and intellectual Sinan Antoon. We see many more children in this film, perhaps because so many adults have died at the hands of Saddam Hussein, the Iranians, or the Americans. Half of all Iraqis are 15 or younger. Sweet and playful in spite of everything, Iraqi children must grow up amid bombings, shootings, and many other everyday terrors.

Between one and six million Iraqis lost their lives during Saddam Hussein's despotic reign. Understandably, the survivors find it hard to trust anyone, whatever promises are made. *Voices of Iraq* and *About Baghdad* are important attempts to present a true picture of the lives and hopes of Iraqis. The Iraqi people deserve our sympathy and our support. But we can share their suspicion, after a quarter-century of American-subsidized oppression, that the Americans may have reasons besides Christian charity to stabilize and occupy their country.

Our sampling of American political documentary films since the 1950s shows that filmmakers offered a narrative for the political developments of recent decades that was often at odds with the official version of events—nothing less than an alternative history. Disenchanted by government dissembling in Vietnam, U.S. media were briefly emboldened to challenge propagandistic lies and to hold public officials accountable. But the press was soon brought to heel by corporate media owners eager to placate their political cronies, achieve deregulation, and maximize profits.

The independent filmmakers who are not tame enough for television, even if they find funding, are considered too marginal to worry about, playing in small venues to small audiences. They work beneath the radar of political orthodoxy and media conventions, developing strong, idiosyncratic voices. As mass media fail—now more than ever—to fulfill their watchdog role over public officials and policies, the importance of documentaries committed to telling the truth increases. Such films bear visual witness to important events, sharing them with those who have eyes to see and ears to hear. Their makers dare to refute the falsehoods passing for conventional wisdom, sometimes risking their lives or reputations to reveal the nature of those lies and the interests behind them. Documentaries have become an essential component for making sense of our time.

Before we explore the unprecedented role of documentary films in the 2004 presidential election, we look at four individual makers of documentaries whose work is indispensable for comprehending the versatility and significance of modern nonfiction film. Each of these artists has built from the tradition we have outlined here, taking it to new levels of political purpose. In very different ways, each has found a style with which to tell stories that undermine or refute the sociopolitical consensus proposed by majoritarian media. Their work enriches our culture with new and generative possibilities, considerably enlarging the range of our aesthetic and political discourse.

Chapter 4

BARBARA KOPPLE: INTREPID PIONEER ON THE FRONT LINES

If you want to do documentaries, you must not be persuaded to wait until you have the money, or be afraid to do it because you've never done it before. You just have to go for it.

—Barbara Kopple

New Year's Eve at the Baltimore Police Department's homicide unit is much too quiet. "The only thing dead in this joint are the phones," says a detective. But the cops know as soon as midnight strikes and the ball falls in Times Square, the bodies will start falling too. To pass the time before then, a man named Brodie plays a tape of the documentary film he shot about the homicide unit during the past year. His opening sequences reveal the self-conscious reluctance of the homicide detectives to being filmed. But soon enough, Brodie has them addressing the camera.

"You commit a crime of violence, whereupon you are jacked up, dragged down to police headquarters, and deposited in a claustrophobic anteroom," one detective explains. "And there you sit . . . until a homicide detective, a man who can in no way be mistaken for a friend, enters the room." One after another, the detectives counsel the camera to remain silent, to wait for a lawyer, even as they demonstrate their skill at cajoling suspects to open up and start talking. This is only one of many discrepancies the documentary reveals—the actualities behind pretended truths. Brodie's film shows the police lying to each other and faking written reports, engaging in illicit romances, and telling jokes over dead bodies. These filmed revelations anger and embarrass various members of the homicide unit. As the indiscretions pile up, the chief of the unit moves to confiscate the tape. But Brodie tells him it's too late. He's already sold the film to PBS.

"But we're all going to appear on national television behaving like. . . like. . . ."

"Like you actually are," says Brodie. "I made this documentary not because I wanted to embarrass anybody, but because I wanted to tell the truth. And when you're after the truth, then, yeah, privacy goes out the window." Brodie compares his filming to police work, sifting through the lives of victims and suspects for the facts. "You guys are detectives. You live in other people's lives. And no, it doesn't bother you. It's not about the privacy. It's about the work. And about pushing past all the lies . . . getting to what's real. And that's what I learned from you guys. And that's what this film is all about."

Brodie and the other homicide detectives are fictional characters on the 1990s television series *Homicide: Life on the Streets*. Based on a book by David Simon, who spent a year with Baltimore's homicide unit, *Homicide* strove for realism, eschewing TV cop-show clichés like car chases and gunfights. "The Documentary" episode, directed by documentarian Barbara Kopple, won her a 1997 Director's Guild award. It was a dizzying mix of fact and fiction: a real-life documentary maker directed an episodic TV program about a "documentary" of a fictional homicide unit based on a nonfiction book. Compounding the irony, Brodie's "documentary" shows police chasing a suspect into an alley where Hollywood director Barry Levinson is shooting his own cop feature. "Reality" colliding with fiction on a movie location is an inside joke, since Levinson was the executive producer for the television series.

Kopple is not afraid to dig beneath our culturally operative clichés to locate more complex human realities. Our society uses polite—or at least, accepted—fictions that allow us to function without undue thought or fuss. Kopple unpacks some of these fictions, especially those dealing with the American social and economic class system. She eschews superficial stories of the sort confected for the nightly news, and facile portrayals of "good" or "bad" people. Kopple prefers to unmask and illuminate the tensions of opposing impulses that war within each of us. She knows our choices forge our identity and determine our fate. Her genius as a filmmaker is to enable us to see the dilemmas her subjects face and to be there when they make their choices. Her superb timing is partly a great patience, sniffing out the crisis and then allowing it to unfold.

Barbara Kopple, a child of privilege, risked her life—and made her reputation—to direct a documentary film about a violent coal miners' strike in rural Kentucky. *Harlan County, USA* got inside the strife, revealing the history of the miners and the perils they faced, from cave-ins to black lung disease to death threats from hired thugs. The film won the 1977 Oscar for best documentary and was designated an American Film Classic by the Library of Congress.

Kopple won a second Oscar in 1991 for her insider's view of a meat-packer's strike in Minnesota during the Reagan years, a brilliant juxtaposition of personal stories and the larger national political context. *American Dream* reveals the long odds against workers looking for equitable treatment in the "greed is good" era of downsizing and does not flinch from showing the devastating consequences for the individuals—and their communities—who dare to take a stand.

Kopple's prolific output since then is hard to categorize. She examined the controversy surrounding Oliver Stone's 1991 movie about the Kennedy assassination in *Beyond "JFK": The Question of Conspiracy*. She directed several fictional television series episodes of *Homicide* and *Oz*, and a biographical documentary about boxer Mike Tyson, then serving a six-year prison term for rape. In the wake of Woody Allen's separation from Mia Farrow and subsequent engagement to his stepdaughter, Soon-Yi Previn, Kopple documented the couple's trip through Europe on tour with Allen's Dixieland jazz band in her film *Wild Man Blues*. She later crafted an intimate portrait of the reclusive movie star Gregory Peck.

Kopple directed two concert films—*Woodstock '94* (1998) and *My Generation* (2000)—exploring continuities between the original Woodstock generation of 1969 and more recent music and attitudes. She directed a TV mini-series, *The Hamptons*, about the lives of Long Island's rich and famous in the months before September 11, 2001. She produced an HBO film, *American Standoff*, about the political struggles of labor leader James Hoffa Jr. with the teamsters union. *Friends for Life: Living with AIDS*, made for the Disney Channel, profiles children living with HIV or AIDS to dispel myths about the disease for young viewers. *Defending Our Daughters* explores human rights issues and the systematic abuses of women in Bosnia, Pakistan, and Egypt. *Bearing Witness* (2004) follows five female journalists reporting from war zones in Iraq.

Fearless, innovative, sometimes militantly political, and always creatively restless, Barbara Kopple continues to define and challenge the possibilities of documentary filmmaking. She is currently working on a film about Dr. Jack Kevorkian, an advocate for assisted dying, who is now serving a prison term in Michigan for second-degree murder for enabling a voluntary euthanasia.

WHICH SIDE ARE YOU ON?

Born in 1946, Kopple grew up in a politically liberal, nonreligious family in the wealthy New York suburb of Scarsdale. She learned her craft by working with Albert and David Maysles on *Gimme Shelter* (1970), about the ill-fated 1969 Rolling Stones U.S. concert tour that ended in murder. This cinèma vèritè classic shows the Stones rehearsing bad boy music that seems to summon up dark energies the musicians cannot control. The brutal violence of the Hell's Angels at the jammed Altamont Speedway concert confounds Mick Jagger's pop star power, rendering him effete and impotent. Footage of the Stones watching the film of the murder is a powerful metaphor for the idealistic 1960s energy turning against itself, devouring its own young.

Kopple also co-directed *Winter Soldier,* about the 1971 Detroit hearings where Vietnam veterans described their war experiences. None of the crew was paid but, "It was stupendous for me because it was a way of looking at these young, beautiful, innocent boys who had gone through so much in their lives," she said later. "I was highly motivated by meeting people and have them open up in such an incredible way, simply because we'd have a camera. Their stories were sometimes sad or extraordinary. The whole essence of storytelling is what motivates me."

During a struggle for control of the United Mine Workers Union in 1969, the reform candidate for the union presidency, Jock Yablonski, was murdered in his Pennsylvania home along with his family. After Yablonski's murder, Miners for Democracy formed to take up his causes of safety and health issues for coal miners. Kopple read about the group and decided to try to tell their story on film.

Harlan County, USA opens with a montage of coal miners entering and leaving mines on conveyor belts. Interior shots reveal the mines as dark, cramped, and claustrophobic. Merle Travis sings, "where the rain never falls and the sun never shines; it's dark as a dungeon, way down in the mines." An old man in a rocking chair sings and talks about his 18-hour days working the mines. He recalls his boss telling him, "Don't take the mule into any bad place." "What about the men?" I asked him. "We can always hire another miner. We have to *buy* another mule."

"In 1973, workers of Brookside, Kentucky, joined the United Mine Workers. Duke Power refused to sign the contract and the workers went on strike," says a graphic. Like her documentary mentors, the Maysles, Kopple does not rely on narration. But she does make effective use of music. Soulful Appalachian folk laments color the narrative, especially the recurring dirge by Florence Reece "Which Side Are You On?". Reece, the wife of a Harlan County miner, wrote the song during another violent strike, in 1931, when the area earned the nickname "Bloody Harlan." The song gathers power through repetition, as we witness more and more scenes of miners' oppression and determination.

> "My daddy was a miner/And I'm a miner's son,
> And I'll stick with the union/'Til every battle's won.
>   Which side are you on? Which side are you on?
>   Which side are you on? Which side are you on?
> Don't scab for the bosses/Don't listen to their lies.
> Us poor folks haven't got a chance/Unless we organize.
>   Which side are you on? Which side are you on?
>   Which side are you on? Which side are you on?

There is no doubt which side Barbara Kopple is on. She attends the workers' meetings and shoots her film from their side of the picket lines. "I definitely had a passion for these miners, although we tried to include as much as we could of the coal owners and operators," Kopple said, decades later. "So yes, the film totally sided with the coal miners because they were the people I'd spent time with, the people whose lives were at stake, and the people who were willing to give up anything for what they believed in." Thugs shot up the homes of pro-union workers. Kopple and her crew carried guns after dark. "We were machine-gunned. A gun was held to my head by a strike-breaker. You can hear me yelling, 'Don't shoot!'" Kopple felt that the presence of her film crew offered some protection to miners who were being threatened with death. In fact, as her film documents, one young man was shot and killed by a scab.

Kopple weaves the back story into her coverage of the current conflict: the United Mine Workers (UMW) under John L. Lewis, the history of Harlan County, the history of black lung disease, the murder of Jock Yablonski, and the defeat and arrest of UMW president Tony Boyle. She follows the pickets to New York City and gets inside a stockholders' meeting where Carl Horn, the president of Duke Power, confronts union employees. We learn that company profits rose 170 percent in 1975, while miners' wages were up 4 percent and the cost of living rose by 7 percent. Back in Harlan County, we witness the armed intimidation of the striking miners. Women take the lead at the meetings, organizing and goading the community to get up before dawn to confront the armed strikebreakers, despite almost no support from local law enforcement. Miners from West Virginia, Illinois, and Indiana come to offer their support for the strikers.

And then a young man is shot point-blank in the face with a shotgun and killed. In this small town, everyone knows who killed him. Some want revenge. But cooler heads prevail. The murder has only strengthened the miners' resolve and sobered the owners. Some feel the murdered man was the requisite martyr, the sacrifice, the blood that had to be paid for a final resolution of the strike. A contract is signed. The Brookside miners return to work. But three months later, in November 1974, the national union contract expires, causing 120,000 miners to strike. Strikes and unrest continue in 1975 and 1976, we are informed, as the film ends.

Harlan County, USA celebrates the indomitable courage of exploited, impoverished workers and their families, who dare to stand up for their rights despite terrible odds, including a justice system in league with their oppressors, and a sometimes corrupt union as their only support. As one union organizer says, "it's a feudal system" in the Harlan County coal mines, a shameful remnant of an exploitative past. Using stark, eloquent regional music, Kopple's film manages to poeticize the struggles of the miners without romanticizing them—a delicate, difficult task.

Eight years later Kopple began to document striking workers of another industry, in a different part of the country, in *American Dream* (1990). The early 1980s were the Reagan years, a time of antiunion fervor. When air traffic controllers struck for better wages and benefits, Reagan fired them all. In Austin, Minnesota, home of the Hormel Meat Packing Company, the workers strike. After reporting a 1984 profit of $29.5 million, Hormel cut hourly wages from $10.69 to $8.75 "to remain competitive." Workers hand out leaflets at the home of a Hormel executive, whose wife tells them, "Lots of people would love to have your jobs." "We just want a fair shake," one replies.

Hormel's chief legal counsel, Charles Nyberg, tells the press that company founder "George Hormel would do what we are doing." But Kopple shows us Hormel promotional films of the late 1940s or early 1950s, boasting of Hormel's innovative guaranteed annual wage and the first profit-sharing plan. Hormel used to take a protective, progressive attitude toward its employees. It seems infected now with the 1980s drive for unprecedented profits and returns for company stockholders, even at the workers' expense. As a union leader says late in the film, "Hormel changed because it was in their interest to change. They're not paternalistic anymore. They're barracudas, like everyone else." When the local union hires a consultant, Hormel president Richard Knowlton says, with a smile, that the union "can say a lot, but they can't do much."

Again, Kopple seems to side with the workers against management. But the issues are not as clear-cut for the Minnesota meat packers as they were for the Kentucky coal miners. Here there are not just two sides, but three, or maybe four. The national union disavows the actions of the local chapter in Austin. National union president Lewie Anderson says the workers "deserve $10.69-plus, believe me." But he fears that the tactic of their consultant, Ray Rogers, to create a massive publicity campaign for the workers against the company, is likely to backfire. Jim Guyette, head of the local, says, "We pleaded with the national union, either help us or get out of our way." Guyette thinks the international union is afraid "we'll find out they're unnecessary." We begin to know these three men and to see how their egos and personalities affect their positions. Kopple also introduces us to a number of men and women who work for Hormel or are affected by the company. In Austin, a town of 22,000 people, that's everyone.

Kopple constantly personalizes the complex social and economic issues at stake. She is able to set the particulars of the Hormel strike in the larger context of the era. Kopple manages to be there, in the tense meetings at the local union hall and at the national headquarters in Washington, in bargaining sessions with Hormel executives and out on the frigid picket lines, showing us the raw emotions of workers laying their jobs and lives on the line. The months-long strike begins to tear families apart. Kopple interviews scabs about why they're crossing the picket lines. One man refuses to consider going back to work without a union contract. His brother decides he cannot honor the strike anymore without endangering the health of his family.

American Dream shows us the agony of longtime union workers eager, even desperate, to work but who feel honor-bound to respect the picket lines. The company is playing for keeps. Hormel fires hundreds of workers at other plants who honor the local union's walkout. As the strike wears on, more and more workers capitulate and trickle back across the picket lines to their jobs without a contract. The conflict is tearing the community apart, wrecking lifelong friendships, rupturing families. The company begins to hire replacement workers, and the Minnesota governor calls out the National Guard to keep the Hormel plants open.

To break the stalemate, the international union takes over the local and negotiates directly with the company. They secure a wage of $10.25 an hour for the workers who crossed the picket lines to return to work. But no provisions exist in their contract for the workers who honored the picket lines. The long strike dooms many small businesses in Austin. Former workers pack up to leave the town where they have lived their whole lives. At a union meeting, a woman plays the guitar and sings the union anthem, "Solidarity Forever" (to the tune of "The Battle Hymn of the Republic"). With the union bitterly divided, union stalwarts working as scabs, and the local superseded by the larger organization, the song has an ironic feel. A final graphic announces the bitter news: "In 1989, Hormel leased half its plant to a company that pays workers $6.50 an hour."

Barbara Kopple's two Academy Award–winning labor films chronicle the ongoing feudal mistreatment of coal miners and a retreat from the "American Dream" in Minnesota, where meat plant workers were forced to yield part of their wages—and their way of life—to maximize profits for companies and their stockholders. If Harlan County, Kentucky, feels like an exotic backwater, nothing is more mainstream than the meat-packing plants across the American Midwest. Kopple sees the longtime struggle for equality and dignity infringed by a new era of government-sanctioned corporate greed. Reagan and Bush, bought and paid for by society's proprietors, shilled for their masters against the common people whom their campaigns pledged to uplift. Between the two documentaries, Kopple directed her first fictional feature, with Danny Glover, James Broderick, and Carol Kane, about the attempt of textile workers in a small southern town to unionize. No other American filmmaker knows the pathos of the modern labor movement as well as Barbara Kopple. But she has other stories to tell as well.

THE WILD, THE FALLEN, THE WEALTHY, THE OPPRESSED

In 1991, Oliver Stone released *JFK*, a fictionalized account of how New Orleans District Attorney Jim Garrison prosecuted a prominent local businessman for conspiring to kill President John F. Kennedy, the only criminal proceeding ever held in connection with the assassination. Stone's film reignited the dormant debates surrounding Kennedy's death and the mixed feelings of many about Garrison, incarnated in the film by the handsome, apparently reasonable, Kevin Costner. Was Garrison a megalomaniacal publicity hound, looking to advance his political career? Or a courageous public servant, taking on a federal bureaucracy bent on concealing the truth? Critics accused Stone's faux-documentary film of muddling the historical comprehension of a generation too young to remember either Kennedy or Garrison. Barbara Kopple and Danny Schechter decided to make a film about the controversy surrounding Stone's movie, a complex proposition, with decidedly mixed results.

Beyond "JFK": The Question of Conspiracy (1992) takes off from Oliver Stone's assertion that November 22, 1963—the day Kennedy was assassinated in Dallas— "changed everything." We see a montage of JFK inauguration and assassination footage and hear media accusations that Stone is creating "propaganda" and "twisting history." Unlike Kopple's earlier and later films, *Beyond "JFK"* has a "voice of God" narration, supplied by former CBS newsman Ike Pappas, who is also among the many journalists interviewed in the film. This documentary is never quite certain where it's going, digging up witnesses to the original event, then interviewing actors who played parts in Stone's movie. Briton Gary Oldman, who plays Lee Harvey Oswald in Stone's *JFK*, is a brilliant actor and a credible Oswald, but a poor choice as an "expert" commentator on the events of November 22, 1963.

Emile de Antonio was the first filmmaker to investigate questions of cover-up and conspiracy in the JFK murder, in *Plot to Kill JFK: Rush to Judgment* (1967), based on Mark Lane's book. *Judgment* was only De Antonio's second film, and the first one he actually shot. His earlier *Point of Order* (1963) was compiled and edited entirely from "found" network recordings. De Antonio and Lane interviewed witnesses in Dallas, some of whom had testified to the Warren Commission. Static, primitive, and amateurish in many ways, *Judgment* remains a valuable, riveting film, the first to challenge the Warren Report. Shocked by the shooting, and their treatment by the Warrren Commission, the men and women speak haltingly but bravely about what they saw. Some tell how the FBI pressured them to change their accounts to fit the official version. A few look as if they fear repercussions for telling the truth.

Kopple's and Schechter's film revisits the shameful performance of the Warren Commission, which Lyndon Johnson created to forestall more thorough inquiries by other state or federal bodies. Arlen Specter's absurd magic bullet theory and J. Edgar Hoover's lying denials about the FBI's longstanding relationships with Lee Oswald and Jack Ruby appear hollow and transparently false thirty years later, and so does the bizarre mantra of mainstream media that the commission's findings prove "the system works." Kopple shows us Gerald Ford, Hoover's spy on the commission, attacking Stone's film. *Beyond "JFK"* shuttles between the real Jim Garrison, saying, "The CIA killed Kennedy," and "The Warren Report is a fairy tale," to Kevin Costner, in character as the Hollywood Garrison, and then out of character as a politically concerned actor. It's difficult to know what's going on, let alone What's Going On?

Kopple's next project seemed an unlikely change of pace: a TV documentary about a heavyweight boxer. NBC commissioned *Fallen Champ: The Untold Story of Mike Tyson* (1993), while Tyson was serving a six-year prison term for raping a teenage beauty contestant. Kopple's treatment of Tyson's life is thorough and artful, but the tale it tells, a kind of American parable, is terribly sad. Kopple takes us to the mean city streets where Tyson grew up, a tough kid in a very tough neighborhood. Violence was everywhere, including home and school. At 12, he already weighed 190 pounds.

Arrested for assault, Tyson was sent to a youth center, where he caught the biggest break of his life. The boxing coach brought Tyson to the notice of the longtime trainer of championship fighters, Cus D'Amato. More than a trainer, D'Amato was a worldly-wise guru and protective father figure who genuinely cared about the tough, talented, emotionally immature Tyson. But in 1985, the year Tyson turned pro, D'Amato died. Tyson was alone: talented, clueless, and very vulnerable.

He became the youngest heavyweight champion in history at 20. As one of his admiring managers says, "He fights everybody like they stole something from him." The sharks began to circle. First came the "shrewd, greedy" Robin Givens and her mother. Givens married Tyson, and then divorced him eight months later, taking a chunk of his fortune. "Givens was the jab that set him up for the right hook of Don King," in the words of one ex-associate. King, "a gangster from Cleveland," moved in, got rid of everyone close to Tyson, and took control of his finances. A disconsolate, out-of-shape Tyson was knocked out in Tokyo in 1990.

Then Tyson attended the Miss Black America Pageant in Indianapolis. Women had always been among the perks of his celebrity. At a rally of Tyson supporters, the execrable Louis Farrakhan cackles that bringing Tyson to a beauty pageant is "like bringin' a hawk to a chicken house." His young accuser, Desiree Washington, was apparently one of the few women who refused his advances. Perhaps he did not believe her, or care. If Givens and King were after Tyson's money, others—like Farrakhan— were out to use him for their own ends. Desiree Washington was a victim. Without absolving Tyson of his crime, Kopple's film shows Tyson victimized by the machinery that set him up as champ, a golden goose to be plucked and an idol ripe for smashing.

Kopple continued to profile celebrities, following Woody Allen on a tour of sold-out European capitals with his jazz band in *Wild Man Blues* (1998). Allen had recently endured a tabloid tempest, breaking up with his longtime companion, actress Mia Farrow, and taking up with Farrow's adopted Korean daughter, Soon-Yi Previn. "The heart wants what it wants," said Allen. Farrow then accused Allen of molesting their two biological children and took him to court. Perhaps Allen hoped Kopple's film would rehabilitate his image and win back some alienated fans. The couple—who married in Venice at the end of this 1997 tour—appear comfortable together.

Previn looks more relaxed and mature than Allen, though he is thirty-five years her senior. She often seems more maternal toward him than romantic, calming his neurotic fears of gondola rides or tiny glitches in their five-star traveling arrangements. The best scene is their visit to Woody's aging parents in New York, when his mother wonders aloud whether he might not have had more success as a pharmacist. The hip, sophisticated comic writer here appears spoiled and infantilized. If Kopple finds unexpected tragic depths and strength in blue-collar America, then among society's privileged, golden celebrities she identifies a surprising pathos and vulnerability.

In March 1998, the Lifetime cable network showed Kopple's *Defending Our Daughters*, a powerful and disturbing chronicle of entrenched cultural injustices against women in various countries, a strong political return to form for the director of *Harlan County, USA* and *American Dream*. Kopple finds articulate informants in Pakistan, Egypt, Bosnia, and the United States to explain the painful and dangerous prejudices women face simply on account of their gender. Victims of rape and genital mutilation speak out bravely against their oppressors. Intrepid as ever, Kopple takes her cameras into small villages, police stations, and courts to interview the men who perpetrate crimes against women in the names of justice, tradition, war, or religious instruction.

A Conversation with Gregory Peck (1999) was the name of the actor's one-man show, in which he reminisced on stage and invited questions from the audience. At the behest of Peck's daughter, Cecilia, Kopple's collaborator on several projects, Barbara Kopple chronicles Peck's national tour and snatches of his personal life. Peck won an Academy Award for incarnating Atticus Finch, a small-town southern lawyer and single father in the 1930s, who defends a Black man falsely accused of raping a White woman in *To Kill a Mockingbird* (1962). That role became a touchstone for his life and for audiences who identify him with it. In one lovely scene, Kopple catches Peck and his French wife at an intimate bistro supper with French President Jacques Chirac, as everyone speaks English in deference to Peck's rudimentary French.

Trails of the rich and famous led Kopple to the wealthy Long Island suburbs of New York, where she tests out F. Scott Fitzgerald's proposition that "the rich are different from you and me." *Once upon a Time in the Hamptons* (2002), a four-hour mini-series, proves instead that individuals with enough money to lead any life they wish more often than not choose triviality over substance. For all its length, *The Hamptons* offers up superficial slices of largely superficial lives. Kopple arrives like many another summer visitor to the Hamptons, on a quest for love or meaning or experience that is foredoomed by its own desire.

As one catty commentator notes, since John Kennedy didn't go down in his plane that summer and Princess Diana didn't die in Paris, local gossip has to make do with Lizzie Grubman. A wealthy party girl, Grubman backed her Mercedes SUV into a group of people waiting outside a Hamptons nightclub on July 7, 2001, injuring 16 of them. She was charged with assault, drunk driving, and leaving the scene of an accident. But Grubman is no Daisy Buchanan. And the Hamptons are not the decadent Weimar Berlin of *Cabaret*. Their suburban sorrows and tepid pleasures bear no fin de siÉcle relevance to the darkness wrought on September 11, which brings this summer to an end. Otherwise, George W. Bush might have proclaimed, "They hate us for our shallowness."

Bearing Witness (2005), a film by Barbara Kopple, Marijana Wotton and Bob Eisenhardt, chronicles a year in the lives of five female war correspondents and photographers as they cover Iraq in 2003–2004, before, during, and after the U.S. invasion. Most are also veterans of wars whose names bespeak some of the worst horrors of recent times: Rwanda, Sri Lanka, Kosovo, Chechnya, and Sierra Leone. Bright, intrepid, and uncharacteristically inchoate when asked about their chosen profession, each woman has stared death in the face. Marie Colvin lost an eye from a grenade in Sri Lanka. Saddam's army arrested Molly Bingham for spying and locked her in Abu Ghraib prison. May Ying Welsh had a grenade dropped on her in Baghdad but escaped injury. Some deep emotional connection draws them, like moths, to the flames of war.

All are Americans, but only Mary Rogers of CNN works for U.S. media. Janine di Giovanni and Marie Colvin write for British newspapers. Bingham takes photos for World Picture News, an international photography consortium. Welsh is a producer for Aljazeera. Each must reconcile her fears and constricted personal life with her deep desire to bear witness and separate truth from illusion. Di Giovanni says, "War is like a greedy woman who wants everything." But the rush of their addiction compensates them for their physical and emotional scars. Presumably, Barbara Kopple can identify. These women and their comrades deserve our gratitude. As we learn at the start of this film, "152 journalists were killed on assignment in the past four years." *Bearing Witness* lets us sample the terror, brutality, and dislocation these women face every day.

NEWS AS A WEAPON, WAR AS A PRODUCT

Barbara Kopple also served as an executive producer of *WMD: Weapons of Mass Deception* (2004), a meticulous, thoroughly damning analysis of the media role in the run-up to the Iraq war, the U.S. invasion, and the ongoing U.S. occupation of Iraq. Danny Schechter, Kopple's occasional collaborator, directed *WMD*, which ought to be required viewing for every journalism student, if not every news consumer, in the United States. More clearly than any other documentary, *WMD* defines our current information dilemma, illustrating the collusion among the Bush administration, the Pentagon, the news corporations, and individual journalists to promote war for their own selfish reasons, against the will and the welfare of the overwhelming majority.

A former network news insider, Danny Schechter makes a credible media critic and narrator for *WMD*. He knows how journalists think and why media corporations act as they do. One of the original producers at CNN, he also worked eight years as a producer at ABC's *20-20*. Schechter says he always wanted to be part of the news media, to spotlight the world's problems. Working in television news, he realized mass media themselves are among those problems.

Looking at coverage of the Bush administration's Iraq policy before, during, and after the 2003 invasion, *WMD* makes a strong case that all major U.S. broadcast media—not just Fox News—acted as mere instruments of the state, akin to the old Soviet propaganda machine Americans used to deride as unfree. The U.S. media no longer represent a range of opinion. They merely repeat and trumpet the government party line as concocted on a daily basis by specialists in the White House and the Pentagon to manipulate public opinion. Polls reveal that most Americans have no clue that the news coverage they saw about Iraq was limited and slanted. That fact only emphasizes the importance of this film, and the need to add media literacy programs to school curricula. The ability to understand and decode media images is increasingly critical in our postliterate era. But Bush is cutting aid to education, not enlarging it.

The desire of all the other TV networks to look just as patriotic as Rupert Murdoch's Bush mouthpiece is what Schechter calls "the Fox effect." As we shall see in Chapter 7, Robert Greenwald's *Outfoxed* details how the network's news policies and story spins are dictated from the top and implemented to harmonize with the White House point of view. It's enough to say here that the Fox effect drove all coverage to the right, ensuring little variation in the approaches of the U.S. TV networks to Iraq. The exhaustive coverage—with reporters embedded among U.S. troops and retired military officers embedded at network studios—obscured as much as it revealed.

As former MSNBC journalist Ashleigh Banfield says in the film, "There's a big difference between coverage and journalism . . . getting access does not mean you're getting the story." Embedded reporter Ted Koppel, who looked as foolish in his military gear as did Michael Dukakis, says, "Live coverage makes for bad journalism." Schechter says, "How wars are covered—or covered up—is key to rallying public support." Schechter and his sources point out that U.S. media coverage was "at its worst when it mattered most," in early 2003, when the public was making up its mind about the war.

The U.S. media allowed Bush to manipulate the truth about the danger Iraq posed to the West. Media cheerleading helped him achieve a consensus.

The *New York Times* later apologized for its pre–Iraq War coverage. But not the TV networks. When Schechter asks NBC's Tom Brokaw if his network might have been more critical, Brokaw denied that NBC had stifled critical voices. But antiwar marches in the United States and worldwide—the largest since Vietnam, and some larger than any in history—were poorly covered. Media did not analyze the reasons for the massive protests or discuss what they meant. And they largely failed to question or challenge the government's assumptions, all of which later proved false. Antiwar activists tried to buy commercial time to air their messages, but the networks refused them.

Schechter provides a quick history of official media manipulation, beginning with Vietnam, where, as journalist Peter Arnett says, "Reporters did not get on the team." After Vietnam, the Pentagon increased their outreach to journalists while limiting their access. CNN—known as "the Chicken Noodle Network" when it started—"won" the 1991 Gulf War by covering the Pentagon news conferences, which highlighted U.S. successes. But CNN correspondent Christiane Amanpour says, "media sold out" to gain their access. American TV viewers never learned, for example, that only one out of five "smart" bombs ever hit targets or that most U.S. troops were killed by "friendly fire."

How the United States set up Saddam Hussein in power and supported him, what the results of the decade-long sanctions were on the Iraqi people, and how and why the Gulf War Syndrome afflicted many U.S. veterans were all stories that failed to get "the full coverage they deserved" in the U.S. media, as Schechter says. Counting sources on U.S. television in the months before the U.S. invasion of Iraq, the organization Fairness and Accuracy in Reporting (FAIR), found that 71 % were pro-war, and only 3 % were antiwar. The U.S. media offered no debate and no platform for dissent.

Journalists embedded with U.S. troops remained uncritical of U.S. military actions, in order not to be "kicked off the team." Naturally sympathetic to the troops on whom their own lives depended, journalists had a clear conflict of interest. Many of them saw the Iraq war as a great career opportunity, a chance to make a name for themselves. The Pentagon intimidated journalists and apparently decided to target some of them as a warning to the rest. An Aljazeera correspondent was murdered by a U.S. missile, though the American military knew the network's location. A U.S. tank shelled the journalist-filled Palestine Hotel—without provocation—killing two and wounding several others. The U.S. military has not investigated these incidents.

For the media corporations, war was a product like any other. They sold it—with high-tech digital imagery, dramatic music, and saturation coverage—and we bought it. TV has become a propaganda system, designed to sell things, including war. But the media corporations had other reasons besides ratings not to rock the boat over Iraq. They had business before the Federal Communications Commission, which subsequently relaxed already lenient media ownership rules, allowing the large corporations to expand their holdings even further. "Did the FCC waive the rules if media agreed to wave the flag?" Schechter wonders.

FCC chairman Michael Powell, son of Secretary of State Colin Powell, adopted a deregulatory style of regulation, deciding in favor of expanded media ownership. So the corporate owners of media have their own conflicts of interest. Their networks back an administration that rewards them handsomely for their support. And the American viewing public—as Danny Schechter says—is "left with jingoism instead of journalism."

The war and the run-up to it were covered differently outside the United States, "and in many cases, more accurately." Donald Rumsfeld and others criticized Aljazeera and other Arab networks for bias, but U.S. networks bought a lot of bombing footage from them and replayed it, stripped of narrative. The U.S. media fees helped finance the Arab networks' coverage. For the rest of the world, watching the war on TV outside the United States, the addition of the Arab networks to the world mix in 2003 was "as important as CNN in 1991" during the Gulf War, according to one British journalist.

WMD not only chronicles U.S. media coverage of the Iraqi war, what Schechter rightly calls "a shameful chapter in journalism," but it also describes the alarming insularity of the most powerful nation on earth, cut off by a totalitarian media from the rest of the world and from reality. Like Barbara Kopple's labor films, Danny Schechter's *WMD* is muckraking journalism in the best sense, an exposure of corruption and a call to action. If we ignore its message, our democratic society, based on an informed citizenry and the free flow of information, cannot long survive.

In all her work, Barbara Kopple engages her iconoclastic urge to get beyond personal and cultural illusions to the way things really are. We cannot—as individuals or as a society—afford to entertain those illusions, or, in the case of media, allow them to entertain us. As the children in *Friends for Life* know, who live with AIDS, illusions can be fatal.

Chapter 5

MICHAEL MOORE: AMBUSH ARTIST

Who among us wouldn't love to go to the movies and split a gut laughing; be surprised, shocked, reduced to tears . . . blown away?
—Michael Moore

When Michael Moore's *Bowling for Columbine* won an Academy Award in 2002, it was the most financially successful documentary ever. Two years later, Moore's *Fahrenheit 9/11* surpassed that success on its opening weekend. Released in the summer before the 2004 U.S. presidential election, the anti-Bush administration film became a powerful rallying point for both Bush detractors and Bush supporters. That it arrived in American theaters with the imprimatur of the Cannes Film Festival's Palme D'Or award only spiked the controversy. No film has ever played such a prominent role in U.S. electoral politics.

The movie's potency can be measured by the prodigious outpouring of oppositional films, books, Web sites, and media denunciations directed against its messages and, especially, against its maker. Many on the right were incensed by Moore's Oscar acceptance speech in March 2003, during the Iraqi invasion, when he called George W. Bush "a fictitious president" from "a fictitious election" who was leading us to war for "fictitious reasons." In *Fahrenheit 9/11*, Moore highlighted the Bush family's Saudi connections and characterized George W. Bush as a corrupt clown and serial deceiver, rendering his critics apoplectic. The outrage and vituperation against Moore continued well after the election and shows no signs of abating anytime soon. The man and his film became widely recognized icons of a deeply polarized country.

In the fierce contentious heat that now surrounds Michael Moore, it is difficult to summon the surprising impact of his first film, *Roger & Me*.

Part of the surprise was that Moore arrived out of nowhere in American theaters in 1989, a full-blown, accomplished filmmaker. Moore's first movie surveyed the devastating effects of General Motors plant closings on his hometown, and GM's birthplace, Flint, Michigan. He accused GM of betraying longtime employees to make larger profits by producing their products overseas. The "Roger" of the title was General Motors CEO Roger Smith.

As Moore says in the film, "My mission was a simple one, to convince Roger Smith to spend a day with me in Flint, to talk to some of the workers laid off by General Motors." Of course, Moore knows that will never happen, but that premise provides a focus for his righteous anger and his withering wit.

Moore introduces himself ("I was kind of a strange child . . .") with snapshots and home movies of himself as a small boy, old black-and-white GM promotional films, and 1950s GM television commercials featuring Pat Boone and Dinah Shore. He shows us the "great day" when GM staged its fiftieth-anniversary parade in the streets of Flint, with marching bands, floats, beauty queens, and dancing AC sparkplugs. He tells us his father worked on GM's AC sparkplug assembly line for 33 years. Many members of his family were GM employees, including his grandfather and an uncle, who took part in the 44-day strike in 1936-1937 that helped create the United Auto Workers union.

He flashes photos of famous escapees from Flint, including the rock group Grand Funk Railroad, Casey Kasem, and TV game show host Bob Eubanks. "I thought if Bob Eubanks could make it, so could I." Moore briefly mentions his journalism career, as editor of an alternative weekly newspaper, which led to a job offer from "a California millionaire" to edit the leftist monthly magazine *Mother Jones*. A quick touristic montage of San Francisco streets and coffee houses and a *Mother Jones* cover featuring a Flint auto worker flash by as Moore tells us he soon returned to Flint, followed by a 1940s homecoming scene of a soldier being welcomed back by his tearful family and Moore saying, "Okay, so maybe it wasn't exactly like that."

These opening minutes of Moore's first film tell us a great deal about him as a filmmaker and a person. We quickly see that Moore is smart and funny, with a wonderful sense of irony and pacing. Moore tells us, "I never went to film school. I learned about movies from watching them." But he is clearly a skilled compilation filmmaker, using bits of stock footage as artifacts of earlier times to convey nostalgic, naïve beliefs and as hilarious slapstick counterpoint to his deadpan narration. He knows where to find this vintage film and how to use it.

His wit allows him greater license to make broad claims and accusations without leaving a sour aftertaste. The sight gags and the ironic juxtapositions of the visual and narrative tracks sugarcoat the sometimes bitter pill of social criticism that lies at the heart of his presentation. When the lush, upbeat harmonies of the Beach Boys hit "Wouldn't It Be Nice" burble beneath a long panning shot of wrecked, dilapidated houses in Flint, block after block, the laughter is meant to catch in your throat.

Moore has honed and refined his techniques over the years. In *Fahrenheit 9/11*, when Moore notes that George W. Bush was suspended as a National Guard pilot for refusing to take a medical exam, four musical notes sound, with no explanation. Only those who recognize the opening guitar riff from Eric Clapton's song "Cocaine" will get the musical accusation.

It is also clear early on in *Roger & Me* that Michael Moore intends to keep himself front and center. Though he appears only briefly as a child in the initial sequences, his imposing adult personage fills many of the frames in this and subsequent films. Whether masquerading as a TV newsman to get into an auto plant, interviewing little people about big issues, or trying to push past corporate flunkeys to beard white-collar miscreants in their aeries, Moore largely remains in character as a shambling, slovenly—if bright and relentless—Everyman, out to confront the heartless Corporate Beast. Moore's persona incarnates blatant buffoonery and righteous indignation. He's a *faux-naïf* whose apparently simplistic questions tease out the hypocrisy and greed behind the feel-good surfaces of modern corporate flummery.

Unlike documentarians who simply point and shoot or else supply off-camera narration, Moore stars in his films as an on-screen provocateur. Seldom content merely to observe the action unfolding before him, he wants to push it and shape it, to reveal what's behind it. Moore's prominent on-screen presence caused immediate controversy that continues today. Critics accused him of egomania and deception. Unhurried and apparently unflappable, Moore lets others (including the film's viewers) experience the discomfort of his cheeky trespasses. Asked to leave the corporate premises by GM flacks, in lieu of his business card Moore offers his Chuck E. Cheese frequent diner card.

Moore aims to surprise us one way and another, with film clips we haven't seen, statistics we never knew, or stunts we'd never have dreamed up. He wants to amuse us or appall us, or both. Flint achieved notoriety as the unemployment capital of Reagan's America, designated by *Money* magazine as the worst place in the country to live. Moore shows Reagan himself taking laid-off GM workers out for pizza and advising them to move to Texas. The mayor of Flint paid TV evangelist Robert Schuller $20,000 to preach inspiration to city residents. "Tough times don't last, but tough people do," Schuller advises. "Turn your hurt into a halo. . . . Just because you've got problems is no excuse to be unhappy." Schuller delivers these bromides with ministerial pomp. But knowing the size of his paycheck renders his words empty and hypocritical.

When Moore asks the lovely Miss Michigan for her message to the people of Flint, she replies with a deer-in-the-headlights grin, asking them to "Wish me well in the Miss America contest"—which she won, Moore lets us know. He sometimes edits with a heavy hand, showing Roger Smith reading a Charles Dickens message of good cheer at a lavish corporate Christmas party while former GM employees, unable to pay their rent, are being evicted from their shabby apartment on Christmas Eve, their Christmas tree dumped on the curb. Subtle it's not, as Yoda might say, but effective it is.

Moore gives audiences lots of information, but makes no pretense of practicing "objective" journalism. He uses TV news clips primarily to mock their formulaic limitations. Media superficiality is simply one more ingredient in the layered, emotional impingement of national trends on personal pathos that Moore wants to show us, the radical reality of absurdity and heartbreak most of us live with but that media largely fail to engage. Moore is making an emotional case as well as a factual one. He wants us to care, to indict, and to convict not just Roger Smith, but also the system he represents, the enshrined greed of capitalism that enriches so few and exploits so many while media nod and say "and that's the way it is."

Seeing *Roger & Me* at the New York Festival, before the film found a distributor, *New York Times* critic Vincent Canby thought Moore's "rude and rollicking documentary" made him "an irrepressible new humorist in the tradition of Mark Twain and Artemus Ward." Canby relished the moment when Moore got the microphone at a GM stockholders meeting only to be cut off, and then caught Roger Smith on the dais, not realizing his own microphone was still on, bragging how he had deftly avoided embarrassment. "*Roger & Me* is stuffed with such remarkable 'found' moments, which are not really found at all. They may be unplanned, but only a filmmaker thoroughly at ease with his subject, and aware of various possibilities, is going to be in a position to find those moments." Warner Brothers bought the film for $3 million and showed it nationwide. It became the most financially successful documentary film of all time, the start of a Michael Moore tradition.

Roger & Me attracted several festival awards and a lot of favorable comment, but also fierce attacks, inaugurating another Moore tradition. *Film Comment* ran a cover story on Moore tagged "Motor Mouth Michael Moore," with tire treads across his shirt. The article inside accused Moore of compressing the events of many years and manipulating the time sequence for his film, deceiving viewers about when things happened. Pauline Kael went further in *The New Yorker*, calling the film "shallow and facetious, a piece of gonzo demagoguery that made me feel cheap for laughing."

Kael accused Moore of making "brutal fun" of the people he interviewed, setting them up as "targets for the audience's laughter." She judged the movie "very offensive . . . like the work of a slick ad exec" using "its leftism as a superior attitude. Members of the audience can laugh at ordinary working people and still feel that they're taking a politically correct position." Chicago film critic Roger Ebert disagreed that Moore was ridiculing his subjects. "I think he is looking at the infinite goofiness of human nature—at the things people will say—with the same deadpan astonishment that I sometimes have when I watch the TV news." As for playing fast and loose with the sequence of actual events, Ebert thought Moore was simply "taking the liberties that satirists and ironists have taken with material for generations." His movie offered something "more important and more rare than facts. It supplies poetry, a viewpoint, indignation, opinion, anger, and humor. When Michael Moore waves his sheaf of *New York Times* clippings in the air and defends the facts in his film, he's missing his own point." Or as Vincent Canby put it, "Mr. Moore makes no attempt to be fair. Playing fair is for college football. In social criticism, anything goes, as it goes triumphantly in *Roger & Me*."

The surprising popular success of Moore's first film and the ferocious backlash against it would be surpassed by his later work, as his targets broadened, his techniques sharpened, and the stakes increased. With the same zeal that he pursued Roger Smith, Moore charged ahead with his career, armed with a deep moral certainty, an irreverence for authority, and a gift for improvisation that would propel him from the margins of social criticism to the center of national politics.

THE MOORE YOU KNOW, THE MOORE YOU DON'T

Born in 1954 and raised in Davison, Michigan, a suburb of Flint, Michael Moore grew up in a pro-union working-class Irish Catholic family. A self-confessed "good kid," Moore was an altar boy, a seminarian, and a National Rifle Association marksmanship award winner. As an 18-year-old longhair, Moore was elected to the school board. He ran on a platform to get rid of the school principal and assistant principal. Both resigned less than a year after Moore took office. He dabbled in college at the University of Michigan's Flint campus, but soon dropped out. At 22, he started an alternative weekly newspaper, the *Flint Voice*, later the *Michigan Voice*. Moore's journalistic mission was to "stay on top of General Motors and get people to think about what it was doing to the town." To help defray expenses, Moore exhibited alternative movies, hosted "Radio Free Flint" on a local station, and contributed occasional essays to National Public Radio.

Ten years after launching his career as a muckraking journalist, Moore was hired to edit *Mother Jones*, a well-produced leftist California monthly magazine with a national readership. "Maybe I was having someone else's hallucination," Moore wrote in his first *Mother Jones* editorial. "After a lifetime of 32 years in Flint, Michigan, I was on a plane to my new home in San Francisco." Moore had wanted to make his newspaper "'the *Mother Jones* of Michigan.' Now I too am in California, editing the magazine that once inspired me to start a paper in my hometown."

Moore admired the magazine's political values but admitted he had not been "entirely satisfied with *Mother Jones* in the past." He planned "to return *Mother Jones* to its muckraking, hell-raising roots with the kind of hard-hitting journalism that is sorely lacking in the U.S. media these days." Moore charged TV journalists with helping apply a Teflon coating to Reagan's presidency, which he promised to scrape off with "a metal spatula . . . although it will be a few months until *Mother Jones* reflects my humble contributions." But by the following month he was gone.

Mother Jones founding editor Adam Hochschild said he fired Moore not over "differences of political vision" but for "more mundane" reasons:

Moore's "ability to perform a demanding job at the level required, to manage a staff effectively, and to work well with others." After a few months, "it was clear to almost all of us who had to work with him most closely that there was a real mismatch between Moore and the editorship of *Mother Jones*." Hochschild deplored the way writers with their own agendas had misrepresented the dispute in other leftist periodicals. And he excoriated Moore for holding "a press conference on the steps of San Francisco City hall, announcing that he was filing a $2 million lawsuit against me and *Mother Jones*'s parent foundation."

By the summer of 2004, Moore could afford to chuckle about the experience and opine that "everyone should be fired at least once in their life." But in the winter of 1986-1987 he was forced to live on unemployment benefits in Flint while he contemplated his next move. Moore had become friends with Kevin Rafferty, a talented compilation filmmaker, who (with his brother Pierce, and Jayne Loader) had created *The Atomic Café* in 1982. The film featured hilarious clips of 1950s educational films, government propaganda, and (mis)information about the atomic bomb and atomic energy. It became a festival favorite and a cult hit.

In the late 1980s, Kevin Rafferty, Anne Bohlen, and *Village Voice* writer James Ridgeway were shooting a film about right-wing militia groups, neo-Nazis, and the White Power movement called *Blood in the Face*. Like *The Atomic Café*, the film would be both funny and disturbing. But instead of assembling a pastiche of vintage film clips, *Blood in the Face* relied on original footage and interviews. Moore agreed to line up radical right-wing fringe groups for the filmmakers in Michigan. Moore appears on camera in the film, interviewing an attractive blonde female member of Aryan Nations. He tells the woman she ought to be in a Coppertone ad instead of at a White Power rally. Playing the rube, violating the proprieties of an interviewer, Moore is sloppily dressed, asking pushy, irreverent questions.

In his book, *Stupid White Men*, Moore credits Kevin Rafferty—a cousin of George W. Bush—with teaching him how to make films. Rafferty worked as a cinematographer on *Roger & Me*. To bankroll his film, Moore used his $58,000 out-of-court settlement from *Mother Jones*, ran bingo games, and exhibited alternative films. It took Moore; his wife, Kathleen Glynn; and their crew three years and a quarter of a million dollars to make *Roger & Me*.

"Our intent was to finish it, hop in a van, and drive around the country showing it in union halls, community centers, and church groups,"

Moore and Glynn wrote later. "We silk-screened some T-shirts and took them to sell at our first film festival so we could afford the trip back home. Instead, our film was bought by Warner Bros., and eventually shown in nearly two thousand theaters."

Moore tried to follow this success with a feature film. In 1991, he wrote the screenplay for *Canadian Bacon*, which he thought of as "a farcical take-off on the Gulf War." But Warner Brothers and other Hollywood studios judged the film "too political." According to Moore, he had no thought of producing a television show until NBC solicited a pitch from him. Bob Simon of CBS's *60 Minutes* later characterized Moore's *TV Nation* as a cross between *60 Minutes* and *Saturday Night Live*. But the program more closely resembled *Candid Camera* with a political agenda and the anti-corporate in-your-face attitude of *Roger & Me*. NBC gave Moore a million dollars to produce a pilot program, but did not include the show in its 1993–1994 season.

Moore loaned the *TV Nation* pilot to John Candy and Alan Alda, along with the script of *Canadian Bacon*. When both actors agreed to star in the film, Moore quickly got studio backing and made the movie. Alda plays a U.S. president who decides to invade Canada to improve his popularity polls. Candy plays a laid-off defense plant worker turned cop in Niagara Falls, who leads an impromptu raid north across the border. Often silly, the film offers some gentle political commentary. When the president says to his advisor, "Canada? The American people will never buy it," the advisor responds, "Mr. President, you know the American people will buy whatever we sell them." *Canadian Bacon* proved a precursor to Barry Levinson's sharper, darker comedy on the same theme, *Wag the Dog*.

TV Nation premiered on NBC in the summer of 1994 as a summer replacement series of eight episodes. It featured Moore's sometimes inspired, sometimes insipid stunts designed to embarrass bigots, corporate wrongdoers, and social miscreants. In the first episode, Moore traveled to the Mexican border city of Reynosa, pretending to investigate the possibility of outsourcing his own show to save money under NAFTA. He found Mexican workers at U.S. firms earning 75 cents an hour and living in crumbling shacks with no running water while their American managers lived in huge homes across the border in McAllen, Texas. Tugging on his GM Mexico baseball hat, Moore asked an American Whirlpool executive in Reynosa, "How would you say in Spanish, 'As soon as you get your arm out of that machine, you're fired?'"

Also on the first show, Moore demonstrated that a prominent, well-dressed Black actor has more trouble getting a cab in New York than a convicted White felon. Cabs zipped past actor Yaphet Kotto to pick up a White man half a block away. Cabbies told the show's interviewers they didn't see Kotto, so Moore shined a spotlight on him, had him hold flowers and expensive-looking gifts, and finally rolled out a huge sign with a pointing arrow that read "I need a cab." Even a decked-out circus clown got a ride before Kotto. Few beside Michael Moore thought to court laughs by highlighting racist reality on American TV. *Time* magazine called Moore "a hybrid of two Ralphs—Kramden and Nader."

Between segments, "TV Nation" ran authentic but quirky poll results, such as "65% of all Americans believe that frozen pizza will never be any good and there's nothing science can do about it." Or "70% of American women have never had an emotionally satisfying relationship with a Republican." Viewer reaction was positive enough for NBC to commission a "*TV Nation* Year-End Special" in December. Moore offered donations to corporations who had paid stiff fines in 1994 for various misdeeds, such as Kodak, fined $8 million for dumping toxic waste, and DuPont, fined $200 million for fungicide pollution. He held a Corps-Aid concert on Wall Street to raise money for Exxon, fined $5 billion for its Alaskan oil spill. Offering the proceeds to an Exxon executive, Moore said, "Accidents happen. Who hasn't spilled something?"

Reviewing U.S. military invasions of 1994 (in Haiti, Somalia, and Kuwait), Moore asked viewers where we should send our troops in 1995. Given the choice of invading Belize or France—or spending the money on our schools—viewers chose France. Uneven as usual, the show ranged from lame bits—hiring a private security guard for the White House—to hilarious ones—Steven Wright asking professionals in various fields for their New Year's predictions. (Wright to a dentist: "Is there a chance in 1995 that you'll say to someone, 'This won't hurt a bit,' when really you know it will?")

NBC declined to renew Moore's contract, but Fox ordered a summer's worth of *TV Nation* for 1995. On "Love Night," Moore took a mariachi band to sing love songs at a KKK rally in Georgia and African American cheerleaders to an Aryan Nations conclave in Idaho. Moore had a Gay Men's Chorus serenade the homophobic Senator Jesse Helms and took leaders of the gun-toting Michigan Militia to an amusement park to mellow them out. The Militia would later figure prominently in *Bowling for Columbine*.

Moore's Fox program took up racial profiling with the case of Brian Anthony Harris, a law-abiding Washington, D.C., television network technician who had been stopped more than twenty times by the D.C. police. *TV Nation* printed up "Not Wanted" posters, rented billboards on buses and roadsides, bought TV time, and hired an airplane trailing a banner to proclaim Harris's innocence, finally getting an off-camera apology from the police. At the end of the segment, Moore gave a 900 number for African American men to call if they had been stopped without reason by police and wanted their names placed on a billboard near the FBI building. According to Moore and Glynn, "The phones rang off the hook."

TV Nation introduced Crackers, the Corporate Crime-Fighting Chicken, a seven-foot-tall "superhero" who specialized in bringing white-collar criminals to justice. One of his first visits was to a large bank. New York City had given First Boston Bank a multimillion-dollar tax break to keep jobs in the city. Thirty days after getting their tax break, First Boston laid off more than a hundred employees. Crackers demanded that either the workers be reinstated or the people's money returned, but was quickly hustled out of the bank by security. Mayor Rudolf Giuliani refused to take any action. On the same show, Crackers also visited a manufacturer of unsafe baby strollers.

TV Nation gave Crackers an RV to travel the country seeking out wrongdoers. He confronted corporate malfeasance in Philadelphia, Detroit, and St. Louis. The program set up an 800 number for people "to report corporate crimes in progress. Over forty thousand calls were received the first weekend."

Some *TV Nation* segments proved too controversial for the networks to broadcast. NBC axed a piece about radical antiabortion activists who harass women entering abortion clinics. Fox refused to air a "where are they now?" segment about the men responsible for the savings and loans scandals of the 1980s. Nor would Fox permit a Civil War–style reenactment of the Los Angeles race riots that followed the Rodney King beating trial. Fox also suppressed an episode showing a man braving the snickers of clerks as he searched New York drugstores for a small-sized condom, and another about a high school in Topeka, Kansas, that gave extra credit to a student picketing funerals of AIDS victims with a sign that read "GOD HATES FAGS!" Fox did not renew *TV Nation*, but the program won an Emmy Award in September of 1995 for Outstanding Informational Series.

DISARMING MOSES

After *TV Nation*, Michael Moore embarked on a prodigious synergistic production of books, movies, and television that dramatically increased his cultural visibility. Moore published *Downsize This!: Random Threats from an Unarmed American* in 1996. He turned his book promotion tour into a series of confrontations with corporations nationwide that were firing workers and moving plants overseas to increase their already high profits. His film of the tour, *The Big One*, was released in 1998, the same year he and his wife published *Adventures in a TV Nation*, presaging his return to television with *The Awful Truth*. Moore's prolific output was only gathering momentum. He would follow his second TV series with two best-selling books, *Stupid White Men* and *Dude, Where's My Country*, achieving a new, more ambitious level of social comment—and controversy—with the 2002 Academy Award–winning *Bowling for Columbine*.

Fahrenheit 9/11, "the first film ever made to justify an Oscar acceptance speech," as Quentin Tarantino suggested to Moore, thrust the documentary filmmaker into the maelstrom of a contentious presidential election. Media oversimplified the 2004 race as being between "red" Republican states and "blue" Democratic ones. In the mediacentric popular press, Mel Gibson's *Passion of the Christ* supposedly represented core red values as opposed to the blue values of Moore's film, a win-win contest for Hollywood. Moore instantly spun two books off his movie—one containing the script, his evidence for the film's charges, and media reactions, and the other with letters about the film from U.S. servicemen—and found himself battling hostility on the right and jealousy on the left.

"Friendly fire" at Moore began soon after *Downsize This!* appeared. Moore's book revealed its author to be Crackers the Corporate Crime-Fighting Chicken at heart. Juxtaposing a photograph of the federal building in Oklahoma City destroyed by domestic terrorists with a photo of a building being demolished in Flint thanks to GM's economic pullout, the book equated corporate greed with terrorism. Moore widened his indictment of corporate immorality. He suggested that if GM really wanted to maximize profits for shareholders they ought to produce crack instead of cars. He presented enough research to argue persuasively that corporate crime is far costlier, more pervasive, and less publicized than street crime.

"There is little here that *Roger & Me* didn't say first and more memorably," wrote Roger Ebert in his review of *The Big One*. James Berardinelli found it "a little troubling how much grief he gives the average working guys who stop him (they are, after all, ordinary men and women trying to hold down a job—the kind of people Moore proclaims to be a voice for)." Many of the corporate security guards could be temps engaged by Manpower, which is now, as Moore points out, the country's leading employer. Moore's alleged mistreatment of working people—that Pauline Kael complained of years earlier—would continue to bother critics of his later films.

As Ebert noted, Moore in *The Big One* is still dressed in "the gimme caps and the blue jeans with the saggy seats," but he is a celebrity now, not an unknown, and is recognized everywhere. We see Moore doing political stand-up comedy for college audiences along with his bookstore appearances. His celebrity has advantages. Striking workers at Borders Books seek him out for his advice about forming a union. In fact, he's a lightning rod for disaffected workers wherever he goes.

Nike CEO Phil Knight agrees to meet with Moore on camera and donate $10,000 to help laid-off workers in Flint. But Knight declines to build a shoe factory in Flint or to accompany Moore on a visit to Indonesia, where Nike sweatshops employ children and pay miserable wages. Decidedly minor Moore, *The Big One* combined shtick from his first film with stunts from his television show. But Moore's working class identity had begun to clash with his growing wealth and fame. Berardinelli claimed he could not tell whether *The Big One* referred to "the United States of America or Michael Moore's ego."

Before the film's release, a *Salon* article attacked Moore as "loud-mouthed, self-serving, and not funny." The author, Daniel Radosh, claimed that Moore's book—like his film and his TV show—"was mediocre at best, but progressives championed it and propelled it onto the best-seller lists" because they liked his politics. Radosh accused Moore of being a self-promoting egomaniac who humiliated people on camera, treated his own employees badly, and flaunted working-class values while living in a million-dollar Upper West Side Manhattan apartment.

Moore accused *Salon* of attacking him because he supported an employees' union at Borders, a major *Salon* underwriter. He also thought *Salon* editor David Talbot, who resigned from *Mother Jones* in 1986 when Moore was hired, was still jealous of Moore's ascent there. Moore defended his films and insisted that all his *TV Nation* writers were union members at his own urging.

The Big One surfaced in 1998, along with Moore and Glynn's book, *Adventures in a TV Nation*, recapping the episodes and reactions to the show's two summer seasons. Moore's second television program, *The Awful Truth*, premiered on Bravo and the BBC as a late-night series in 1999. *The Awful Truth* was *TV Nation* with a larger budget, fewer constraints, more showmanship, and greater authority. Moore no longer hosted his show on the street in Times Square but in a well-appointed theater. Crackers now took on the Disney Corporation's unfair labor practices, showing the sweatshops where Disney products were made and visiting Walt Disney World in Orlando to debrief the workers who played the costumed characters there under difficult conditions.

Moore drove a pink bus he labeled the Soddomobile, full of prancing, scantily clad gay men on a tour of all the states with anti-sodomy laws. He finally confronted the homophobic bigots in Kansas who held up signs saying "God Hates Fags" as he could not do on his earlier network show. He toured the corporate offices of Philip Morris and R.J. Reynolds tobacco companies at Christmas, leading carolers who had lost their larynxes to throat cancer due to smoking. These were among his better-conceived and more memorable stunts. A number of others fell flat. Though relegated to a late hour on a cable channel, *The Awful Truth* made for edgy, exhilarating, often hilarious TV.

When *The Awful Truth* wrapped its run, Moore went to work on a book about the administration of George W. Bush, the Thief-in-Chief, as Moore labeled him. Moore characterized Bush's takeover of the White House as a coup. "Old white men wielding martinis and wearing dickies have occupied our nation's capital. . . . Launch the SCUD missiles!" Moore recounted the Republican theft of the presidential election in Florida and retailed the lies and corruption of "the Bush family junta" and friends like Enron's Ken Lay. But his book, *Stupid White Men*, was almost not published.

As Moore wrote later, "By the morning of September 11, 2001, the HarperCollins printing presses . . . had already printed 50,000 copies of an announced 100,000-copy first printing . . . when the world . . . came to a standstill." His publisher wanted Moore to change the title and the cover and rewrite huge portions of the text. Moore balked. Learning of the controversy, a group of librarians lobbied HarperCollins, which finally relented, publishing the book in February 2002. *Stupid White Men* quickly climbed to the top of the best-seller list and remained there a year.

In Michael Moore's golden spring of 2002, his just-finished film, *Bowling for Columbine*, was invited to compete at the Cannes Film Festival, the first documentary so honored in almost fifty years. The film won a prize, great applause, and worldwide distribution, arriving in American theaters in October on a tidal wave of buzz, assuring wide distribution and large audiences. With his deft blend of comedy and anger, his sharp eye for quirky detail and his weakness for glib generalizations, Moore explored America's obsession with guns and its peculiar penchant for gun violence.

Taking the 1999 shootings at Columbine High School in Colorado as his jumping-off point, Moore tries to understand why Americans shoot each other in far greater numbers than do citizens of any other country. He visits a bank that gives a free gun to anyone who opens a new account. The bank conducts its own, on-the-spot background check and Moore walks out waving a rifle. But easy access to weapons does not explain the disproportionate U.S. murder statistics. Moore later finds it equally easy to buy weapons and ammunition in Canada. But Canadians don't resort to gun violence as Americans do. They aren't as fearful as Americans. They leave their doors unlocked, even in Toronto, as Moore discovers by opening some. Canadians have guns aplenty—ten million families own seven million guns—but they don't use them on each other. Moore points to the calm presentation of news on Canadian television as one reason. Missing are the hysterical pace and inflection of U.S. media reports, which emphasize photogenic violence and operate on the principle that "if it bleeds, it leads."

Moore's film is literally all over the map, but he returns again and again to Columbine High School and to Flint, Michigan. Moore calls Michigan—where both he and actor Charlton Heston grew up—"a gun lover's paradise." Moore earned an NRA marksman award as a teen. Heston became the NRA president in 1998. Moore talks to members of the Michigan Militia; one of them says, "It's your job to defend you and yours. If you don't do it, you're in dereliction of your duty as an American."

Clever editing and a rapid-fire pace help to smooth the transitions, which aren't always logical. Several set pieces jump out of the movie. Moore presents "A Brief History of the USA," a hilarious animated saga of racism and paranoia that lays out the violent American past for those with the shortest attention spans. Later, an official at Lockheed Martin near Littleton, Colorado, tells Moore that the missiles his company makes are for deterrence, not aggression. "We don't hurt or kill people just because we don't like them," he says. In rebuttal, Moore offers a horrifying montage of bloody U.S.-sponsored coups and assassinations around the world since

1953. His newsreel-like survey cuts from Iran to Central America to Vietnam to Chile, piled high with the bullet-riddled bodies of people the United States killed because it didn't like them, while, in ironic counterpoint, Louis Armstrong sings "What a wonderful world." Moore knows he cannot count on the historical knowledge of audiences, especially in the United States.

When politicians and parents blame shock rockers like Marilyn Manson for stimulating violent attitudes in teens, Moore talks to Manson, who articulates the cultural dynamics of violence precisely. Like Moore, Manson blames U.S. mass media for "a campaign of fear and consumption. Keep everybody afraid and they'll consume." Moore repeatedly indicts the news media for creating fear. As he learns from University of Southern California professor Barry Glassner, author of the book *Culture of Fear*, although murder rates are down in the United States, murder news coverage is up. Whereas crime rates are dropping, the fear of crime is rising. Walking with Glassner in South Central Los Angeles, Moore concludes there is less to fear from racial violence than from the pollution that disfigures the city. "Will you arrest the polluters?" he asks a cop, who turns away.

In a hyper *TV Nation* moment, Moore confronts officials of K-Mart with two disabled Columbine victims who still carry bullets in their bodies from the massacre. Those nine-millimeter bullets were sold by K-Mart. Moore gets the two boys to demand that K-Mart stop selling the bullets. Within days, K-Mart promises to stop selling all ammunition in their stores—a small but stunning victory.

The film's final set piece—an interview with Charlton Heston—turned out to be the most controversial. Moore enters the electronic gate at Heston's home to the strains of "It's a beautiful day in the neighborhood," from Mr. Rogers. In previous clips, Moore has shown Heston on the scene in Denver ten days after Columbine, holding a rifle aloft at an NRA meeting, proclaiming, "From my cold dead hands!" Denver's mayor had asked him not to come, but Heston replied, "Don't come here? We're already here!" Heston also led an NRA rally in Flint, Michigan, shortly after a six-year-old boy there shot and killed his first-grade classmate with a gun he found at home.

Moore asks Heston why *he* thinks so many Americans kill each other with guns. "Well, American history has a lot of blood on its hands . . . ," says Heston. "More than Germany? Japan? England?" Moore retorts.

"We have more mixed ethnicity . . . ," Heston says. "Do you think it was at all insensitive of you to come to Denver and Flint so soon after those tragedies?" Moore asks an incredulous Heston. "Would you like to apologize to the people of Flint? Or Columbine?" "You want *me* to apol- . . .?" When Moore pulls out a photo of the six-year-old gun victim, Heston scuttles away.

Bowling for Columbine represented a quantum leap for Michael Moore, a major achievement. He uses his evolving skills as a filmmaker to grapple with a serious social problem from various angles. His mix of humor and pathos, stock footage and creative interviews, personal stories, and national trends works better here than ever. If the answers to his questions about American violence prove as elusive in the end as those about GM's Roger Smith, the point of the journey is the journey itself, getting us to think in new ways about the world we take for granted, and to ask whether it's the one we really want.

Critical reception varied, with *New York Times* reviewer A. O. Scott of at least two minds about the film, finding it "disturbing, infuriating, and often very funny," though full of "slippery logic, tendentious grandstanding, and outright demagoguery." Hoping Moore's film would stir debate, Scott feared it would merely elicit "uncritical support from his ideological friends and summary dismissal from his foes." Andrew Sarris deplored Moore's "cheap shots," especially against Charlton Heston. Sarris's prediction that "Michael Moore is not likely to be nominated for an Oscar for Best Documentary Feature anytime soon" proved spectacularly off the mark. Online critic Ned Depew found the film "inconclusive, fragmentary, confusing, and upsetting—which is to say . . . everything Mr. Moore hoped it would be . . . a powerful contribution to the national dialogue on violence." Audiences voted with their record attendance for a non-concert documentary. The film grossed more than $20 million and won an Academy Award.

THE TEMPERATURE OF TREACHERY

"Was it all just a dream?" asks Michael Moore, as fireworks burst over Al Gore's Florida victory celebration in 2000 at the opening of *Fahrenheit 9/11*. "God bless you, Florida! Thank you!" yells the doomed Gore, beaming amid a clutch of movie stars. "Did the last four years not really happen?" A hurry-up banjo riff à la *Deliverance* signals a sinister redneck mafia at work in the background. Moore recaps election night 2000 as the TV networks call Florida for Gore, and then recant. Bush's cousin, John Ellis, at Fox, led the turnabout. We flash from Florida Governor Jeb Bush, George's brother; to Florida Secretary of the State Katherine Harris, chair of the Bush campaign in Florida and the one charged with counting Florida votes; and then to former Secretary of State James Baker, longtime crony of the candidate's father, who says: "I think all this talk about legitimacy is overblown."

These well-coiffed, well-spoken, and impeccably dressed scoundrels—with illegal help from their Supreme Court cronies and passive Democratic opponents—pulled off a massive electoral fraud while the whole world watched and did nothing. We then see the joint session of Congress meeting to certify the election, with Al Gore presiding. One by one, members of the Black Caucus in the House of Representatives move to challenge the election results, which were based, in the words of Congressman Alcee Hastings, on "the overwhelming evidence of official misconduct, deliberate fraud, and an attempt to suppress voter turnout." But congressional rules require at least one U.S. Senator to join the challenge, and such a person cannot be found. The camera pans the gallery filled with Senators sitting on their hands. None of the so-called liberals—Kennedy, Biden, Leahy, Murray, Feingold—or the men personally defrauded—Gore and Lieberman—stand up against the official misconduct and fraud. The shameful procession continues as Black congressmen and -women appeal for support, only to be graveled down by Gore.

Cut to Inauguration Day. On the rainy Washington streets, tens of thousands of demonstrators have come to vent their anger at the coup. The jeering crowd stops the presidential motorcade, pelting Bush's limo with eggs, waving signs of protest. "No President had ever witnessed such a thing on his Inauguration Day," Moore says. And we realize that we never saw this shocking event on television, as we did not see the appalling spectacle of the U.S. Senate abetting the theft of the presidency. Why not? American media corporations chose to conceal these events from their viewers.

One of the valuable services *Fahrenheit 9/11* performs is to rescue and exhibit important, even crucial, images of recent reality suppressed by the U.S. news media. In these early scenes, and especially with later footage from Iraq, Moore shatters the censorship imposed upon Americans by the U.S. government and its media allies in order to manipulate

public opinion. In sequence after sequence, Moore graphically demonstrates that we have not been given all the information we need to judge
the true merits of our leaders and their conduct of events.

Moore makes no secret of his critical stance toward the Bush administration, reiterating and updating his tirades in *Stupid White Men* and *Dude,
Where's My Country?* Unlike his previous films, *Fahrenheit 9/11* does not
center on Moore's own persona. He narrates the film but largely remains
in the background, especially at the start. He puts the early focus on
George W. Bush. When Bob Simon later charged Moore on *60 Minutes*
with humiliating people in his movies, Moore said, "I drag people in
front of the camera who have made millions miserable and they humiliate themselves."

The film portrays Bush as a "lame duck president," on vacation more
than forty percent of his first eight months in office, hiding out in Craw-
ford, Texas. In a long, hilarious sequence reminiscent of the film *Feed*,
Moore shows Bush, Rumsfeld, Cheney, Powell, and Rice being made up
for TV. Paul Wolfowitz licks his comb and grins. Ashcroft primps and
chortles. Then comes the terror of September 11, 2001. Moore does not
show us the attacks. He knows we have all seen them repeatedly. He leaves
the screen dark, letting us fill it in, leaving only the sounds of fear and confusion from that day.

Though informed that a plane had hit the World Trade Center, Bush
decides to go ahead with his planned visit to a Florida elementary school.
As Bush sits in the classroom, his Chief of Staff Andrew Card whispers in
his ear that a second plane has hit the World Trade Center: "The nation is
under attack." Bush continues to sit with the children as they read *My Pet
Goat*. Seven minutes tick by on the clock.

Many reviewers found the scene of Bush paralyzed and apparently
clueless in the classroom the most devastating moment in the film. Critics
responded with fury, disputing the time frame and rejecting Moore's
voiceover that speculated what might be running through Bush's mind as
he sat there. Because Moore publicly expressed hope that his movie would
help drive Bush from the White House, partisan critics assailed the movie
with unusual vehemence. Nearly every scene was ripped apart, debunked,
and reviled in a torrent of books, blogs, articles, and movies, often on ideological grounds. As White House Communications Director Dan Bartlett
remarked when the film was released, "We don't have to see it to know it's
full of factual inaccuracies."

Moore's elevation from filmmaker to spokesman for the political opposition in an election year bothered some on the left as well, who found him a grandstanding gadfly. We shall consider Moore's political impact and look at some of the objections and rebuttals to Moore's film—including the movies *FahrenHype 9/11* and *Celsius 41.11*—in Chapter 8, in the context of the 2004 presidential election. Such was the polarizing power of *Fahrenheit 9/11* that strong emotional opposition to the film—on the left and the right—continued long after the election.

On September 13, as the film recounts, 142 Saudis, including 24 members of the Bin Laden family, were allowed to fly out of the United States. Moore looks at the Bush family's longstanding intimate connections with the Saudis. "Okay, let's say one group of people, like the American people, pay you $400,000 a year to be President of the United States, but then another group of people invest in you, your friends, and their related businesses $1.4 billion over a number of years. Who ya gonna like? Who's your daddy?" The Saudis are long-term benefactors of and investors in Bush family enterprises including George W.'s mismanaged Texas oil ventures and his father's war-profiteering Carlyle Group.

Like all of Moore's films, *Fahrenheit 9/11* jumps from topic to topic, often with only the thinnest threads of transition. We bounce from the Saudis to former official Richard Clarke's denunciations of Bush's policies to an overview of Taliban connections to U.S. oil companies to mindless terror alerts in the United States to John Ashcroft singing his own composition, "Let the eagle soar," complete with an MTV-like graphic. Moore shows up onscreen to pull a couple of stunts, but they are pointed, funny, and effective. When he learns that no one in Congress actually read the USA Patriot Act before voting for it, Moore hires an ice cream truck to drive near the Senate as he reads the Patriot Act out loud to legislators over the loudspeaker system. His camera follows Marine recruiters in Flint, picking off the young men with no futures, like wolves culling strays from the herd. Later Moore himself approaches Congress members in Washington, trying to solicit their pledges to send their children to fight in Iraq. Of the 535 members of Congress, only one now has a child in military service there. Watching the legislators trying to dodge Moore and his petition is one of the film's more delicious moments.

Fahrenheit 9/11 shows us bloody footage of Iraqi civilians and U.S. soldiers in Iraq that never made it to the sanitized American news programs. As Moore allows us to see, the damage for everyone involved has been horrific. Thousands of Iraqi women and children have been killed and maimed for no reason. And many U.S. GIs, conditioned to "shoot at anything that moved," as one of them says, by listening to heavy-metal rock blasting in their helmets, seem to be waking as from a trance to realize the extent of their own brutality. This is the real Vietnam syndrome, which we did not overcome in the 1991 Iraq War, despite the claim of the first President Bush. As Moore reminds us once again—letting Bush and Cheney rant against Saddam—this wretched, obscene violence was built on lies: that Saddam had stockpiles of weapons and a relationship with al Qaeda.

Moore finds a heroine in Flint to personalize his indictment and provide a strong moral center to bring his film home. Lila Lipscomb—executive assistant at the Career Alliance, a nonprofit agency helping the unemployed—lost one of her sons, Sergeant Michael Pedersen, in the Iraq war. She reads aloud the last letter he sent from Iraq, a week before his death: "How is everyone? I'm doing fine. We are just out here in the sand and windstorms, waiting. What in the world is wrong with George 'trying to be like his dad' Bush? He got us out here for nothing whatsoever. I am so furious right now, Mama. I really hope they do not reelect that fool, honestly." Lila Lipscomb's pain is palpable. Her anger is righteous. Her grief is insupportable. Lila's husband, Howard, wonders what his boy and other Americans boys are dying for. Moore then cuts to a hotel conference where corporations have gathered to figure ways to profit from the war.

Thanks to Cannes and the publicity surrounding Disney's refusal to distribute *Fahrenheit 9/11* in the United States, for fear of alienating the Bush clan, record crowds turned out for the film's opening weeks and months. It became the "largest grossing documentary ever, beating the previous record holder (*Bowling for Columbine*) by 600 percent." The film earned more than $119 million in U.S. theater ticket sales alone. And Moore made sure the DVD version came out before the election. Critical reaction was so divided and so emotional that *Salon* published companion positive and negative reviews of the film.

Salon's Stephanie Zacharek joined the chorus of critics who thought liberals forgave Michael Moore's crude excesses because they liked his politics. Though Zacharek found *Fahrenheit 9/11* "occasionally effective," she thought Moore undermined his own case with "his jokey, faux-populist self-righteousness . . . and by the slapdash connections he makes between various facts and events. The issues at stake are too serious for a

spotlight-hungry manipulator like Moore to be mucking around with."
But *Salon*'s Andrew O'Hehir considered the movie "an enormous film . . . .
It contains multitudes. In its bigness and rage, its low humor and its
sentimentality, it has something of Whitman, something of Twain,
something of Tom Paine. Love him or hate him, Michael Moore is
becoming one of the signal artists of our age."

Reviews tended to be as mixed as Moore's film was judged to be. *The
New Yorker*'s David Denby pronounced *Fahrenheit 9/11* "Moore's most
powerful movie—the largest in scope, the most resourceful in means." But
Denby also thought Moore "doesn't challenge or persuade an audience,
but tickles or irritates it. He's too slipshod intellectually to convince many
except the already convinced." Here Denby touched on the most crucial
political question surrounding the film: would seeing it persuade voters to
withdraw their support for the Bush administration? O'Hehir thought that
"for better or worse the vast majority of those who see the film will be predisposed to agree with his interpretation of events. (We do not live in a
time when pop culture is likely to change anybody's mind.)" Asked if he
weren't simply preaching to the choir, Moore responded, "Well, the choir
needs a good song to sing."

"In 20 years of writing about film, no movie has tied me up in knots
the way Michael Moore's *Fahrenheit 9/11* (Lions Gate) has," wrote David
Edelstein in *Slate*. "It delighted me; it disgusted me. I celebrate it; I lament
it." Groping to express what the film meant to him, Edelstein called it "a
blend of insight, outrage and sniggering innuendo . . . threaded with cheap
shots . . . an act of counterpropaganda . . . a boorish, bullying force . . . all
in all, a legitimate abuse of power." *The Hollywood Reporter*'s Kirk Honeycutt judged the film to be Moore's "weakest," whereas the *San Francisco
Chronicle*'s Mick LaSalle believed it easily Moore's "best."

While many reviewers argued whether *Fahrenheit 9/11* was really a
documentary or an act of political propaganda, a few thought the film con-
founded such categories. For Andrew O'Hehir, Moore's "mind-bending"
movie was "more like a drug experience than a political documentary."
David Tetzlaff, a professor of film studies at Connecticut College, con-
curs. For Tetzlaff, *Fahrenheit 9/11* "presents a vision, not an argument."
Moore offers a "dystopian narrative" in the mode of *1984*, or *Brazil* or *The
Matrix*, to demonstrate that "we have come to inhabit a false, constructed
consciousness." Moore's "radical film" is all about "altered consciousness," beginning with Florida as a dream and ending with an incantation

from Orwell: "Victory is not possible. The war is not meant to be won, it is meant to be continuous." For Tetzlaff, the filmmaker is playing the role of "Michael Morpheus," for whom red and blue are not the colors of states but of different pills, offering different realities. (In the *Matrix* films, the resistance leader Morpheus—named after the Greek god of dreams—offers a red pill to those who wish to know the truth about the Matrix and a blue pill to those who wish to believe what they will.) *Fahrenheit 9/11* "is not asking which side you are on but which reality do you want to be in."

Republicans were content—after failing to stop the film's release—to make campaign issues of Moore's perceived lapses of taste and logic in *Fahrenheit 9/11*. Running against the unseemly Michael Moore and his "unpatriotic" film was preferable to running on the Bush administration record of economic and military failures. But Moore's narrative power had reached a new, courageous level. He used his anger and humor and filmmaking talents to expose the high crimes and misdemeanors of his own government, his own president, and their venal media lapdogs in the midst of a vicious war launched "for fictitious reasons." He vindicated his Oscar remarks and put the right on notice that their false claims would not go unchallenged. He placed a nonfiction film at the very center of the culture. Moore triumphed in 2004 even if the Democrats did not.

Chapter 6

ERROL MORRIS: THE POLITICS OF PERSONALITY

Unfortunately, we believe things not because they are true, but because to believe otherwise would damage how we are accustomed to seeing the world.

—Errol Morris

"I think the human race needs to think more about killing, about conflict," says the 85-year-old Robert McNamara. "Is that what we want in this 21st century?" Errol Morris's camera probes the old man's face from different skewed angles, moving in close, then backing off—sparring like a boxer, looking for an opening, an insight, a glimpse of McNamara's soul. His words seem mildly, if not wildly, ironic.

As secretary of defense for Presidents Kennedy and Johnson from 1961 to 1968, McNamara presided over the prosecution of the American war in Vietnam. The greatest buildup of U.S. forces in Southeast Asia took place on his watch. From 1968 to 1981, McNamara was president of the World Bank. Why in the world is he talking to Errol Morris, a well-known connoisseur of human strangeness, whose cinematic gaze tends to linger the longest on the oddest people?

"I developed this two-minute rule during the making of *Gates of Heaven*," said Morris, speaking of his first film, "that if you leave people alone and let them talk without interrupting them, in two minutes they will show you how crazy they really are."

Robert Strange McNamara is no exception to Morris's two-minute rule. Bright, eloquent, charming, thoughtful, and elusive, McNamara endures the Morris gaze—and ours—for an entire movie. The interview is never static or boring. *The Fog of War: Eleven Lessons from the Life of Robert McNamara* reflects Morris's own restless character, antic and meditative, moving back and forth in time to the slick young McNamara lecturing Congress or the news media with maps and a pointer, to the slightly incredulous old man on the film set, whose bulging basset hound eyes seem to ask, can you believe it?

When McNamara mentions getting cables from Khrushchev during the Cuban missile crisis, we see a tight close-up on a teletype machine, robotic and relentless, pounding out prose we only catch glimpses of, just enough to get the gist, like skimming a quick text for an overdue book report. The words are concrete but their import is mysterious, requiring translation. McNamara, Kennedy, and other officials argue whether these words portend unavoidable nuclear war, or offer some way to avert the conflict. Over and over we return to images of bombs dropping—photographed from the plane above as they fall in graceful arcs and slow-motion tumbles, pregnant with disaster, accompanied by the Byzantine throb of Philip Glass's music, and unstoppable on their destructive trajectories. It's too late to call them back. Too late to stop hell from raining on the earth. Too late for McNamara's doubts to change the course of the war in Vietnam.

"My earliest memory is of a city exploding with joy." McNamara remembers the end of World War I in 1918, when he was two, growing up in San Francisco. The people in the streets were "celebrating the belief of many Americans and particularly Woodrow Wilson—that we'd fought a war to end all wars." The party was premature and tragic, considering that 160 million human beings were killed by conflict in the twentieth century. The naïve, paradoxical notion of a war to end all wars proved to be ironic foreshadowing for McNamara's career. He spent significant portions of his adult life making strategic plans for war, during World War II and Vietnam. Bombs seemed to follow him and to fall from him, across Europe and Asia.

With dispassion and a kind of wonder, McNamara describes how he helped plan the firebombing of Tokyo in March 1945 that "burned to death 100,000 civilians: men, women, and children" in a single night. "Were you aware this was going to happen?" Morris asks, from off camera. "Well, I was part of a mechanism that in a sense recommended it. I analyzed bombing operations and how to make them more efficient." McNamara advised bringing B-29 bombers down from 23,000 feet to 5,000 feet to increase their bombing accuracy. Fifty square miles of Tokyo, a wooden city, was burned. Morris presents this anecdote as #4 of the lessons from McNamara's life: "Maximize efficiency."

"Lesson #5: "Proportionality should be a guideline in war." McNamara served as a colonel under the command of General Curtis LeMay. LeMay did not believe that firebombing 100,000 Japanese civilians was excessive because he figured it saved American lives. "And he went on from Tokyo to firebomb other cities. Fifty-eight percent of Yokohama. Yokohama is roughly the size of Cleveland. Fifty-eight percent of Cleveland destroyed. Tokyo is roughly the size of New York. Fifty-one percent of New York destroyed. Ninty-nine percent of the equivalent of Chattanooga, which was Toyama." LeMay's command firebombed 67 Japanese cities, killing 50 to 90 percent of their inhabitants, *before* dropping atomic bombs on Hiroshima and Nagasaki. No wonder LeMay felt the United States was too inhibited in Vietnam. He had operated without restraint in World War II.

"LeMay said, 'If we'd lost the war, we'd all have been prosecuted as war criminals.' And I think he's right," says McNamara. "He, and I would say, I, were behaving as war criminals. LeMay recognized that what he was doing would be thought immoral if his side lost. But what makes it immoral if you lose and not immoral if you win?" McNamara stares at the camera as we try to read his expression. Do his eyes betray remorse? It's a quintessential Errol Morris moment—a lovely, brutal philosophical conundrum. We understand their collaboration better now. Morris values McNamara's ability to abstract these large moral questions from his own experience, in almost surgical fashion. And McNamara gets his chance to vent in a far more personal mode than in the written memoirs he has churned out over the last decade.

McNamara claims to admire T. S. Eliot's lines from "Little Gidding":

> We shall not cease from exploration
> And the end of all our exploring
> Will be to arrive where we started
> And know the place for the first time.

In his 1995 memoir, *In Retrospect*, McNamara wrote, "I have not yet ceased from exploration, and I do not yet fully know the place, but now that I have traveled this journey of self-disclosure and self-discovery, I believe I see Vietnam far more clearly than I did in the 1960s." Morris says McNamara's memoir is "the main reason I made the film."

To understand America's Vietnam War years better, McNamara might have chosen other lines from Eliot's poem, lines that appear earlier in the same stanza:

We die with the dying:
See, they depart, and we go with them.
We are born with the dead:
See, they return, and bring us with them.

Many died with the dying on both sides of the Vietnam War, thanks largely to decisions taken by McNamara. That the dead return, bringing us— and McNamara—with them, should be no surprise. But was McNamara born with the dead? That, he will not say.

In Robert McNamara, Morris has found a person whose political and historical stature is large enough to bear the weight of the epistemological questions Morris—the former philosophy grad student—likes to pose. He has moved beyond the existential absurdities of pet cemeteries and naked mole rats here, into "a shadow history of the twentieth century," as one critic called the film. With McNamara, Morris explores the Emersonian notion that "There is properly no history, only biography."

His other films have been rehearsals for this meaty, consequential subject, honing his craft and sensibility to debrief McNamara, who drifted toward Morris perhaps to unburden himself in public, only to find that, at the deepest level of his psyche, he can't do it. The Academy of Motion Picture Arts and Sciences awarded *The Fog of War* an Oscar for the best documentary of 2003. In his acceptance speech, Morris said, "I'd like to thank the Academy for finally recognizing my films. . . . I thought it would never happen."

True, Morris might have won an Oscar for *The Thin Blue Line* (1988), a wildly innovative film that revealed—and helped correct—a case of criminal injustice. Certainly, *A Brief History of Time* (1992) deserved recognition for rendering British physicist Stephen Hawking's cosmic questions comprehensible in terms of Hawking's own physically debilitating limitations. Even *Mr. Death* (1999), whose subject and protagonist are oddly similar to *The Fog of War*, offered the cautionary tale of a technocrat devoted to humane executions, who paid a high price for revising history. All these films show the Morris tendency to be, as one critic put it, "both detached and frantically intense." The Morris style is viscerally engaging yet emotionally distant from the people and events in his films, however horrendous, heartwarming, or hilarious. Of course, at a Morris film, what warms one heart may chill another and tickle a third. So why an Oscar for this film? Because, with a kind of faux-random Jungian synchronicity, Morris and McNamara collided with the prevailing zeitgeist.

Almost a year into the U.S. occupation of Iraq, *The Fog of War*—the ruminations of one old man—displayed a shocking relevance. Morris himself acknowledged this when he told the Academy Awards audience, "Forty years ago this country went down a rabbit hole in Vietnam and millions died. I fear we're going down a rabbit hole again. And if people can stop and think and reflect on some of the ideas and issues in this movie, perhaps I've done some damn good here." Some critics attacked Morris for going too easy on McNamara, letting him off the hook. *Salon*'s Charles Taylor faulted Morris for an undue emphasis on the "aesthetics" of the film, "blurring" the basic issues "with artistic ambitions." But Morris cannot be blamed if an essential mystery remains at the core of McNamara's personality and thus, of the Vietnam War.

In some ways McNamara remains an enigma to himself, hidden behind the charts and graphs of his own rationality. (At one point Morris shows mathematical symbols falling instead of bombs on targets below.) As close as McNamara comes to admitting guilt is when he says, "I'm very proud of my accomplishments, and I'm very sorry that in the process of accomplishing things, I've made errors." That vague, bloodless remark hardly suffices for the 25,000 Americans killed in Vietnam on his watch, or the millions of Vietnamese killed, or the Japanese incinerated in World War II. But it's as far as he will go. Morris tries to follow up, in the film's epilog, by asking him directly, "Do you feel in any way responsible for the war? Do you feel guilty?" But McNamara stonewalls, retreating to his decades-long silence. The interview, the film, is over.

REALITY SANDWICHES

Errol Morris grew up in a Long Island suburb of New York. After earning a degree in history from the University of Wisconsin in 1969, he started graduate work in the history of science at Princeton, but soon withdrew. In 1972, Morris began a doctoral program in philosophy at the University of California at Berkeley, where he became interested in film at the university's extensive, eclectic Pacific Film Archive. He also developed an interest in "the metaphysics of mass murder" and the insanity plea.

"When we say someone is insane, we're either saying, one, 'that person could be mentally ill,' or, two, 'I don't *know* why that person does what he does.' Rather than expressing a knowledge, we're expressing a lack of knowledge. I wrote an essay on the insanity plea and movie monsters and certain mechanistic fantasies we have about criminal behavior. I very much wanted to write a doctoral thesis on this stuff, and it hurt my feelings when Berkeley just sort of kicked my ass out of there."

At the Pacific Film Archive, Morris met the German film director Werner Herzog. The two men shared an interest in human oddities and the cultural fringe. Morris told Herzog about Ed Gein, a Wisconsin mass murderer notorious for robbing graves, cannibalizing his victims, and making artifacts from their remains. Morris interviewed Gein at the "maximum-security institution for the criminally insane" in Wisconsin, where he was confined. Morris thought about writing a book or making a film about Gein.

"My mother was worried about what I was doing," said Morris. "She has this wonderfully euphemistic way of talking to me. At one point she said, 'Errol, can't you spend more time with people your own age?' And I said, 'But, Mom, some of these mass murderers are my own age.'"

Herzog met up with Morris in Wisconsin and shot some scenes for a film he was making. Morris, who had no filmmaking experience, had "a chance to observe a master." Herzog paid Morris enough for him to take a trip he'd been planning to a town in the Florida panhandle with the nickname "Nub City," because some residents there had tried to collect insurance benefits after "accidentally" losing limbs. The citizens of Vernon, Florida—a.k.a. Nub City—did not give Morris a warm welcome. Someone told him, "down here, people don't get murdered—they just disappear."

Morris returned to Berkeley and began writing a feature film script entitled "Nub City," pitching it as a film about people who "literally become a fraction of themselves to become whole financially." One day he saw a headline in the *San Francisco Chronicle*: "450 Dead Pets Going to Napa Valley." That headline would appear, along with others, like "They're digging up dead pets, old griefs on Peninsula," in his first film, *Gates of Heaven*. Ostensibly about two pet cemeteries, one defunct and the other successful, *Gates of Heaven* is really, like all Morris films, about dreams and delusions, the inchoate longings and bizarre beliefs that lurk in apparently normal human heads and hearts.

Though Morris understood the conventions of documentary films, he decided "instead of being as unobtrusive as possible," to be "as obtrusive as possible." "Instead of hand-held cameras using available light, I lit everything and the camera is on a tripod." Rather than simply observe events, Morris directed his interview subjects to speak directly to the camera. "You could even say in some real sense they're performing for the camera. They are real people but they are delivering a performance." Morris has never changed his approach. He has worked to perfect it, inventing a device he calls "the interrotron," to help focus the gaze of his interview subjects on the camera.

Gates of Heaven begins with the stocky, balding paraplegic, Floyd McClure, whose collie was run over by a car when Floyd was ten. Burying the dog was important for him. So when he saw "a nice piece of land" available near a freeway in northern California, he got "kind of a kismet idea" to build a pet cemetery there. Morris alternates between Floyd, who loathes the "glue factories" that boil dead animals down, and Mike, who runs just the sort of rendering plant Floyd despises, and who can't believe how attached some people get to their pets. "I get some real moaners on the phone," Mike confides. Floyd offers a sample eulogy for a hypothetical dog: "Little Toby was put on this earth for two reasons—to love and be loved." For reasons not entirely clear, Floyd's pet cemetery failed. "The only thing that I'm guilty of is compassion," says Floyd. "I was not only broke but broken-hearted."

With no transition, Morris shows us an unidentified old woman in a doorway, her cane propped next to her, just talking. "I've been through so much I don't know how I'm alive." And on she rambles, like a refugee from a Beckett play, offering a self-canceling monolog that bears only peripherally on the rest of the movie. "I like the irrelevant, the tangential, the sidebar excursion to nowhere that suddenly becomes revelatory," says Morris. "That's what all my movies are about. That and the idea that we're in possession of certainty, truth, infallible knowledge—when actually we're just a bunch of apes running around. My films are about people who think they're connected to something, although they're really not."

Morris follows the exhumed pets to their reburial site at the Bubbling Well Pet Memorial Park in Napa County, run by Calvin Harberts, his wife, and two sons. Calvin explains how the birth control pill is responsible for America being "in the middle of a pet explosion." Calvin encourages bereaved pet owners to talk about their dead animals at their interment. The Harberts started a church with their own chapel, complete with their own stained-glass windows, and teaching that "the Creator extends His benevolence to all species."

"Listening to what people were saying wasn't even important," according to Morris. "But it was important to *look* as if you were listening to what people were saying. Actually, listening to what people are saying, to me, interferes with looking as if you were listening to what people were saying."

Gates of Heaven opened at the 1978 New York Film Festival and later that year in Berkeley. Werner Herzog, who apparently told Morris, "If you ever make a film, I'll eat my shoe," was filmed eating his shoe at the Berkeley premiere. Morris's movie drove the usually sober and reliable film critic Roger Ebert gaga. Ebert loved the layers of "comedy, pathos, irony, and human nature. I have seen this film perhaps 30 times and am still not anywhere near the bottom of it. All I know is, it's about a lot more than pet cemeteries. . . . When I put it on my list of the 10 greatest films ever made, I was not joking; this 85-minute film has given me more to think about over the past 20 years than most of the other films I've seen."

Morris returned to Vernon, Florida, but could not overcome the hostility toward his "Nub City" film idea. Having obtained financial backing, under pressure to do something, Morris simply turned his camera on various town residents, including a worm farmer, a turkey hunter, the town cop, and other old geezers and just let them talk. And that is *Vernon, Florida*. Nub City is never mentioned. Critic John Nesbit thought "even the 'semi-normal' people appear to be alien beings when Morris records them." After its New York Film Festival premiere in 1981 and its PBS showing in 1982, *Vernon, Florida* became a video store rarity, though Morris's recent fame ensures its re-release on DVD.

Morris began and then abandoned a number of projects in the early 1980s. His main source of income then was his investigative work for a private detective agency. But his next completed film—*The Thin Blue Line* (1988)— achieved a new level of depth and complexity, creating a unique, far more polished and controversial "documentary" style. Morris went to Dallas, Texas, with a tentative film idea for *Dr. Death*, about Dr. James Grigson, a Dallas psychiatrist. Grigson testified frequently for the prosecution in capital cases, invariably pronouncing the person on trial "an incurable sociopath," certain to kill again. Morris spoke with Grigson, and with several death row inmates whom Grigson's testimony had helped convict. Some of the prisoners proclaimed their innocence, including Randall Adams, who was convicted of murdering a police officer in 1976. The deeper Morris probed, the more he believed that Randall Adams was indeed innocent. Rehearsing the Adams case became the new focus for his film.

Calling himself a "director-detective," Morris relied on his investigative skills to prove that Dallas police and the district attorney railroaded

Adams to death row for a crime they knew he did not commit. Morris was able to impeach the witnesses who testified against Adams and identify the real killer. He called *The Thin Blue Line* "the only murder mystery to solve a real murder." The film begins with Adams recounting events around the time of the murder, as we see them reenacted. As other witnesses and police officers tell their different versions, Morris varies his presentation to fit their tales.

"I've been told that I am the progenitor of a host of reality-based shows with reenactments because of the reenactments of the crime which appeared in *The Thin Blue Line*," said Morris. "But . . . they were intended to be ironic . . . illustrations of untruth, of confusions, deceptions, error. They were part of an extended essay on the theme of how believing often can be seeing and not the other way round—illustrations, not of reality, but of phantasmagoria."

Back and back we run through the disputed events, with a focus on a gun, or a clock, a car door, a milkshake, a movie marquee, as the Philip Glass soundtrack—relentless, repetitive, obsessive—leads us in circles around and around the crime.

Glass's brilliant score gives emotional texture and dimension to this tabloid *Rashomon*, making it an almost operatic saga of lies and treachery. We feel tense confused, and paranoid—caught in the dark, oxymoronic hell of Texas justice. With the Glass score, the reenactments, the random/ crucial fetishized objects, and the interviews focused on a single life-and death event, Morris's filmmaking powers made a quantum leap here. He was ready to take on the universe. So he did.

LIONS, ROBOTS, THE BIG BANG, AND A HONEYMOON AT AUSCHWITZ

"Stephen Hawking is arguably the most important scientist since Einstein," Errol Morris tells the camera. The BBC filmed Morris making *A Brief History of Time* (1992), his movie of Hawking's unlikely bestseller. Isn't a film version even more unlikely? Morris admits, "I've been told by a lot of people this was impossible. . . . We can't hire actors to act out the book." The BBC account of how Morris fashioned his film about Hawking's cosmic theories makes a fascinating epilog to Morris's own documentary.

"Which came first, the chicken or the egg?" asks the mechanical computerized voice of Stephen Hawking. A huge chicken pops his head up before a starry background. So we know this won't be a boring physics lecture. But hold on to your thinking caps, folks. That guy in the wheelchair has a few other questions on his mind, such as Where did the universe come from and where is it going? How real is time? Will it ever come to an end? Did anything exist before the Big Bang? Why do we remember the past, but not the future?

Morris tells us his film has "two objects of inquiry: Stephen Hawking and the universe around him." Morris conducts his stylized interviews first. Depending on what people say, he decides what visuals to use. "Hawking uses everyday objects in his book to illustrate his concepts," Morris says. "We'll try to do the same."

"I gave up playing games with Stephen when he was about twelve because he took them too seriously," says his sister. She tells us her brother knew eleven ways to get into the house. We see photos of Hawking as a boy. He says: "I learned the universe was expanding, but I didn't believe it. Expansion of the universe suggested that it had a beginning sometime in the past." Young Stephen knew the Bible well. He won a school divinity prize one year. Hawking says, "An expanding universe does not preclude a creator, but it does put limits on when he might have done the job."

Morris tells us that because Hawking spent most of his life in environments with gothic architecture, at St. Alban's, Oxford, and Cambridge, he decided to use that in the movie. Hawking was a brilliant student at Oxford, but lazy. "My attitude was, there was nothing worth making an effort for," he says. Then, at 21, Hawking was diagnosed with a progressive, degenerative disease that eventually rendered him unable to walk or speak. The doctors gave him two-and-a-half years to live. It was then that Hawking shook off his ennui and plunged seriously into the research that has helped to change our understanding of the universe.

Philip Glass says Morris gave him a list of words to think about as he composed his music for the film, such as *science*, *black hole*, and *wheelchair*. The music has a poetic, not a precise, relation to the material, Glass tells us. Stephen Hawking is "a powerful symbol of human fragility, but with the capacity to ask amazing questions. This is really a movie about hope," says Morris. Hawking says, "The public wants heroes. I fit the part of a disabled genius." You know if he could shrug his shoulders, he would. "Einstein said God does not play dice with the universe. Not only does God play dice, he sometimes throws them where they can't be seen." That's the kind of physics—and metaphysics—Errol Morris can endorse.

For his next movie, Morris fabricated a collage of wildly disparate elements from the lives and work of four dedicated craftsmen: a lion tamer, a topiary gardener, a robot scientist, and an expert on naked mole rats. According to Mark Singer, Morris shot footage of the lion tamer, Dave Hoover, in 1985, but did not know what to do with it. "Then I got interested in the mole rats. What's the connection between the lion tamer and the mole rats? I don't know if there even is one." Morris had also acquired a short 1903 Thomas Edison film called "Electrocuting an Elephant," which he ultimately used in a later, darker film.

He ended up adding a scientist who built sophisticated robots, and a topiary gardener who had spent a lifetime trimming trees and shrubs into elaborate animal shapes. With a score by Caleb Simpson, incorporating elements of circus music, Morris shuffles back and forth among his four artists, sometimes letting each man ramble on about his specialty, sometimes cutting quickly from the robots to the mole rats to 1930s Clyde Beatty jungle adventure film clips, bridging the changes with Simpson's bubbling music, as if willing connections among the four men. After the relatively sober single focus in each of his two previous films, *Fast, Cheap, and Out of Control* (1997) was an antic symphonic romp, with a kind of Kurt Vonnegut sensibility, as if Morris were adding his own cinematic "Calypso" to *The Books of Bokonon*:

> Oh, a mole rat expert
> At the Philly zoo
> And a lion-tamer
> With a scar or two
> And a topiary artist
> And a robot geek—
> All fit together
> In the same mystique.
> Nice, nice, very nice;
> Nice, nice, very nice;
> Nice, nice, very nice—
> So many different people
> In the same device.

The title of the film comes from an idea of the robotics expert to send a large group of small robots into space to survey planetary surfaces: they would be fast, cheap, and out of control. Morris must have felt some kinship with these men, each dedicated to whacky work and utterly absorbed by it. He communicates his fascination with artistic obsession; however, whereas the film is lively, witty, occasionally thoughtful, and never dull, it has an arbitrary feel, as if he might have thrown in a snake charmer and an ice hotel architect in place of, or with, the subjects he chose. But even Morris Minor is good fun.

Morris ventures back into deeper waters in *Mr. Death: The Rise and Fall of Fred A. Leuchter, Jr.* (1999). The film opens with Leuchter, a middle-aged White man with large glasses and a broad Boston accent, speaking directly at us: "I became involved in the manufacture of execution equipment because I was concerned with the deplorable condition of the hardware that's in most of the states' prisons, which generally results in torture prior to death." Leuchter tells us his equipment allows for a more "humane execution." He has built electric chairs, lethal injection machines, gas chambers, and even gallows. His clients, state prison authorities, "pay for the parts, the labor and the installation, and a 20% markup, which is more than fair."

While making *Mr. Death*, Morris tried out his new invention, a modified teleprompter he calls the *interrotron*. For network newscasters and politicians who want to maintain eye contact with their audience, teleprompters display the text "right over the lens on a half-silvered [two-way] mirror." For his invention, Morris uses two prompters. "And you cross-connect them, so the video feed on the B-camera goes to the A-prompter, and vice versa. So they're both connected, and we're both looking at each other's video images on a half-silvered mirror, in front of the lens." Morris wants his filmed interview subjects to keep eye contact with the viewers. "I have this need to create a stream of consciousness narration, rather than an exchange between two people."

Morris cuts back and forth from Leuchter's monolog to shots of the Tennessee electric chair he designed. We learn that Leuchter's father was a prison worker and took young Fred with him to his "office," allowing Leuchter to visit the execution chamber where Sacco and Vanzetti were put to death. Leuchter recounts a number of grotesque execution disasters due to malfunctioning equipment. Here at last Morris is able to use the macabre 1903 Edison film, "Electrocuting an Elephant." Wired up and juiced, enveloped in a cloud of smoke, the elephant finally topples over in a heap, still moving.

Leuchter's earnest recitation of his efforts to improve execution apparatus recalls McNamara's credo: "Maximize Efficiency." Both men devised logical, ingenious "improvements" for methods of killing people. Both are technicians of death, who believe that somehow their work will improve the human condition. Both might have prospered in the hierarchy of the Third Reich. And suddenly, *Mr. Death* goes there.

Leuchter is hired by Ernst Zundel, a German convicted in Canada of making false statements that could "cause injury or mischief to a public interest." Zundel, the author of books like *Did Six Million Really Die?* and *The Hitler We Loved and Why* denies that the Holocaust took place and employs Leuchter to help him prove it. Zundel paid for Leuchter—and his new bride—to travel to Poland and visit several Nazi death camps, including Auschwitz. "Morris, who followed Leuchter's journey ten years later, briefly toyed with calling his film, *Honeymoon in Auschwitz*."

Zundel's cameraman shoots Leuchter spelunking through the crematoria of Auschwitz, illegally bagging stone samples from the walls and floor. Based on the lack of hydrogen cyanide in his samples, Leuchter would testify on behalf of Zundel—and issue a detailed report of his findings— that millions of people could not have been gassed to death at Auschwitz. Morris carefully retraces Leuchter's odyssey and analyses the faulty science that led to his conclusion. The chemist who performed the tests for Leuchter tells Morris that "Leuchter's sample have no meaning" because the cyanide would remain only in the surfaces of the rock, which were smashed to bits for analysis.

Leuchter's bogus science made him a pariah in some circles, a hero in others. His wife left him, and no prison authorities would hire him. Holocaust survivor groups brought a criminal action against him in Massachusetts for practicing engineering without a license. He is welcome only at revisionist history conferences, speaking to other Holocaust deniers. His report has been translated into many languages. In what has become a sort of signature ending, Morris shouts at him from off-camera: "Have you ever thought that you might be wrong, or do you think you could make a mistake?" "No, I'm past that," Leuchter replies.

When Morris showed Leuchter *Mr. Death*, Leuchter asked, "What is the film about to you?" In reply, Morris said, "It is about my curiosity— how you got yourself into this fix." Morris remained sympathetic to Fred Leuchter, despite or perhaps because of his illusions. Morris said, "In the end, I'm left with the question, 'Do I know who Fred is?' Plus, one other question, which I assume will stay with me for awhile: 'Do I know who I am myself?'"

THE HAZE OF POLITICS

Errol Morris took his interrotron to television in 2000, interviewing quirky individuals for a series called *First Person*, on Bravo. He aired a second year of *First Person* in 2001 for the Independent Film Channel. Shows on the Independent Film Channel, without commercial breaks, lasted longer than the Bravo programs, but Morris still pronounced himself frustrated by the time constraints. He invariably had much more material available on each of his subjects.

"Stairway to Heaven" featured Temple Grandin, an autistic designer of slaughterhouses, famous for her ramp that used optical illusions to lead livestock calmly from the holding pen to the bolt gun. Grandin relaxes at home in her own "squeeze chute," usually used to immobilize cattle for inoculations. "I Dismember Mama" profiles Saul Kent, who ran away from the police with his dead mother's cryonically preserved head. "Eyeball to Eyeball" debriefs former lobster fisherman Clyde Roper, who has spent three decades hunting for the mythical giant squid.

After finding and filming these and other exceptional individuals, Morris claimed, "I'm often annoyed by people who somehow think that what really interests me is just the odd, the eccentric, the bizarre. I think that it's really quite different than that. I like there to be some underlying context, some set of issues or problems that is expressed in the material, that goes beyond the material itself. . . . Yeah, I like eccentric stories, I like oddball stories. But they have to be something more than just that." It may be that context—rather like beauty—resides in the mind's eye of the beholder.

Morris has also made many television commercials over the years, for United Airlines, Miller Beer, Volkswagen, American Express, Quaker Oats, Kodak, and others. A Morris ad campaign for Apple Computers "consisted of vignettes about real people who had abandoned PCs for Macs. And, while although he had never before been involved in electoral politics . . . Morris decided to make a series of documentary political ads featuring Republican switchers, people who voted for George W. Bush in 2000 but had decided to vote for John Kerry" in 2004.

Morris found financial backing for his idea at MoveOn.org, the online nonprofit organizer for progressive politics that helped support Robert Greenwald's anti-Bush films in 2004. "MoveOn sent out an e-mail and questionnaire seeking 'authentic American voices committed to change.'" Of the 20,000 responses they received, five hundred came from Republican switchers, of whom Morris selected forty-one to interview. MoveOn posted seventeen of Morris's thirty-second spots with switchers on its Web site, asking members to vote for their favorite. One hundred thousand respondents gave first place to Lee Buttrill, an ex-Marine who fought in Iraq. MoveOn quickly raised money to place several of the Morris ads on television in swing states.

Perhaps Morris's prolonged exposure to Robert McNamara, reprocessing the horrors of Vietnam—and even those of World War II—and his belief that the United States might be "going down a rabbit hole again" in Iraq, motivated his newfound political activism. Besides filming the "switch" ads, Morris and his wife went to Wisconsin to monitor a swing-state precinct on election day as part of the Election Protection campaign to make sure voting procedures were free and fair. Perhaps to prolong his "bully pulpit" moment at the Academy Awards, and to spend the capital of his new prestige, Morris op-ed pieces began to appear in the *New York Times*.

"All of life seems to be about denial—the denial of death, the denial of reality, the denial of everything that it is convenient for us to deny." Morris wrote about a videotape of a U.S. Marine shooting a wounded Iraqi insurgent in Fallujah. In trying to comprehend it, "We are involved. What do the images mean? What do they show?" Morris repeated his axiom that: "Believing is seeing and not the other way around." Yes, he said, he realizes Iraq is not Vietnam. "The geopolitical situations are very different. And yet, there is a common element—our capacity for self-deception, for denial and for evasion."

When George W. Bush was inaugurated for a second term as president, Morris wrote that John Kerry's campaign had "failed because of his inability to tell his own story." He had edited out his opposition to the Vietnam War, leaving a blank space in his biography that opened him to attack. "That was a mistake." It gave people the impression that he had something to hide. "To me, John Kerry's heroism encompassed both his actions in combat and his willingness to change his mind and stand up for what was right." On the other hand, Bush "never pretended to be anything but a ne'er do well who turned his life around when he became a born-again Christian." His life story was . . . "recognizable and easy to understand" even if his evasion of military service "was not honorable." Kerry had committed the literary, and cinematic, sin of constructing a faulty narrative. "Mr. Kerry was forthright about almost everything except himself—and in this election that was not enough."

In his 1995 memoir that piqued the interest of Errol Morris, Robert McNamara found "eleven major causes for our disaster in Vietnam." They were not *The Fog of War*'s "eleven lessons." McNamara's conclusions were largely tactical: "We failed . . . to recognize the limitations of modern, high-technology military equipment" and "we had not prepared the public to understand the complex events we faced." The lessons Morris drew from McNamara's life were largely epistemological: "Rationality Will Not Save Us" and "Belief and Seeing Are Both Often Wrong." Morris was acting on a variation of a strategy McNamara described in the film for press conferences and Congressional inquiries: "Never answer the question asked of you. Answer the question you *wish* had been asked." Morris structured his film around the lessons he *wished* McNamara had drawn from his experiences.

By getting beyond and beneath the specifics of Vietnam to the core of hubris and error ("Lesson #11: You can't change human nature"), Morris tries to penetrate the "fog of war," with the recognition that, as McNamara said, "We're rational but reason has limits." Morris "hated McNamara" during the Vietnam War and clearly despises Holocaust deniers. Yet he sympathizes with Fred Leuchter and with McNamara's quixotic—because limited—quest for self-knowledge. We are all deluded in some way. Instead of presidential debates, candidates should be required to babble to the interrotron about their deepest beliefs. Then we would at least know the brand of insanity on offer.

Of course, one person's sanity is another's madness. George W. Bush's religious beliefs seem righteous and reasonable to some, yet shallow and bigoted to others. As Morris suggests, our opinions, even our ability to apprehend phenomena, most often follow from our predispositions. Seeing depends on believing, not the other way around. But of course, both are "often wrong." Our political system—like every human enterprise—depends for its efficacy and meaning on individuals whose unstable, unpredictable sensibilities may subvert our society's aims and values instead of forwarding them. Morris savors these paradoxes, like the physically debilitated physicist Stephen Hawking upending our understanding of the universe or like obsessed, deluded individuals attempting to construct reasonable, efficient institutions.

Fred Leuchter does not deny the Holocaust because of anti-Semitism, but because of his misplaced faith in faulty scientific procedures. He sees himself as a rational human being, pursuing objective truth, like each of us. His path is as blind and narrow as McNamara's at Defense, calculating the cost efficiencies of making war in some part of his brain that remains hermetically compartmentalized from the incalculable, obscene consequences of his decisions. Leuchter applies his ingenious engineering skills to the task of making execution machinery more humane, while never questioning the need for such devices. Randall Adams was appointed to die in one, victimized by a justice system dependent on unreliable witnesses and officials indifferent to the truth. As a filmmaker, Morris has evolved from spotlighting human oddity for its own sake to illuminating the intersections of personal and national delusions, exploring the ways in which human failings translate into political follies. He's never going to lack for work.

Chapter 7

ROBERT GREENWALD: GODFATHER OF "UN"BELIEVABILITY

Democracy is not a spectator sport.

—Robert Greenwald

In the overheated political summer of 2004, while *Fahrenheit 9/11* boomed at the box office, other movies assaulted candidates and issues in theaters, on television, and on videodiscs. As one journalist put it a month before the election, "If DVDs really were guns, the country would look like Dodge City this week." On the digital front line against Bush administration policies stood Robert Greenwald with his own documentary triple threat: *Uncovered*, *Outfoxed*, and *Unconstitutional*. Greenwald directed the first two films and produced the third. His movies challenged the Bush administration's rationale for the Iraq war, revealed Fox television news to be a White House mouthpiece, and showed how the USA Patriot Act infringed various freedoms guaranteed to American citizens by the United States Constitution.

To make films tackling such big issues quickly enough to appear before the election, Greenwald pioneered new production and distribution techniques. He found financial support from MoveOn.org, a liberal Internet advocacy group, and the Center for American Progress (CAP), a progressive Washington think tank started by former Clinton Chief of Staff John Podesta. Because of time constraints, "I never considered the traditional gatekeepers," wrote Greenwald. Instead he and his backers created "an alternative distribution concept" for the film. CAP hosted screenings of *Uncovered* in several major U.S. cities. Using their extensive electronic community, MoveOn promoted hundreds of house parties nationwide for its members to view the film. A full-length version with additional

material was released to theaters in selected cities and entered in film
festivals. The DVD was sold over the Internet through MoveOn and on
its own Web site. Greenwald repeated this distribution plan with *Outfoxed*. He produced *Unconstitutional* with help from the American Civil
Liberties Union (ACLU). Greenwald also founded Public Interest Pictures, a nonprofit corporation "organized to produce socially active
documentaries."

Robert Greenwald seems an unlikely cinematic crusader, having
built his long and successful career on feature films. His prolific
filmography, dating from the 1970s, includes many television movies of
the week, from the titillating (*Katie: Portrait of a Centerfold*) to the comic
(*How to Murder a Millionaire*). One of his best-known TV movies was
The Burning Bed, starring Farah Fawcett as an abused housewife who
sets her husband on fire as he sleeps. Based on a true story, the 1984 film
also capitalized on publicity from Fawcett's own turbulent private life.

Despite Greenwald's pulpy past, his more recent work does have some
political content. In 2000, he directed a biopic about 1960s radical Abbie
Hoffman, *Steal This Movie*. He also produced a satirical television miniseries,
Crooked E: The Unshredded Truth about Enron. Then Greenwald seemed to
undergo a conversion experience. Like a cinematic Saul on the road to some
political Damascus (or perhaps Armageddon), Greenwald suddenly turned
his career into a high-gear assault upon Bush administration malfeasance
and other wrongheaded public policies.

Greenwald may have been pushed into his new career phase by the
2000 election. Shocked by news of electoral irregularities in Florida, Joan
Sekler and Richard Ray Perez, of the Los Angeles Independent Media
Center, made several trips to Florida to find out what was happening. As
their filming process lengthened, Sekler asked Earl Katz to help finance the
project. Katz called Greenwald. When they saw Perez's and Sekler's footage,
Katz and Greenwald agreed to become executive producers for *Unprecedented: The 2000 Presidential Election*. Sekler and Perez wrote, directed, and
produced the film. Released in 2002, *Unprecedented* shocked film festival
audiences with its detailed, but easily understandable chronicle of precisely
how the Bush forces sabotaged the democratic process in Florida, thus
stealing the election and the U.S. presidency.

The film opens with the inauguration of George W. Bush, quickly
backtracking to Election Day 2000 in Florida. "At 7:05 when the polls
opened, we knew we had trouble," says a poll worker. Florida was a multi-

faceted disaster, including threats against voters by police and polling staff and a lack of bilingual personnel. "But," as we are told, by the familiar voice of narrator Peter Coyote, "the story of the 2000 election started long before." The film reminds us that Jeb Bush first ran for governor of Florida in 1994. When asked what he would do for African Americans in the state, he candidly replied, "Probably nothing." Bush lost the election. In 1998, he kept a tighter rein on his arrogance and won the statehouse with only 10 percent of Black support. Governor Bush quickly moved to abolish affirmative action programs in Florida.

The Black community mobilized against the Bush cutbacks and increased voter turnout by 65 percent in 2000. But African Americans in Florida met a series of obstacles designed to limit their vote. Bush decided to make aggressive use of an 1868 law denying convicted felons the right to vote in Florida. Bush and his secretary of state, Katherine Harris, hired Database Technologies (DBT) to create a "felon purge list" to eliminate convicted criminals from the voter rolls. The state of Florida instructed DBT to create the list with "loose parameters." If a voter's name only partially resembled a name on the list, he or she was designated ineligible to vote. DBT executives warned the state that their criteria would result in many "false-positive" matches. But the state replied that they wanted broad categories. Katherine Harris, who oversaw the felon purge, was also the co-chair of the Bush for President Campaign in Florida, a clear conflict of interest. The film shows us Harris in New Hampshire, campaigning for Bush.

African Americans, who voted 90 percent Democratic, made up 50 percent of the felon purge list. The film interviews a number of Blacks, including several prominent citizens, who were erroneously targeted by the list. The U.S. Commission on Civil Rights ultimately concluded that a disproportionate number of African Americans had been denied their voting rights in Florida. But their report was published too long after the election theft to make a difference. Greg Palast wrote the voter purge list story for the British press, but he was snubbed by U.S. media. He shows us that several of the so-called felons were listed for crimes committed in the future. Palast alleges that 95 percent of those on the purge list did not belong there. Florida also illegally purged thousands of ex-felons who had moved there from other states.

Unprecedented reviews other voting problems, such as the confusing "butterfly" ballot in Palm Beach County, which caused elderly Jews to vote unintentionally for the anti-Semitic Pat Buchanan. Other counties had equally confusing "caterpillar" ballots. More than 175,000 ballots were unread by the machines set up to tabulate them. In Duvall County alone, 27,000 votes were trashed. As Palast points out, Florida is one of the few states that identifies voters by race, making it easy for polling officials to see precisely who is being eliminated.

Gore asked for manual recounts in only four Florida counties, where he believed he could gain votes. He did not request a statewide recount, which proved to be a decisive tactical error. Hand recounts are always more accurate than machine counting. Recognizing this—while governor of Texas—George W. Bush signed a liberal manual recount law for the state. Only machine error can cause so-called dimpled chads, ballots not completely punched through. But in Florida, Republicans mocked the idea of manual recounts. We see James Baker inveighing against manual recounts for the press, playing a slick Sean Hannity to Warren Christopher's mumbling Alan Colmes.

Katherine Harris required county officials to justify their recount requests, and then denied them. Democrats appealed to the Florida Supreme Court, which ruled that the vote recount deadline must be extended. Republicans tried delaying tactics to stall the recounts until they could appeal to the U.S. Supreme Court. In the film's most disturbing footage, we see the congressional aides who were flown into Miami to demonstrate against the recount. These Republican staffers staged a "mini-riot" that shut down the Miami-Dade recount. *Unprecedented* shows us the pandemonium, and then stops the action to circle and identify the faces of the troublemaking interlopers. Aides to Senator Fred Thompson of Tennessee, several Republican representatives, and the National Republican Congressional Committee screamed and shook their fists in mock populist outrage. Neither the media nor the government took any action against these disgraceful tactics. Of course, Republican officials were the ones who sent the demonstrators. As Texas Congressman Tom DeLay said when he was told the cigar he was smoking in a restaurant was against government regulations, "I *am* the government."

And so is the U.S. Supreme Court, which ruled five to four to stop the Florida recount, giving Bush the election. Two of Antonin Scalia's sons worked for law firms representing the Bush campaign during the recount. One of them was later rewarded with a high-level appointment to the Labor Department in the Bush administration. Clarence Thomas's wife had a job vetting résumés for Bush administration job seekers. Yet neither "justice" recused himself from deciding *Bush v. Gore*, the quid for the quo of their appointment. The Court decision was delivered unsigned, late at night, with the provision that it did not apply to any other case—a bloodless, cold-blooded coup d'ètat.

More than a year after the 2000 election, a recount sponsored by the *New York Times*, *Washington Post*, and *Los Angles Times* concluded that if all the ballots had been counted, Gore would have won. Of course, by then it was much too late. Those newspapers and most other American media failed the story when it was unfolding.

The *Unprecedented* DVD expands and updates the 2002 theatrical version. Digital technology allows political documentary makers dealing with topical subjects to augment and follow up on their original material, to reflect subsequent events or even reactions to their original productions. Just as the "Making of . . ." segment of a DVD may shed important light on a feature film, sometimes surpassing the feature itself in terms of technical ingenuity or cultural comment, the extended interviews or "special features" of nonfiction films may add the critical information that viewers need to put issues into perspective. Of course, many "extras" are frivolous and pointless, for all but the most devoted fans. Most "deleted scenes" deserve to be cut. But some are crucial.

The supplementary DVD material for *Unprecedented* reveals the movie's strengths and weaknesses. The passage of time and the emergence of new information alters the movie's function from an expression of outrage to a bellwether for electoral reform. Ralph Neas of People for the American Way tells us that *Unprecedented* serves as a good organizing tool for registering voters and recruiting polling monitors. People for the American Way formed a broad coalition with other groups to sponsor Election Protection in response to the 2000 electoral debacle. Providing limited coverage for the 2002 elections, the Election Protection program expanded in 2004 to monitor polling places around the country, finding different sorts and degrees of voter disenfranchisement nationwide.

Perhaps inevitably, Sekler and Perez got much of their material from journalists who had covered the Florida drama since before the election. Thanks to television shows like *Meet the Press* and *Washington Week in Review* we are long accustomed to journalists speaking as experts. *Unprecedented* relies heavily on John Lantigua, Greg Palast, John Nichols, Jake Tapper, and others to explain the action. The reporters do provide valuable context for the unfolding events, but the film is much stronger when it shows us the principal players speaking or acting. Unlike the films of Errol Morris or Michael Moore, *Unprecedented* concentrates on making its case, paying scant attention to cinematic style. The film's narrative tone of controlled rage trumps any chance of wit.

Greg Palast enjoys a rare comic moment with Clayton Roberts, Florida's Director of Elections. When Palast asks him about Database Technologies, Roberts abruptly rips off his microphone, calls for the state police, and hurries away. The moment is so delicious that Palast uses it again in his own movie, *Bush Family Fortunes: The Best Democracy Money Can Buy* (2004). The film's subtitle is the name of Palast's best-selling book, which included his original stories about the Florida election heist.

Palast's movie recaps the 2000 Florida election yet again, along with quick looks at Bush family connections to Enron and the Saudis. This BBC pastiche is a grab bag of antiadministration bits and pieces first explored elsewhere. Posing in his trench coat in various locations, his bald head hidden under a felt fedora, and walking toward the camera as he talks, Greg Palast—an enterprising and courageous journalist—here approaches self-parody. After his starring role in *Unprecedented*, it must have been tempting to write and direct his own investigative epic. But timing is everything and his timing is off here.

In the deluge of anti-Bush documentaries before and during the 2004 election, some cannibalizing and piggybacking was perhaps inevitable. Many journalists, academics, and politicians, unknown before their documentary cameo careers, pop up in film after film to join the chorus of critics against Bush, the war, or the media. But filmmakers seeking a benediction from Noam Chomsky, Michael Moore, or Mark Crispin Miller to add weight to their efforts risked a certain predictability.

LIES AND THE LYING LIARS

The idea for *Uncovered* began with "pure rage" according to Robert Greenwald. Reading an article about Iraq in June 2003, Greenwald found a quote from a Bush administration official about "programs of mass destruction." "I got a knot in my stomach and a feeling of deep concern," he wrote. "We did not go to war for a program. A program can be a paper, a blueprint, some notes. We went to war because we were told there were weapons . . . and that the threat was imminent and dangerous." Greenwald immediately began work on *Uncovered*, intending to juxtapose the new revisionist line with the original speeches from Bush officials about weapons of mass destruction. As he researched, he discovered deep divisions within the CIA and the government.

Greenwald found two dozen impressive witnesses against the Bush administration policy, not the usual liberal suspects but instead high-ranking intelligence analysts with long careers at the CIA, the Pentagon, and the State Department. These experts explain that charging Iraq with possessing "weapons of mass destruction" was "a convenient way to trick Congress" into approving military action. Invading Iraq was a political decision, they tell us, not a strategic or defensive one.

Uncovered is most effective when it shows us the orchestrated, clearly scripted lies erupting from the mouths of Bush, Cheney, Rumsfeld, and Rice. "We don't want the 'smoking gun' to be a mushroom cloud," they say again and again, about why they can't wait to invade Iraq. CIA analyst Ray McGovern analyzes Colin Powell's "embarrassing" speech to the United States. With CIA Director George Tenet seated behind him as a prop, "a potted plant," Powell's performance was "masterful, but none of it was true." Powell used sketches of "mobile labs" in Iraq, not photographs, because "the labs may not exist." Powell's charge that Iraq had 100 to 500 tons of chemical agents stockpiled was not "a conservative estimate," says McGovern, "but a neoconservative estimate."

Former weapons inspector David Albright tells us that the post–Gulf War inspections of Iraq were "the most intrusive weapons inspection program in history—and it worked. That's another reason why we went to war for nothing." The experts conclude that by invading Iraq we are likely to produce the terrorism the president says he wants to fight. Polls show that few outside the United States believe the Bush administration's reasons for invading Iraq. It's as if the Vietnam War had never happened.

The *Christian Science Monitor* called the film "mandatory" viewing for its "astounding array" of facts and perspectives "invisible in newspapers, TV reports, and everywhere else." If Greenwald could find these prominent dissidents inside the intelligence establishment, why couldn't the journalists? Owen Gleiberman of *Entertainment Weekly* pronounced *Uncovered* "smashingly effective . . . more resonant than *Fahrenheit 9/11*." But Gleiberman also thought the film blended "into the white noise of media overkill . . . preaching to a microscopic sliver of the converted." Jack Matthews in the *New York Daily News* judged it "a crisp historical document that is worth your time, even if the information in it was not worth the President's."

Uncovered was not the only film dedicated to exposing Bush administration fictions. *Hijacking Catastrophe: 9/11, Fear & the Selling of American Empire* makes a similar case, with more historical context. Jeremy Earp and Sut Jhally assemble a largely familiar cast of talking heads to explain the Wolfowitz doctrine—the call for regime change in Iraq a decade before the 2003 invasion. *Hijacking* argues persuasively that the 9/11 terrorist attack merely provided a pretext for this longstanding plan. For Earp and Jhally, it is not the failure of intelligence but the manipulation of it that constitutes the Bush administration's greatest sin.

The updated DVD release of *Uncovered* includes a short documentary by feature film director David O. Russell called *Soldier's Pay*. Russell directed *Three Kings*, a 1991 tragicomic action adventure about the Persian Gulf War with George Clooney, Mark Wahlberg, and Ice Cube. For a planned re-release of the film, Russell and co-directors Tricia Regan and Juan Carlos Saldivar interviewed U.S. soldiers who had apparently lived out a version of the fictional theft of Saddam's fortune portrayed in *Three Kings*. When Warner balked at pairing the films, Cinema Libre, Greenwald's distributor, agreed to include Russell's new work with *Uncovered*.

Soldier's Pay betrays the haste and low budget with which it was made. But the film demonstrates how the Army's lower class recruits quickly learn to degrade and humiliate an enemy they are trained to regard as less than human. The U.S. soldiers are encouraged to loot civilian homes in Iraq, for necessities as well as souvenirs. When members of the Third Infantry Division stumbled upon boxes stuffed with $100 bills, totaling millions, some of them held on to some of the money. Staff Sergeant Matt Novak was court-martialed and dishonorably discharged, though his superiors, who were present at the looting, were not punished. "Where did that money go?" asks Novak. "Did it go to rebuild Iraq?"

The film details the huge disparities between the U.S. troops and the much better equipped, better paid mercenaries who work for Halliburton's Kellogg, Brown, and Root. Though it blurs too many issues, Russell's film adds to the indictment of a poorly managed war, in which GIs bear an unfair share of the fight and the spoils. As Andrew O'Hehir wrote in *Salon*, "this film captures the sense that the U.S. has wandered down a dark alley and now finds itself with no way out."

"While working on *Uncovered* it became clearer and clearer to me what an enormously important part the media had played in the President's ability to convince us to go to war and how Fox was the leader of that," said Greenwald. He decided to focus on Fox News as "an example of what happens when we have extreme media control." Greenwald assembled leftist media critics, ex-Fox employees, and hundreds of clips from the Fox News Network to tell his story. Greenwald also got copies of Fox News Editorial Chief John Moody's internal memos, instructing Fox employees what to report and what not to report and how to spin each day's events.

Moody's "issue of the day" coordinated a media echo chamber with the White House that resonated throughout America. Greenwald uses Fox clips that show how catch phrases and buzzwords enter the lexicon of all Fox News personnel at once. When Moody decides—along with the Bush White House—to paint John Kerry as a flip-flopper, we see host after host of Fox shows using the phrase. In order to introduce opinions without any proof or corroboration, Fox program hosts use the phrase "some people say." "Some people say John Kerry looks French." Greenwald bombards us with dozens of examples, which would be funny were they not a clearly programmed propagandistic onslaught. Similarly, when Fox News bully-boy Bill O'Reilly tells a complaining viewer that he has only ever told one guest to "shut up," Greenwald rams the lie down O'Reilly's throat with a dozen or more clips of him using that schoolyard expression. O'Reilly's no ordinary liar. He's a sanctimonious one.

O'Reilly figures in another memorable *Outfoxed* segment, badgering a young man named Jeremy Glick, whose father was killed in New York on September 11, 2001. O'Reilly berates Glick for signing an antiwar petition and tells him his father would be ashamed of him. Glick tells O'Reilly he doesn't want his father's death exploited as a pretext for war, but O'Reilly tells him to "just shut up!" and cuts off Glick's microphone. Glick says O'Reilly's aides then rushed him out of the building, claiming they were afraid O'Reilly might attack him. O'Reilly's ugly, boorish behavior apparently appeals to many viewers. He's one of Fox's most popular "commentators."

If, as media critic Jeff Cohen says in the film, "media is the nervous system of a democracy," then Fox News is like a right-wing electroshock to that system. Fox themes pander to the fears of its viewers, keeping them alarmed and tuned to Fox. Their slanted, simplistic presentation of issues misinforms their viewers, as surveys show. Many more Fox viewers thought Saddam was connected with the events of September 11 and al Qaeda than people who got their news elsewhere.

The intimacy of Fox News with the conservative Republicans' agenda runs deeper than just the longstanding connection of Fox News chief Roger Ailes with the Nixon, Bush, and Reagan campaigns. Fox White House correspondent Carl Cameron jokes with George W. Bush before a televised interview. Cameron talks about his sister, who works for the Bush campaign. Bush chuckles and says, "She's a good soul." Jeff Chester, of the Center for Digital Democracy, calls Fox "nothing more than a 24/7 political ad for the Bush campaign." Britt Hume, whose interview guests are 83 percent Republican, spins the Iraq war toll by saying that, with 277 Americans killed, the odds of a soldier dying there are the same as a Californian's chance of being murdered. Since the U.S. death toll has inched toward 2000 (as of this writing), it would be enlightening to catch Hume's well-spun update.

Especially during coverage of the 2003 Iraqi invasion, the rampant jingoism of Fox News's talking heads appealed to viewers, thereby increasing the network's ratings. Iran-Contra perjurer Oliver North was an embedded correspondent for Fox in Iraq. Because television popularity breeds imitation, Fox News competitors like MSNBC, CNN, and CNBC try to out-Fox Fox. When Bush cousin John Ellis first announced on Fox that Bush won the 2000 election in Florida and nationally, ABC, CBS, and NBC went along with that verdict in minutes, well before they could have conducted their own independent investigations of the polls. Fox drives television news further to the right, even as Sean Hannity and other conservative pundits excoriate the "liberal media."

The *New York Times* film critic A. O. Scott thought that *Outfoxed* showed "The on-air Fox personalities . . . to be a prize collection of blowhards and hyenas, with little regard for either journalistic niceties or basic good manners." Describing Bill O'Reilly's attack on Jeremy Glick, Scott wished "that the ghost of Joseph Welch would enter the studio and inquire, at long last, after Mr. O'Reilly's decency. But those days—when Welch undid Senator Joseph R. McCarthy on live television, and when that medium was new enough to bring a promise of transparency and truth telling into the public consciousness—are long past." *Washington Post* media critic Howard Kurtz accused Greenwald of doing what he accused Fox News of doing, making "no effort at fairness or balance himself." Kurtz did not evaluate the substance of Greenwald's charges. Kurtz practices the sort of gutless, on-the-one-hand, on-the-other-hand "objectivity" that Fox News easily trumps with the decisive slant it labels "fair and balanced."

Near the end of *Outfoxed*, the film briefly shifts its focus from Fox News to the larger corporate media environment and the problem of ownership consolidation. But this last-minute swipe at "the whole system" of U.S. media diffuses the precision of Greenwald's attack on Fox. Several media experts whom Greenwald interviews—such as Jeff Cohen and Robert McChesney—also appear in a film that does attempt Big Picture criticism of American media, namely, *Orwell Rolls in His Grave*, written and directed by Robert Kane Pappas. Preachier and not as flashy as *Outfoxed*, *Orwell* offers a two-hour course in media awareness.

Thanks to professors like McChesney and Mark Crispin Miller, *Orwell* has an academic feel. Danny Schechter (who directed *WMD: Weapons of Mass Deception*), tells us that "Media, which are supposed to check political abuse, are now part of the political abuse." Schechter made his remarks long before conservative commentator Armstrong Williams revealed that the Bush administration had paid him $240,000 to plug its policies in his newspaper columns and on his talk shows. Vermont Congressman Bernie Sanders describes media as "a subsidiary of corporate America." He summarizes Rupert Murdoch's successful Fox formula as "taking the working class to the right with violence, sensationalism, and super-patriotism." New York University Professor Mark Miller quotes Nazi propaganda chief Joseph Goebbels: "The job of media is to create an ostensible diversity that conceals uniformity." Miller clearly sees the fascist model as applicable to the increasingly concentrated ownership of U.S. media.

Orwell shows us meetings of the Federal Communications Commission, presided over by Michael Powell, son of Colin. Powell comes off as a classic "reluctant regulator," hoping perhaps for a cushy post-FCC position in the industry, willing to give corporations unfettered access to broadcast outlets in order to maximize their profits. The FCC treats media corporations as individuals, granting them First Amendment rights of "free speech" to rationalize their unlimited acquisition of broadcast outlets. Powell shows no concern about diminishing the range of public discourse. As Bernie Sanders opines, "It's not a matter of conflicting opinions but a question of whether ideas matter at all anymore in America."

If Fox News viewers are unlikely to watch *Outfoxed*, to whom does *Orwell* appeal? Pappas may not be preaching to the converted, but to the wind. *New York Times* reviewer Dave Kehr found Pappas's "rambling screed . . . almost quaintly beside the point" in this era of personal computers and camcorders, Web bloggers, and the commercial success of Michael

Moore. But does Kehr believe that the corporations that own newspaper, magazine and book publishing chains, radio and television station groups, movie studios, and communication satellites will leave the Internet wide open for the expression of alternative views? Not likely.

U.S. Marine Lt. Josh Rushing compares Fox News with the Arab news network Aljazeera. A military press spokesman at U.S. Military Headquarters in Qatar—or Cent Com HQ, in military jargon—during the U.S. invasion of Iraq, Rushing achieved unexpected notoriety in Jehane Noujaim's *Control Room*, a look inside Aljazeera. Unlike his belligerent bosses, Rushing seems open and reasonable. United States Secretary of Defense Donald Rumsfeld would only concede half of Rushing's point: "We know Aljazeera has a pattern of playing propaganda over and over." Aljazeera carried the U.S.-Iraq war to 40 million Arab viewers worldwide. Aljazeera journalist Hassan Ibrahim found it "amazing that the United States has galvanized support for the hated Saddam" by its invasion. Aljazeera showed captured and killed coalition troops, which brought protests from the United States and the United Kingdom. Bush called the network "the mouthpiece of Osama bin Laden" even as U.S. General Vincent Brooks ladled out disinformation at Cent Com on a daily basis.

As *Control Room* shows, soon after Rumsfeld strongly rebuked the Arab network, a U.S. bomb struck Aljazeera's Baghdad bureau, killing a journalist. Aljazeera had been careful to inform the United States about the location of its bureau. And since Rumsfeld often brags about the accuracy of U.S. bombing strikes, the attack would seem to be less an accident than a warning.

Hassan Ibrahim laughingly tells the story of a BBC reporter who saw children chanting "Goddamn Bush! Goddamn Bush!" The reporter did not know Arabic, so he reported that the kids were cheering Bush. The truth of the war eluded even those who sought it sincerely, beyond the incoming propaganda from every side.

THE WAR AT HOME

"We created *Unconstitutional* to show Americans the extent to which our civil liberties have been trampled upon by our government since 9/11," wrote Robert Greenwald on the film's Web site. Written, produced, and directed by Nonny de la Peña, and backed by the ACLU, *Unconstitutional:*

The War on Our Civil Liberties explores ways in which the Bush administration's response to terrorism has diminished the freedoms of American citizens. It's another parade of talking heads, but what they have to say is frightening and not widely known. The USA Patriot Act was passed 45 days after 9/11, rushed through Congress largely unread by legislators and without debate. "This is what happens when federal legislators respond in panic," says the ACLU's Laura Murphy.

"No member of Congress read this bill," says Oregon congressman Peter De Fazio, echoing Michigan's John Conyers in *Fahrenheit 9/11*. Conservative Bob Barr and liberal Barney Frank hammered out an anti-terrorism bill that Congress debated, but the White House substituted its own version at 3:45 AM on the morning of an 11 AM vote, with many new provisions contrary to constitutional law, drastically expanding federal law enforcement powers. The Justice Department used racial profiling to round up Islamic immigrants, holding them for months without charges and without any contact with the outside world. "We have never in U.S. history had investigative detention, until now," says Barbara Olshansky of the Center for Constitutional Rights.

Vincent Cannistraro, former head of counterterrorism for the CIA, points out that indiscriminate arrests based on stereotypes alienate the very informants we need to help us by reporting on suspicious activities within immigrant communities. The 9/11 hijackers already knew enough about how Americans stereotype Islamic terrorists to shave off their beards and avoid mosques when they arrived to carry out their hijacking.

Urging local police departments to enforce immigration laws, U.S. Attorney General John Ashcroft oversaw mass round-ups and deportations of immigrants, many of whom were seeking political asylum. The U.S. government commissioned private airlines to fly these refugees back to their countries of origin, late at night. Immigrants were suddenly snatched from their homes and sent back to Pakistan, Syria, Egypt, and elsewhere, where reports have come back of their torture and death. We meet a family of Syrian refugees in Seattle, U.S. residents for ten years, who were arrested and detained. Though cleared in four days, the family's father was kept ten months in prison. No official deigns to explain. In April 2003, the Inspector General of the Department of Justice issued a report highly critical of the U.S. government abuse of immigrant rights.

Unconstitutional does not penetrate far into Camp Delta at Guantanamo Bay, Cuba. But the suggestive photographic glimpses of this corner of

the American Gulag, combined with harrowing personal stories of some
detainees and the revelations of Abu Ghraib prison abuses in Iraq, render
this portion of the movie the most shocking and dispiriting sequence of all.
Former Congressman Bob Barr calls Guantanamo a symbol of the Bush
administration's war on terror, in which "anything goes." Camp Delta was
selected as a holding tank for terrorism suspects from around the world
because it was outside the United States but under U.S. control and
beyond the world's scrutiny. For a society built on openness, such secrecy
goes against our principles. In the words of Donna Newman, lawyer for
detainee Jose Padilla, "Government secrecy usually means they're hiding
their lack of evidence." The British father of one Guantanamo prisoner
says, of his son: "If he is guilty, he should be punished. But if not . . . why
is he there?"

Because they are not on U.S. soil, Guantanamo prisoners enjoy no
constitutional rights. White House counsel Alberto Gonzalez, chosen to
succeed Ashcroft at Justice, characterized the Geneva Conventions, which
govern the treatment of prisoners, "obsolete." If the Geneva Conventions
are inapplicable, reasoned Gonzalez, then the United States cannot be
prosecuted for war crimes. Hundreds of Camp Delta detainees, including
inappropriate suspects such as old men and children, have been locked up
indefinitely with no charges, no lawyers, no trials. Some are manacled,
isolated, deprived of necessities, and interrogated using torture. More than
thirty detainees tried suicide before the government stopped reporting suicide attempts.

The West used to regard the Soviet Union as a place where indeterminate prison sentences, inhumane punishments, and barbaric values reigned
supreme. Now, for much of the world, the United States has become the
predominant oppressor and violator of human rights. Abu Ghraib and
Camp Delta are symbols of arrogant imperial power, police-state tactics
justified without irony in the name of freedom. Asked when the prisoners
might be released, Donald Rumsfeld said that we can hold these prisoners
until the War on Terror is over. But Bush administration spokesmen have
said the War on Terror may not end in our lifetimes. We ought to be
shocked and ashamed and angry enough to demand change. As the film
points out, 90% of the Patriot Act will remain permanent in law unless we
change it.

Large portions of the USA Patriot Act have nothing to do with
terrorism. The federal government can now scrutinize personal records of

banks and public libraries. The Justice Department can perform searches without warrants and initiate wiretaps without "probable cause," as the Constitution guarantees. The film interviews a scuba shop owner whose list of customers was subpoenaed by the government. Bush and Ashcroft scrapped the restrictions on domestic spying. Police spend an inordinate of time surveilling and disrupting peace groups, simply because that's an easier job than making honest efforts to interdict actual terrorists.

City Councilor David Meserve introduced a resolution to make his hometown of Arcata, California, a civil liberties safe zone, exempt from the USA Patriot Act. "This is not an issue of the left and the right," says Meserve, in the film. "This is an issue of our basic freedoms. America needs to remember not just what we're fighting against but what we're fighting for." Arcata is 1 of 340 communities in 41 states, along with 4 statewide resolutions, opposed to the USA Patriot Act. "These communities represent over 53 million people who believe that the Patriot Act goes too far," Greenwald writes.

Unconstitutional "puts faces and bodies to the nameless numbers victimized by the 'War on Terror,'" as one critic wrote, "whose stories are often buried beneath kinder, gentler photo opportunities and sports scores." De la Peña's film attempts to penetrate behind the camouflage euphemisms of the Bush administration and the great media silence to inform and energize viewers and call them to action. Greenwald's Web sites provide links to organizations with blueprints for various levels of political involvement. Despite the electoral setback of 2004, he appears unwilling to concede the struggle for a just and civil society. Can the great, self-absorbed beast of American opinion, narcotized by obsessive, unquestioning TV coverage of political liars, be stirred from its cynical lethargy? Robert Greenwald is acting on the belief that the truth does matter, that Americans can be made to care. His films are acts of idealism and hope. Late in 2005 he was working on a film about the abuses and excesses of Wal-Mart.

Greenwald displays the zeal and energy of a newly politicized convert. Unlike Barbara Kopple and Michael Moore, whose oppositional stance arises from their commitment to labor and the rights of individuals, or Errol Morris, whose taste for existential absurdity informs his view of politics as a kind of pathology, Greenwald practiced relatively apolitical filmmaking until what he saw as a series of crises challenged him to act. He put his professional expertise to new uses. Instead of creating fictional diversions, he exposed dangerous official fictions posing as fact. With a motivated resourcefulness, Greenwald pioneered methods of production and distribution aimed at getting timely cinematic counternarratives before the American people as the compromised news media would not. He is the film artist as patriot: Citizen Paine.

Chapter 8

POLITICAL THEATER: THE 2004 DOCUMENTARY CAMPAIGN

Politics is ultimately about results.

—Karl Rove

Robert Greenwald and Michael Moore made films intended to influence the 2004 election against George W. Bush. Both filmmakers attacked the legitimacy of his ascent to the presidency and his claims against Iraq to justify war. *Bush's Brain,* codirected by Michael Paradies Shoob and Joseph Mealey, takes a longer view, detailing the dark, eventful career of political strategist Karl Rove, who guided George W. Bush to the White House.

Bush's Brain makes a largely circumstantial case of malicious mischief against Rove. But the preponderance of evidence, based on a book by Texas journalists Wayne Slater and James Moore, gathered from Rove campaigns going back thirty years, with damning testimony from his former friends and allies, makes the case convincing. Like *The Perfect Candidate*, about Chuck Robb versus Oliver North in Virginia, *Bush's Brain* indicts not only the foul tactics of Karl Rove, but also the system that repeatedly rewards him. Rove's phenomenal success is symptomatic of great moral failings within the Bush administration and the American political system.

Rove dropped out of college to work for Republican political campaigns. During a 1970 race for Illinois state treasurer, Rove stole letterhead stationery from the Democratic candidate and sent out 1,000 invitations to come to his campaign headquarters for "free beer, free food, girls, and a good time for nothing."

Professor Robert Edgeworth of Louisiana State University explains how Rove "robbed" him of the national chairmanship of the College Republicans in 1973 with bullying and lies. *The Washington Post* accused Rove, by now friends with personal-attack-artist Lee Atwater, of teaching Nixon-style dirty tricks to college Republicans. The FBI investigated but Rove denied the charge. Impressed with Rove's junkyard dog approach, George H. W. Bush hired him for his political action committee in Houston.

In just over a dozen years, Rove's hardball tactics transformed Texas from a traditional Democratic state into a rightwing Republican bastion. *Bush's Brain* describes the 1986 race for governor. As election day neared, Rove's candidate, Bill Clements, was running slightly behind the Democratic incumbent, Mark White. Then, days before the candidates were to debate, Rove announced he had found an electronic eavesdropping device in his office. Rove's charges obliterated coverage of the debate and all other issues. Clements won. Only after the election did the FBI conclude that someone from inside the Clements campaign had planted the bug.

To oust liberal Jim Hightower from his post as Texas agriculture commissioner, Rove convinced Rick Perry to change parties and run against him. He had the FBI bring charges against two Hightower underlings, for campaign violations neither man had committed or condoned. The charges succeeded in helping Perry win Hightower's job. But Rove pressed ahead with the prosecutions even after the election. The two state officials ended up in prison, their political careers in ruins, in a classic case of Rove overkill. Perry succeeded George W. Bush as governor of Texas.

Above all, Rove is known for orchestrating whisper campaigns to smear his opponents, as he did against Texas Governor Ann Richards in 1994, by spreading a rumor that she was a lesbian. In the 2000 South Carolina Republican primary, after John McCain beat Bush in New Hampshire, leaflets told voters about McCain's "black love child" (McCain had adopted a Bangladeshi orphan), his wife's drug addiction, and his mental imbalance following his imprisonment in Vietnam as a prisoner of war. Texas journalist Molly Ivins calls it a Rove trademark—"the flyers that appear on windshields of cars in fundamentalist church parking lots alleging something unappetizing about Karl Rove's opponent." *Bush's Brain* shows how Rove's attack machine targeted Georgia Democratic Senator Max Cleland in 2002. Televised ads questioned Cleland's patriotism, though he had lost an arm and both legs in military service in Vietnam. Bush visited Georgia five times and spent $14 million to defeat Cleland.

When Ambassador Joseph Wilson criticized Bush's State of the Union speech for saying that Iraq had tried to buy yellowcake uranium in Africa to make nuclear weapons, Karl Rove told the press that Valerie Plame, Wilson's wife, was fair game. Attributing his information to "high administration officials," syndicated columnist Robert Novak revealed Plame's undercover identity as a career CIA agent. Breaking her cover was against the law, as Rove and Novak knew. But Rove wanted revenge. And Novak has long been Rove's media stooge. In 1992, the Bush presidential campaign fired Karl Rove for leaking information to Robert Novak. But neither man has been, or is likely to be, punished for the illegal act of spite that cost Plame her career and could cost some of her international contacts their lives. As former Texas Land Commissioner Gary Mauro said of Karl Rove: "There is no rule he will not break."

Assessing Rove's power, journalist James Moore says flatly, "Karl is now Co-President of the United States. Just as he was Co-Governor of Texas." With Rove running the White House out of Hillary Clinton's old West Wing office, Bush's policies are all "pure politics" says Moore in the film. Rove sees the War on Terror as a "marketing device." He tells Republicans, "War keeps Bush's numbers up." James Moore is appalled: "[Rove] says, 'it's going to cost many lives and much treasure but we can run on it.'" But the 2004 election results seem to support the conclusion of film critic Chris Barsanti about *Bush's Brain:* "If this is all Rove's enemies could muster, he's got nothing to fear."

Bush's Brain is the perfect cinematic complement to *George W. Bush: Faith in the White House* (which is discussed later in this chapter). *Faith* bathes Bush in a religious light, rendering his career a parable about the power of Christian belief. *Bush's Brain* shows us the flip side of the fable, Bush's alliance with a dark operative who slashes and slanders anyone who stands in his way. Bush aims his gaze heavenward as Rove consummates Bush's Faustian bargain for power down in the gutter, consolidating his own hidden but potent sway over policies and people, including the president. Accountable only to his protégé, and then only if he loses, Karl Rove will always subvert the best interests of this country if it serves his own advantage, no matter who gets hurt.

Rove displayed his methods and morality earlier—while remaining characteristically offstage—in the engaging and heartbreaking film, *Horns and Halos* (2002). Filmmakers Suki Hawley and Michael Galinsky follow the story of a best-selling biography of George W. Bush that was recalled by its prestigious publisher, and then reissued by a small, alternative press. St. Martin's Press printed 80,000 copies of J. H. Hatfield's *Fortunate Son,* a biography largely based on previously published materials. For maximum 2000 election year publicity, St. Martin's insisted that Hatfield publish his most original—and sensational—charge against Bush in the Afterword section of the book. Hatfield learned that Bush had been arrested for possession of cocaine in 1972. His father, then a Houston Congressman, called a friendly judge, who agreed to expunge all record of George W.'s bust in return for community service in a Houston rehab program for African Americans.

Fortunate Son reached Number Three on the *New York Times* best-seller list and made Amazon's Top Ten before St. Martin's recalled the book and destroyed it. The Bush camp had attacked the book. They had leaked a derogatory story about biographer J. H. Hatfield to reporter Pete Slover of the *Dallas Morning News.* Slover wrote that Hatfield had served five years in prison for "solicitation of murder," which was true. Then Bush lawyers threatened the publisher with legal action. With Hatfield's credibility impugned, St. Martin's caved and censored its own book. News of the author's sordid past overwhelmed and undermined his account of the cocaine bust, partly because Hatfield refused to reveal his sources.

By the time Soft Skull Press took up Hatfield's cause and printed a second, "revised" edition in 2001, Hatfield decided to reveal his sources for the cocaine story. Of the three he named, the most prominent was Karl Rove. Hatfield realized that Rove had set him up. Rove fed him the story, knowing he could use Hatfield's own background to discredit him. As Hatfield himself says, "Since that book came out, the cocaine issue has been a dead issue, and it's been a dead issue because of that book." It's a brilliant strategy: send out a true story with a flawed messenger; then expose the messenger's flaws to Robert Novak, Pete Slover, or some other media lapdog; and the story will die—though it deserves to live. The CBS story of Bush's National Guard service during the 2004 campaign, fed to CBS by a shaky source, follows this same tried and true pattern. Rove must have been tickled when CBS took the bait, considering the long Bush family grudge against Dan Rather. Again, a true story was put to rest by linking it to an unreliable source. The *Los Angeles Times* concluded, "The roar of condemnation aroused by CBS's use of unverified documents drowned out other news accounts that exposed Bush's spotty service record as a young pilot." Rove knows how to play the media like an accordion. He squeezes, they squawk.

A WASP Sammy Glick, Karl Rove has enough gall to be divided into nine parts, as Budd Schulberg said of Sammy. Rove's political Vince Lombardi persona—"winning isn't everything, it's the only thing"— represents one symptom of our grand national malaise, like politicians making war in the name of religion or abnegating civil rights in the name of freedom. "Victory" is hollow in both cases because the means nullify the ends. Rove is emblematic of modern American politicians who stand for nothing beyond their own political survival.

BUSH VS. KERRY: THE MOVIE CAMPAIGN

Though neither presidential candidate produced or officially sanctioned a documentary campaign film, several 2004 movies served that promotional function. Journalist and biographer Paul Alexander began shooting *Brothers in Arms*, about John Kerry's Vietnam service, before Kerry announced his candidacy. Alexander decided to make a movie about the men who had served with Kerry on Swift Boat 94 in Vietnam. He shot the film in the summer and fall of 2003, as Kerry jockeyed for position among the Democratic presidential contenders. *Brothers in Arms* blends archival Vietnam War–era footage with contemporary interviews of the five veterans (a sixth died in 1997).

Kerry and his crew served on a U.S. Navy patrol boat in the Mekong Delta in 1969. As each man tells us how he got there, we immediately feel the huge class difference that exists between Kerry and the others. His world of private schools and Yale is an alien realm to boys who joined the Navy because they were low on options.

The fast, noisy Swift Boats motored into narrow delta channels on missions that could last five or six days. The enemy was silent, hidden in the bush. There were "moments of intense fear, which you learned how to manage," says Kerry. Sometimes the Vietcong waited until the boats went upriver, then laid mines to blow them up on their return. Swift Boat crews saw death up close every day, in the eyes of their enemies and the bodies of their friends.

In the film, crew members Del Sandusky and Mike Medeiros recount the events leading to Kerry's Silver Star. A Vietcong fighter fired a rocket at them from the jungle. Kerry beached the boat and chased the soldier into the bush. As the man rose to fire another rocket, Kerry shot him. Medeiros, Kerry's backup, says he deserves his medal. Sandusky agrees.

Their direct, graphic testimony contrasts starkly with later campaign charges by the Swift Vets that Kerry should not have been honored. The crew left Vietnam later in 1969. About the war, Kerry says, "We were supposed to be winning the hearts and minds of the people but we were alienating them on a daily basis."

Brothers in Arms then shifts from Vietnam to the Mall in Washington, D.C., jammed with thousands of antiwar protestors. To the strains of "Amazing Grace," the camera pans the mostly young faces, coming to rest on a large American flag with a peace symbol in place of the stars. The mordant voice of Jack Webb, a no-nonsense 1950s TV cop, denounces the protestors as young people who are ignorant of the reality GIs face in Vietnam. This is the movie's only Michael Moore moment, the ironic patriotic entreaty on behalf of our soldiers, many of whom are here on the mall, protesting the war as members of the organization Vietnam Veterans against the War.

We see Kerry's famous witness at the Fulbright Committee's Senate hearings in 1971, saying, "How do you ask a man to be the last man to die for a mistake?" Then, in footage as harrowing as any battle scene, *Brothers in Arms* elicits the postwar stories of Kerry's crew, who were devastated by their return to civilian life. As David Alston says, "They programmed me to kill but they didn't deprogram me." Del Sandusky tells us, "The war never really leaves your psyche." Both men suffered severe posttraumatic stress, becoming alcoholic and suicidal. Gene Thorson spent his time in bars, drinking and keeping quiet about his experiences, feeling there was no one he could tell.

When Kerry's 1996 U.S. Senate opponent charged that his heroism in Vietnam was actually a war crime, the Kerry campaign flew his former crew to Massachusetts to set the record straight. All five came, reuniting for the first time since the war, realizing they still shared a strong bond. As Gene Thorson says, "That's when I finally felt welcomed home." *Brothers in Arms* ends in the fall of 2003, as Kerry's former Vietnam boat mates travel with him to presidential campaign rallies across the country. If Kerry is exploiting his old crew for their political value as patriotic symbols, he is also protecting them from their undeserved ignominy and despair. These men have shown their bravery, not only in battle, serving their country, but also by sharing their struggles for survival in a society still hostile or indifferent to memories of the war that marked them forever.

On May 4, 2004, the newly formed group Swift Boat Veterans for Truth, or Swift Vets, announced their opposition to Kerry, declaring him "unfit to serve as commander in chief." Houston lawyer John O'Neill started the group with Merrie Spaeth, a Texas Republican activist, and Rear Admiral Roy Hoffman, a Vietnam commander famed for his zealous advocacy of high body counts of enemy dead. O'Neill replaced Kerry aboard Swift Boat 94 but did not meet him in Vietnam. He has publicly criticized Kerry's anti-war activism since 1971. Nixon dirty tricks–meister Charles Colson picked and groomed O'Neill to attack Kerry, whose articulate denunciations of the war and Nixon's policies had begun to embarrass the president. Kerry and O'Neill debated each other on TV on the *Dick Cavett Show* in 1971. Spaeth had been involved in a similar effort for Bush four years earlier to discredit Arizona Senator John McCain, a POW in Vietnam.

In August, the Regnery Press published O'Neill's book, written with Jerome Corsi, *Unfit for Command: Swift Boat Veterans Speak Out against John Kerry.* The book quickly became a bestseller, thanks in part to on-air promotion by Robert Novak, who did not mention that his son was Regnery's head of marketing. On August 4, the first Swift Vets television ad, "Any Questions?" aired in several swing states. A chorus of Vietnam veterans denounced Kerry. "I served with Kerry in Vietnam. He's lying about his record. John Kerry lied to get the Bronze Star. I know. I was there. I saw what happened. John Kerry is no war hero. John Kerry dishonored his country."

On August 20, a second Swift Vets ad excerpted Kerry's 1971 testimony to the Senate, in which he summarized atrocities that some U.S. troops had confessed to at the Winter Soldier hearings earlier that year. One veteran ex-POW said that Kerry had thus freely offered the enemy a confession that POWs had been tortured to give. A third ad claimed Kerry had lied about spending Christmas 1968 in Cambodia. A fourth asked, referring to Kerry's return of his Vietnam combat medals, "Can a man who renounced his country's symbols now be trusted?" In all, the Swift Vets produced nine anti-Kerry TV ads for various markets from August through October. The ads made news, becoming a major campaign issue and receiving much more free airtime than paid advertising time.

As *Brothers in Arms* demonstrates, the accusations against Kerry did not come from the men who served on his boat, but from others, many of whom—like John O'Neill—were not in Vietnam when Kerry was, or Jerome Corsi, who was never there. Ironically, the veterans in the TV ads who claimed Kerry did not deserve his medals listed their own medals as their credentials. John McCain and other former soldiers denounced the ads. Some Vietnam vets—including some of Kerry's former crew—rose to his defense in op-ed pieces and interviews.

Debate about the accuracy of the Swift Vets' charges against Kerry continues, but the accusations themselves—regardless of their merit— were enough to put Kerry on the defensive. Did Karl Rove resurrect O'Neill for a well-timed August ambush of Kerry? As Rove tells a TV journalist in *Bush's Brain*: "Sometimes you use negative ads to change the subject." Bush's draft dodging did not compare well to Kerry's service record. Smearing a war hero—however unjustly—made perfect political sense.

George Butler had already completed his own movie about John Kerry when the Swift Vets controversy sent him back to the editing room. Butler, Kerry's personal friend for decades, was not a novice filmmaker. His 1977 movie, *Pumping Iron*, about the culture of competitive weight lifting, made a star of Austrian bodybuilder Arnold Schwarzenegger. Butler also directed *Pumping Iron II*, about female body builders, and two highly regarded films about the ill-fated Shackleton expedition to the Antarctic. Butler's *Going Upriver: The Long War of John Kerry* offers a larger picture of the Vietnam era than does Alexander's film, with much more historical context and period news footage. It is a riveting, well-crafted film about a man coming to terms with the meaning of patriotism in a tumultuous time.

"You can't understand who John is unless you understand what Vietnam meant to him," says his sister as the film opens. Butler show us Kerry at Yale in 1965 saying, "Commitment comes from the individual when he is ready." Kerry's political ambition is already clear and partly explains his motivation for serving in Vietnam.

The Mekong Delta, where Kerry served, was a free-fire zone, meaning that "you could fire at and kill anyone there." Journalist Neil Sheehan says he asked the U.S. Commander William Westmoreland if he weren't concerned about the number of civilian deaths. Westmoreland replied, "Yes, but it deprives the enemy of population, doesn't it?" The Swift Boat sailors tried to kill anyone they saw along the river.

Butler's film rehearses the events for which Kerry was awarded the Silver Star. He also interviews Jim Rassmann, who fell into the river during another incident, laden with heavy gear. Rassmann affirms that Kerry saved his life, pulling him back on board under enemy fire at great personal risk. Kerry earned a Bronze Star for that action, a medal also disputed by the Swift Vets, who said there was no enemy fire that day.

John Kerry returned home to a country divided by the war. He attended the Winter Soldier investigation organized by the Vietnam Veterans against the War. Butler shows us powerful footage from these emotional, seldom-seen proceedings. To the only people capable of understanding them—their fellow vets—young men testify to horrific things they saw or did in Vietnam. In tears, they describe the torture and murder of men, women, and children. These confessions formed the basis for Kerry's Senate testimony, words the Swift Vets described as a betrayal of U.S. fighting men.

In April 1971, thousands of war veterans camped on the Mall in Washington. Butler shows us a CBS interview with a plucky, articulate Kerry, a voice of temperate protest in a crowd of very angry vets. Senator William Fulbright invited Kerry to testify to his Foreign Relations Committee. Instead of the snippet shown by the Swift Vets, Butler gives us a generous portion of Kerry's eloquent testimony. We can see why Fulbright congratulates him on his presentation and why Nixon fears him. This 27-year-old combat veteran understands and articulates the moral dimension of the conflict and the damage it is doing to our own country.

We witness the collective anguish of veterans who now believe their sacrifices—and those of their dead comrades—were for nothing. On April 23, many of these men, including John Kerry, flung their ribbons and medals on the Capitol steps. We hear Chuck Colson gloating to Nixon on the phone that he has found the perfect attack dog to get Kerry: John O'Neill and his ad hoc Vietnam Veterans for a Just Peace. Butler gives us a long look at O'Neill confronting Kerry on the Cavett show, not the quick clip shown in the anti–Michael Moore film, *Celsius 41.11*. The more we see, the better Kerry looks by comparison, as in the 2004 presidential debates. Butler's film gives Kerry the last word: "We haven't finished that confrontation yet. We haven't learned those lessons."

The film *Stolen Honor: Wounds That Never Heal* labels the Winter Soldier confessions "frauds." The Sinclair Broadcasting Group planned to air the film on its 62 stations shortly before the election. Former prisoners of war—including two men seen in Swift Vets ads—say in the film that their captors used Kerry's Senate testimony to demoralize them and prolong their captivity. Controversy surrounding the movie's substance and timing depressed Sinclair's stock price and forced the network to excerpt only portions of it for broadcast on 40 of its stations.

"*Stolen Honor*'s rhetorical strategy goes something like this," wrote Dana Stevens, after watching the entire film: "John Kerry claimed that atrocities were committed by some of the 540,000 troops deployed in Vietnam. Therefore, John Kerry must have committed atrocities." Yet the former POWs interviewed in the film insist no atrocities ever took place in Vietnam. Stevens judged *Stolen Honor* "a document of the lunatic fringe." With the 2004 campaign centered on Vietnam, there was scant mention of health care, the economy, or Iraq.

George W. Bush: Faith in the White House avoids any issues at all, simply asking whether America is better off with a professed Christian in the presidency—a conclusion it assumes. The DVD's cover bills it as "an alternative program to *Fahrenheit 9/11*." But *Faith* fails to engage any issues raised by Moore's film, concentrating solely on the religiosity of George W. Bush. As the cover also says, "See how the power of faith can change a life, build a family, and shape the destiny of a nation." Of course, a presidency is best judged by results, not intentions. But *Faith* is all about how devout Bush is, taking no account of what his first term achieved.

In 1980, Ronald Reagan asked voters, "Are you better off now than you were four years ago?" Fewer Americans could have answered yes in 2004 than when Reagan asked. Luckily for Bush, nobody did. If *Faith* seems a disconnect from reality for the fact-based crowd, its pitch is to the faith-based, for whom a "covenant with Christ" is sufficient, come what may. Frank Rich found it an "unintentional and considerably more nightmarish sequel" to *Fahrenheit 9/11*. He thought the film "must be seen" because it shows "why Mr. Bush feels divinely entitled to keep his job" despite the debacle in Iraq and how "faith, or at least a certain brand of it, counts more than competence."

Evangelical religious leaders like James Robison tell us they are "convinced that Bush has deep convictions." Another religious expert locates Bush's beliefs somewhere "between mainstream Christians and Evangelicals." Bush aide Doug Wead says Bush's faith gives him "a moral clarity befitting a world leader." The film cuts occasionally to Bush in the pulpit of a huge church, telling the congregation that he prays often and stating, "Christ changed my life."

Faith offers up a sanitized biography of George W. Bush that plays like a Biblical parable. Even *Christianity Today*, which found the film "informative and inspiring," thought the "dramatic reenactments" of key moments in Bush's life were "cheesy." The "arrogant kid with the big mouth" consoles his mother when his sister, Robin, dies. The child actor who portrays the boy George tells a friend he can't come out to play because his mother needs him. Narrator Janet Parshall tells us the young Bush spent many years "chasing the good life, smoking, drinking, and cursing."

The film elides inconvenient facts. "Bush started his own oil company— Arbusto," is all it says, without telling us where his start-up money came from or how quickly his business failed. In parable fashion, we learn that in the summer of 1985, George W. took a walk on the beach in Maine with the preacher Billy Graham. "Are you right with God?" Graham asks him. "No, but I want to be," says Bush. His Texas Rangers baseball deal is mentioned briefly as a prescient gamble, not as a handout from his father's friends and a taxpayer rip-off. *Faith* spins his 1994 Texas gubernatorial victory over Ann Richards as a product of his Christian faith over a mean woman—not a gay-bashing, Clinton-hating fiesta of lies and innuendos, pandering to corporations.

In a line that quickly became fodder for Internet humor, one presidential admirer in the film says, "Nobody spends more time on his knees than George W. Bush." But it's no laughing matter. Ted Haggard, president of the National Association of Evangelicals, says that "Bush will be known as the man who stood up to Islamic fundamentalism being used to tyrannize their own people and he'll be seen in another hundred years in the Islamic world as a great liberator." Is that how long the U.S. occupation of Iraq will last?

The Kerry Vietnam movies, made by his admirers, were intended to introduce that elusive demographic—the undecided voter—to a man of principle, who bravely served his country in battle and resolutely spoke unpleasant truth to power. But these films succeed almost too well. Many may wonder where that forthright, outspoken young Kerry went. Did his Senate years cloud his clarity? *Stolen Honor* and the Swift Vets TV ads cast doubt on Kerry's heroism and even his patriotism. Though the charges themselves proved, on closer scrutiny, misleading and much more spiteful than accurate, they cast enough doubt to confuse, if not dissuade, wavering voters.

George W. Bush: Faith in the White House was a bouquet to believers, a pep talk to the base: only a dedicated Christian can lead this country at this perilous moment in history. Never mind that this Christian has lied, sanctioned torture, debauched the U.S. Constitution, driven the country dangerously into debt, and bungled the war in Iraq, which continues to bleed us. Bush has in fact *created* much of our current peril. But none of that matters, compared to the Reawakening of Christian Principles that Bush is leading, according to the film.

After the election, James Dobson revealed one aspect of that Reawakening. Dobson, whom the *New York Times* called "the nation's most influential evangelical leader," threatened to target Democratic senators who block conservative Supreme Court appointments. He named six senators facing reelection in 2006. He intends to rally his forces against all who defy him. Is God a Republican, out to take down the faithless?

Both sides of the movie campaign—like the political campaign—largely failed to address the present reality. Mired in Vietnam or lost in prayer, the candidates nurtured idealized cinematic images of themselves far removed from current social or economic problems—let alone solutions. People go to the movies seeking "mythic solace for reality," according to University of Southern California Professor Leo Braudy. In the election of 2004, movies about the presidential candidates tried to provide that mythic solace. Kerry offered us his youth; Bush, his faith. With politicians pandering to moviegoers' taste for escapism, it was little wonder that by the end of the election, audiences sought to escape politics itself.

INTEMPERATE BACKLASH

Looking back on 2004, *New York Times* cultural critic Frank Rich thought the film that best represented the year was Mel Gibson's hit, *The Passion of the Christ*. "The Gibson conflation of religion with violence . . . its prurient and interminable wallow in the Crucifixion," while largely ignoring what Jesus taught, "reflects the universal order of the day," Rich wrote, especially "the savagery of the actual war that radical Islam brought to our doorstep on 9/11."

Like Gibson's film, the Bush presidential campaign appealed less to the head than to the gut. Michael Moore's attack on the Bush administration in *Fahrenheit 9/11* provoked emotional outcries having less to do with the film's facts than its intentions. In a lengthy, rambling diatribe entitled "Unfairenheit 9/11: The Lies of Michael Moore," Christopher Hitchens condemned Moore's film as "a sinister exercise in moral frivolity, crudely disguised as an exercise in seriousness. It is also a spectacle of abject political cowardice masking itself as a demonstration of 'dissenting' bravery."

Hitchens despised the film's contradictions: "Either the Saudis run U.S. policy or they do not." "Either we sent too many troops [to Afghanistan], or were wrong to send any at all . . . or we sent too few." But these are categorical imperatives of Hitchens's own devising. After writing that Moore "prefers leaden sarcasm to irony and, indeed, may not appreciate the distinction," Hitchens leadenly dismissed the film as a "windy and bloated cinematic 'key to all mythologies.'" His otherwise inexplicable ferocity had less to do with Moore's film and more to do with his own political stance.

By attacking Moore, Hitchens was defending his own public support for the 2003 invasion of Iraq. As his rationale for the ongoing war became increasingly transparently untenable, Hitchens turned his rising anger on those who spotlighted its folly and futility. Like Bush and his cohorts, Hitchens is incapable of admitting his mistake, even though, as the courageous and perceptive author of *The Trials of Henry Kissinger*, Hitchens, unlike Bush, surely recognizes it. Hitchens took a retroactive swipe at Moore as "the guy who thought it so clever and amusing to catch Charlton Heston, in *Bowling for Columbine*, at the onset of his senile dementia. Such courage." Hitchens's gratuitous savagery set the tone for much subsequent anti-Moore invective.

Moore himself took every opportunity to inflame the controversy surrounding his film. In August, he accepted an assignment from *USA Today* to cover the Republican National Convention in New York. Moore made the most of his mainstream journalistic opportunity to make fun of the Republicans. When Senator John McCain addressed the convention and called Moore a "disingenuous filmmaker," he did not know Moore was sitting in the press section. McCain later admitted he had not yet seen Moore's film.

Anti-Michael Moore Web sites proliferated through the summer of 2004 and beyond the election Moore hoped to influence. Broadening their attacks from *Fahrenheit 9/11*, these sites berated and deconstructed Moore's earlier films, and made a specialty of personal attacks on Moore himself. Some people have literally made a career of attacking Moore, like David T. Hardy, the creator of mooreexposed.com. Hardy's Web site begins with headlines: "Should a 400 lb. man advise us on the evils of overconsumption? Should a resident of a million-dollar apartment claim to be a poster boy of the working class?"

He and Jason Clarke (of moorelies.com) co-authored a book: *Michael Moore Is a Big Fat Stupid White Man*, which Clarke called "a thorough examination of a career spent in hypocrisy, pseudo-intellectualism, deception, and deceit." Published by Regan Books, the publisher of Moore's *Stupid White Men*, their book was timed to coincide with the U.S. release of *Fahrenheit 9/11*. The book's thesis is that Moore suffers from Narcissistic Personality Disorder and actually despises himself. Hardy popped up in TV summer sound bytes to denounce Moore's "crockumentary."

At least four full-length documentary films were produced to refute Moore's movie, endowing it with another, unique level of celebrity. First came *FahrenHype 9/11: Unraveling the Truth about Fahrenheit 9/11 & Michael Moore*. Narrated by Ron Silver in a grim, portentous mode, the film selectively deconstructs facts and sequences in Moore's film to reveal his "deceptive" filmmaking practices. Silver assures us that anyone can play such cheap tricks: "You give me enough footage of Michael Moore, I can make him look like an anorexic right-winger." But his producers apparently only gave Silver enough footage to try very hard to make Moore out to be a big fat left-wing liar. As Silver tells us (whether scripted or not is hard to tell), "As a propagandist, I prefer Leni Riefenstahl or Ezra Pound. Tokyo Rose was better looking."

Lacking the wit or the agile editing of Moore's film, *Hype* consists mostly of talking heads, including odd choices, like political gadfly Dick Morris, who acts as a kind of host. Identified as an "ex-advisor to President Clinton," Morris says, about the U.S. lack of preparedness against terrorism, "Bush deserves eight months of blame. But Clinton deserves eight *years* of blame." *Hype* begins by revisiting Bush sitting in the Florida schoolroom after learning that a second plane hit the World Trade Center, insisting that Bush remained there only "five minutes . . . not seven minutes" as Moore claims. Right away, the audience knows that this film is going to be a nitpicker's night out.

"Was it all just a dream?" Silver quotes Moore's opening line. "Michael, I know why you're so upset. You voted for Nader and Nader cost Gore the election. I understand, but, come on, Michael, stop dreaming. Wake up!" Silver tells us that he voted for Gore but supports Bush since 9/11. He equates Moore to Charles Lindbergh and other isolationists of the late 1930s, who resisted a war with the Nazis. Georgia Democrat turned Republican National Committee (RNC) attack dog Zell Miller also invokes World War II. Miller compares fighting terrorists to killing the poisonous snakes in his backyard. Can't wait for em to strike. Gotta get em first. The redneck's guide to international diplomacy.

We see the scene from Moore's film where Bush addresses a posh banquet, saying, "It's nice to be here among the haves and the have mores. Some people call you the elite. I call you my base." *Hype* pulls back to show us that Gore was also at this annual Al Smith Dinner, a fundraiser for Catholic Charities. The politicians were lampooning themselves. Bush was just joking. "Moore's strongest point is simply invalid," says Jason Clarke. We can see that Moore edited the scene for maximum impact, but is this really the extent of *Hype*'s anti-Moore revelations? Well, yes, it is.

But the movie's talking heads offer quotes that no amount of context can render rational, such as Dick Morris's assertion that "When George Bush got Pakistan to fight terror with us—that was monumental. You can take 15 Frances and Germanys. Give me Pakistan if you want to fight terror." Or Ann Coulter asking the liberal stumper, "If we went to war for oil, then why are gas prices so high?" Or Steven Emerson, author of *American Jihad*, explaining: "It's not Norwegian women in wheelchairs that are attacking us in Manhattan—it's Islamic extremists." These moments are not laugh-out-loud funny, but rather perplexing, surreal non sequiturs, much like the movie itself.

Celsius 41.11: The Temperature at Which the Brain Begins to Die, is an even more haphazard cinematic rebuttal to Moore's film, with an even smaller array of conservative talking heads. While aiming to refute half a dozen assumptions of *Fahrenheit 9/11*, *Celsius* also addresses itself explicitly to the 2004 presidential campaign, down to its anti-Kerry theme song: "John Boy, tell us which way the wind is blowing today, Do you believe anything that you say?" This film plays fast and loose with the facts, starting with its opening narration: "We begin with the premise that John Kerry is a decent man with a distinguished record of public service— as is George W. Bush." But since Bush was a draft dodger who shirked even his substitute military duty, this is conceding too much. There is less unintentional comedy here and much more sinister bald-faced lying.

The preternaturally petrified conservative columnist Charles Krauthammer wonders aloud at the "unprecedented level of hostility" directed against Bush. Neither he nor his off-camera interviewer apparently considered that the bloody, obscene Iraq war—based on transparent lies and protested by millions before it started—might have ticked a few people off. Bill Sammon, a *Washington Times* reporter, calls Moore's assertion that Bush stole the election in Florida a "lingering myth." Sammon misrepresents the findings of the U.S. Commission on Civil Rights, which he says did not substantiate charges of voter disenfranchisement. Yet the commission quite plainly affirmed the "disenfranchisement of countless eligible voters in 2000 . . . " that "fell most heavily on the shoulders of African Americans." What part of that does Sammon not understand?

Mansoor Ijaz—who the film labels a "terrorism expert" but who is actually a Fox News and *National Review* commentator, Pakistan lobbyist, and investor in "security technologies,"—states matter-of-factly, offering no proof, that there is "no question that links between Saddam and al Qaeda existed." American Enterprise Institute (AEI) scholar Michael Ledeen, a longstanding but here unidentified advocate of war with Iran, traces the beginning of the current conflict of the West with the Middle East to 1979, when Iranian rebels took Americans hostage. Why not 1953, when the CIA deposed the Iranian regime of Mohammed Mossadegh for nationalizing Iranian oil? Ledeen's AEI cohort Joshua Muravchik claims the U.S. response to Islamic aggression "has been very passive." If *FahrenHype 9/11* is ridiculous, *Celsius 41.11* is malevolent, repeating Bush administration lies, in part because some of its talking heads originated and spread them.

Conservative critic Michael Medved contributes a truly creepy performance, accusing John Kerry of "the grandmother of all flip-flops" for serving in Vietnam, then turning against the Vietnam War. These positions are "irreconcilable" according to Medved. "Is Kerry a hero or a protestor?" He is both of course, but Medved can't grasp it. When he speaks of meeting Kerry at Yale in the 1960s, Medved calls Kerry, "the great JFK; a very, very big man on campus; pompous and portentous even as a student." Medved has never overcome his undergraduate envy of Kerry. He would be pitiable, but for his malign intent. All the critics in this film come off as so many annoying gnats, bugging their betters. The humorless cast and amateurish production values guarantee *Celsius 41.11* the minuscule audiences it deserves.

Michael Moore Hates America adapts Moore's *Roger & Me* mode, as filmmaker Michael Wilson trails Moore around the country trying to interview him for his movie without success. Wilson doesn't really think Moore hates America. He just wants to expose Moore's manipulative methods of filmmaking, which Wilson himself emulates. Interviewing the mayor of Flint, Wilson lies about his own project, telling the mayor he is making a documentary about small towns.

Wilson's biggest coup is getting the venerable documentarian Albert Maysles to characterize Moore as "tyrannized by his method, which is to simplify complex ideas." Lacking Moore's wit and cinematic skills, Wilson is reduced to making "fat" jokes. As one reviewer concluded about Wilson, "He's trying to suck off some of Moore's substantial spotlight to jumpstart his own filmmaking career that, if this unprofessional film is any indication, has absolutely no justification to continue."

Last and certainly least, *Shooting Michael Moore* is promoted on a Web site of the same name by the film's creator, first-time director Kevin Leffler. Leffler grew up in Moore's hometown, graduated from Moore's high school three years after he did, and worked two years with Moore on a Flint crisis hotline. The film's Web site trailer shows Leffler driving an ice cream truck through an African American neighborhood, inviting passersby to party at Moore's posh home on Torch Lake in northern Michigan. Leffler claims he's inviting African Americans because Moore said, "White people scare the crap out of me."

Leffler's prank seems racist and mean spirited, as does his posting a "Help Wanted" sign in Harlem with the phone number of Moore's New York production studio. He razzes Moore about how much money he's made, exposes Moore's ill treatment of his workers and interview subjects, accuses him of being illegally registered to vote in two states, and of having cheated during his Boy Scout survival training. Leffler also hired a roundish dwarf and dressed him up as Mini-Mike. Is Leffler settling a boyhood grudge or merely trying to siphon off some of Moore's celebrity for himself? His movie looks like a hatchet job, grist for a dark meditation on the price of fame in a Stephen King novel, or maybe a psychological case study of a real-life Rupert Pupkin, dressed as an ice cream salesman, handing out frozen bile.

Immediately after the 2004 election, right-wing pundits like Robert Novak blamed the Democratic defeat on Michael Moore. Novak thought Democrats should regret having embraced Moore's values. But the tidal wave of reactionary vitriol inspired by *Fahrenheit 9/11* revealed the fear among Bush supporters that Moore might damage his electoral chances. It was almost as if the Republicans preferred to run against Moore's film, feeling perhaps that Moore's tactics, if not his issues, offered easier targets than John Kerry. Errol Morris expressed the fear "that much of the material emerging from the left or from the Democrats was preaching to the choir. I sometimes look at *Fahrenheit 9/11* as a kind of secular church. You could go to the movie theater and collectively worship against the Bush infidel."

Some on the left disavowed the politics of Moore's film. Progressive critic Robert Jensen agreed that Bush was bad for the country. He defended *Fahrenheit 9/11* from right-wing attacks. But Jensen found Moore's facile anti-Bush stance an incoherent critique of the system of empire. His movie fails to answer the questions it raises about the reasons for the U.S. invasions of Afghanistan and Iraq. Blaming the Bush dynasty and its Saudi cronies does not comprehend larger trends in American policy. "In other words," wrote Jensen, "if we beat Bush and go back to 'normal' then we're all in trouble. Normal is empire building. Normal is U.S. domination, economic and military, and the suffering that vulnerable people around the world experience as a result."

Moore himself thought *Fahrenheit 9/11* had relevance beyond the election. The film was "about the Iraq War and the War on Terrorism and the use of fear to manipulate the public. I started it before there was Bush versus Kerry." Kerry lost the election but Moore easily vanquished his self-styled cinematic rivals. Americans have long enjoyed smashing their own idols. Taking on the White House in 2004, Michael Moore had become an idol worthy of personal and political assaults, which are often indistinguishable in American life.

The artistry of Moore's film dwarfed those of his rivals. But—politics aside—there were deeper reasons not to like the Anti-Moores. There is something unseemly and self-diminishing about individuals who dedicate their careers and lives to denigrating the achievements of another person. Defining yourself in opposition to someone else renders you small and unoriginal. The Anti-Moores are punks by their own definition.

As is John O'Neill. He entered public life as a convenient tool for Chuck Colson and Richard Nixon to use against Vietnam veterans who questioned the war's conduct and purpose. The war finally ended. Regimes changed at home and abroad. But like a supporting player in an unpopular TV series that ended decades ago, O'Neill is associated forever—in our minds and apparently in his—with that one part. He never had another. When John Kerry became the Democratic presidential nominee, O'Neill arose from the dead like a zombie celebrity has-been on the "E! True Hollywood Story," whom we are surprised but not necessarily gratified to find out is still alive. Like David Cassidy or The Monkees playing Vegas, O'Neill made his comeback, reprising his role as the Anti-Kerry in a book, TV commercials, and movie cameos, proving that character assassination—a la Nixon, McCarthy, Novak, and Rove— remains a viable, even lucrative career in America.

Fact-based films took sides during the 2004 election—for and against candidates, issues, and other films—revealing again the vast difference between documentaries that admit to having a point of view and journalism that does not. The documentarians hoped to influence undecided swing voters, a minuscule but mighty minority. If the makers of *George W. Bush: Faith in the White House* were literally preaching to the converted, then Moore and his rivals also appealed largely to audiences predisposed to their points of view. Through various means—including the accumulated testimony of authoritative talking heads; accusatory, exasperated, or ironic tones of voice; and multiple modes of visual corroboration—all the campaign films strove to be believable, while tailoring their data to fit their political preconceptions.

Scientists or scholars who suppress evidence that contradicts their hypotheses are considered unscrupulous by their colleagues. Valid conclusions are supposed to emerge from complete data treated in a responsible, fully reported way. A different standard applies to makers of campaign documentaries, who select and arrange information to shape their narratives and sell their points of view. The truth they seek to present is the one with which they began. Each film offers not only an argument, but also a value system on which it is based. Audiences cannot accept one without the other. It's a package deal. Most 2004 political campaign films reified viewer values, but did not change many minds. Believability is crucial to making their messages persuasive. Ironically, more than ever, filmmakers resort to varying degrees of artifice to achieve that believability.

Chapter 9

ALTERNATIVE REALITIES

We have . . . become an image-obsessed culture, a culture that increasingly doesn't care whether things are real or not.

—Jon Else

Film scholars have devised a number of categories to comprehend the varieties of documentary films. We have avoided discussing those terms because they suggest a rigidity that does not truly reflect the dynamic nature of the documentary form. Classifying a film as "reflexive" or "interactive" does not necessarily increase our understanding of it, either as a political artifact or a work of art. Such academic concepts may make a film less accessible, not more. As film scholar Bill Nichols acknowledged in 1994: "Things change. The four modes of documentary production that presented themselves as an exhaustive survey of the field no longer suffice."

This final chapter will explore in plain terms several important contemporary trends in political documentary films. One of the most significant—and sometimes disturbing—of those trends is the tendency toward what Nichols calls the "blurred boundaries" between factual and fictional films. Nichols recognizes that we prefer to acquire information about our world "in the form of narratives, stories that make meaning" of some sort. "Inevitably, the distinction between fact and fiction blurs when claims about reality get cast as narratives." Nichols describes how fictional films adopt documentary techniques and vice versa. But the boundaries between fact and fiction have blurred in many more dramatic and sinister ways, as we shall see.

A second significant trend in political documentaries is a kind of educational effort—aimed at younger audiences—to show how U.S. policies affect the entire planet. The United States is no butterfly in the rain forest, more like Godzilla. So it makes perfect sense for American documentary films to take up global themes, to transcend the political, mass-mediated barriers erected to divide and conquer us, the world's majority.

A third, related trend is the use of documentary films as a means of empowerment, not simply in terms of sharing important information or vital images with mass audiences, but also by inviting participation in the filmmaking process itself from those who are usually outside it. Democratizing the documentary point of view, or crafting a film from multiple perspectives, subverts the hierarchy inherent in traditional approaches to film construction, allowing us to reveal ourselves to one another. The ultimate political empowerment is a personal transformation of consciousness, a process on which some nonfiction films have begun to focus.

Telling fact from fiction can be tricky at times. And the recognized arbiters of taste and judgment are uncertain how or where to draw the line.

In 2005, the Academy of Motion Picture Arts and Sciences awarded the Oscar for best short documentary to *Mighty Times: The Children's March*, about a 1963 civil rights demonstration conducted by thousands of children in Birmingham, Alabama. A dispute arose about how much of the film was archival, and how much was re-created. Reenactments—a documentary staple since Errol Morris's *The Thin Blue Line*—are "explicitly allowed by the academy." The filmmakers claim that only about 10% of their movie was reenacted. But Jon Else, cinematographer for the 1987 television miniseries about the Black civil rights movement, *Eyes on the Prize*, estimates that at least half of *The Children's March* was reenacted, "using vintage cameras and distressed film stock," to give the sequences an authentic period look. Critics charged the filmmakers with deception.

How much reenactment is too much for a supposed "documentary"? Academy rules state only that a documentary "may be photographed in actual occurrence, or may employ partial reenactment, stock footage, stills, animation, stop-motion, or other techniques, as long as the emphasis is on fact and not on fiction." In other words, the Academy is struggling to stay abreast of new developments in this protean genre, with no real guidelines for what constitutes a documentary film.

Feature films engage reality to add gravitas and edge. For their movie about a married couple abandoned by their dive boat, Chris Kentis and Laura Lau shot *Open Water* (2004) in the open ocean, where real sharks circled the unprotected actors. Elliot Greenebaum made *Assisted Living*

(2004), about the relationship between a nursing home aide and his elderly patient, in actual personal-care facilities and nursing homes, using the real residents for his cast, several of whom died before the film opened.

A better model for how fact and fiction can illuminate multiple meanings of events is Alain Brigand's cinematic pastiche of responses to September 11, 2001, from eleven filmmakers. In Chapter 3, we saw how Mexico's Alejandro González Iñárritu shaped a dark, eloquent poetry from the sights and sounds of the tragedy. And how Britain's Ken Loach seized the moment to remind us that we have long inflicted brutalities upon one another that no ideology can justify. Several other filmmakers crafted fables built upon facts to locate the meanings of that moment.

Israel's Amos Gitai chose to re-create a bloody bombing in Jaffa, whose terrible toll is bumped from the news by the 9/11 media blitz. Bosnia's Danis Tanovic sounds a similar theme, juxtaposing the acknowledged horror of that day against the ongoing invisible grief of exiled widows from Srebrenica, for whom 9/11 only adds to the reasons why the rest of the world has forgotten them. Media coverage is a zero-sum game that poses a riddle: if an event is not covered on the news, did it really occur?

Indian director Mira Nair dramatizes the true story of a young Muslim man in Brooklyn who goes missing after 9/11 and is publicly accused of being a terrorist. Neighbors shun his family. But the young man, Salman Hamdani, was a paramedic who rushed to the World Trade Center to help and was killed. His mother, at the funeral, says, "First they called you a terrorist, now they call you a hero." Stereotypes dehumanize those who believe them, as well as their targets. Against the odds, Idrissa Ouedraogo of Burkina Faso wrought a rare bit of gentle comedy from 9/11. Two weeks after the attack, some dirt-poor children in Ouagadougou glimpse Osama bin Laden there. They plot to capture him for the $25 million reward, but he eludes them. Personal lives, however remote from mediated events, are touched by them and may yet be defined in relation to them. Medialand is a world we have in common.

More troublesome incursions of fiction into the factual media world include those described by a retired intelligence officer, Air Force Colonel Sam Gardiner, in Danny Schechter's *WMD: Weapons of Mass Deception*. Gardiner estimates that the White House and the Pentagon together "created or massaged" fifty to sixty stories in the run-up to the Iraq war and during the invasion in order "to distort and dominate the news agenda." One example was the bogus tale of the "daring U.S. rescue of the heroic U.S. Army soldier Jessica Lynch" from an Iraqi hospital. The authorities did not care that the story proved false and soon disappeared. It served its purpose. The Lynch story "hung around for more than a week," obscuring unpleasant realities that U.S. officials preferred not to publicize, until they concocted their next misleading narrative.

The Pentagon also dominated coverage through sheer inundation. Robert Pelton describes the million-dollar media facility at Doha, Qatar, as a "firehose," where officials bombarded journalists with a surfeit of information, more than they could use, effectively drowning out other sources. As Gardiner warns, "If you didn't like the way this war was covered, you're *really* not going to like the next one" as high-level propagandists and news manipulators hone their ability to commandeer the crisis news agenda.

The Bush administration manufactures some news stories by bribing certain "journalists," such as right-wing columnist Armstrong Williams, who received $240,000 to promote Bush education policies. Another deceptive practice flourishing in the Bush years is the government production of "'video news releases' that look indistinguishable from authentic newscasts and, as ready-made and cost-free reports, are sometimes picked up by local news programs" without disclosing the source of the material. Whether or not these stories are fictions, they are dishonest, policy promotions masquerading as reportage, like the state-run media systems of totalitarian governments.

If coverage of the Iraq war and the Bush administration feature propaganda disguised as journalism, news and entertainment blur when media cover rituals involving celebrity. The 2005 trial of singer Michael Jackson for child molestation was closed to cameras. But E! Entertainment Television and British Sky Broadcasting showed it to worldwide audiences anyway, using trial records and a Michael Jackson impersonator. Transcripts of each day's court proceedings were edited down to a half-hour show, reenacted, and broadcast over a global satellite service. Edward Moss, who has impersonated Jackson in many countries for more than a decade, was engaged to incarnate the singer for the length of the trial. Such news and entertainment hybrids are becoming more common as media consumers become less able to tell the real elements from the fake. Of course, certain types of so-called journalism have always contained fantastic elements.

American tabloid media are direct descendants of the tall tales told on the American frontier. Elvis—along with wise or evil space aliens—

inhabit the territory Paul Bunyan and Davy Crockett once bestrode. Hoax and hyperbole were tools of P. T. Barnum's trade. Barnum hired "experts" to debunk the curiosities he exhibited, to whip up controversy and public interest. The Hearst/Pulitzer era of yellow journalism flooded the media with apocryphal tales and staged stunts, some of which led to social reform, others, to war. Orson Welles revealed the generous American capacity for credulity in his 1938 radio broadcast *War of the Worlds*, scripted to resemble a series of news bulletins and "flash" updates, as thousands panicked and fled their homes to escape a "Martian attack." Late-night cable televangelists and infomercials milk this same reservoir of naïve longing for some form of transcendence. And the epidemic of conspiracy-oriented Web sites demonstrates that even though our technology may be sophisticated, popular appetites for the marginal, the whimsical, and the paranoid remain unsated. Of course, it is much easier to believe in something—no matter how bizarre—than to question everything.

American filmmakers have always combined elements of fact and fiction. The modern, politically purposeful mix of the two elements may have begun with Haskell Wexler's 1969 film *Medium Cool*. Set in Chicago during the summer of the 1968 Democratic National Convention, the film opens with two TV journalists at a car wreck, getting the news footage they need before calling the police to send an ambulance for the injured, bleeding victims still in the car. One of the reporters becomes involved with a woman and her young son. When the boy runs away, during the convention, his mother looks for him along downtown streets that have turned into a war zone, complete with tanks and barbed wire, as war protestors face Chicago police and National Guard troops.

Actress Verna Bloom remains in character as the searching mother, threading her way through actual Chicago crowds of cops, soldiers, and antiwar demonstrators, as Wexler trails her with his movie camera. When the police and demonstrators clash, tear gas canisters are lobbed back and forth. One lands near the camera, prompting someone to yell, "Watch out, Haskell, it's real!" That shout remains on the movie soundtrack. The genuine tension and violence in the streets adds to the sense of menace for the mother seeking her lost child. This sequence remains a powerful one, though the politics of the convention, as shown in the film, and those of the film itself, remain incoherent.

Emile de Antonio mixed fact and fiction much more audaciously and oddly in his little-seen film *In the King of Prussia* (1982), a reenacted political trial, with the actual defendants playing themselves. In September 1980, a group of Christian antiwar activists—including the radical priests Philip and Daniel Berrigan—broke into a General Electric weapons plant in King of Prussia, Pennsylvania. The protestors, who became known as the Plowshares Eight, burned documents, damaged missile nose cones, and poured vials of their blood on files of papers. Banned from the court, de Antonio intercut actual news coverage of the trial with courtroom reenactments. Actor Martin Sheen plays the judge. The Berrigans and other defendants play themselves. De Antonio shot his film as the real trial was finishing up. Just after production ended, the defendants—all of whom were convicted—began serving prison sentences.

Hollywood feature director Robert Altman and cartoonist Garry Trudeau served up a more polished and sustained mèlange of political fiction and reality with their satirical HBO series *Tanner '88*. Shot during the 1988 political season of primary elections and political conventions, the eleven-episode series featured a fictional Democratic presidential contender, Jack Tanner. As played by Michael Murphy, Tanner interacts on the campaign trail with actual politicians like Pat Robertson, Bruce Babbitt, and Bob Dole to give Tanner the candidate, and the series, a sense of immediacy and authenticity.

On the 2004 DVD version, Altman said he considers the series his "most creative work." Altman and Trudeau did not script the real politicians. They just described the dramatic situation, and then asked them to speak with Tanner or other characters as they would in real life. The encounters are superficial, except for the heartfelt conversation Jack Tanner has with Bruce Babbitt, who had recently quit the presidential race.

Topical, spontaneous, and frequently funny, *Tanner '88* combines Trudeau's smart, edgy script and Altman's penchant for loose scene construction and overlapping dialog with superb improvisational acting by Murphy, Cynthia Nixon as his daughter, and Pamela Reed as his campaign manager. The Sundance channel reran the series during the 2004 electoral season, when the DVD came out. The fresh relevance of the sixteen-year-old series moved Sundance to commission a sequel. Unfortunately, Altman and Trudeau's new mini-series, *Tanner on Tanner*, about Alex Tanner's documentary of her father's career, is a stilted, lifeless mess. Altman's attitude defines the problem. In his DVD interview, Altman expresses a lofty disdain: "Most of these documentary films are really about nothing, except the process of making the documentary itself."

Sadly, though many documentaries do attempt more, that *is* the substance of *Tanner on Tanner*. In one overwrought scene, Cynthia Nixon, as Alex Tanner, tries to interview Ron Reagan at the Democratic Convention. Reagan, a commentator for MSNBC, comes to the interview with his own camera crew. He has double-booked the interview with Alexandra Kerry, daughter of the actual Democratic presidential nominee, who really was making a documentary about her father. Of course, Altman's own cameras are there, along with those of an actor playing one of Alex's film students, making a documentary about the making of her documentary. The concept must have seemed funny, but the scene—like the rest of the mini-series—does not work.

With fictional candidates running for real offices and top administration officials cooking up fictional news to control the media agenda, Americans may be forgiven some degree of confusion or cynicism about what constitutes political reality. As Ronald Reagan knew, or rather, as the speechwriters of that heavily scripted president understood, Americans prefer clear, simple storylines with recognizable heroes and villains to messier tales involving shades of gray and having to draw one's own conclusions. Several major Bush administration narratives, such as "free trade" and the "War on Terror," involve the export of American values worldwide through policies that demand the subordination or marginalization of world regulatory bodies, like the International Monetary Fund or the United Nations. Independent filmmakers counter these official stories with alternative versions, aimed at unmasking the corporate greed and capitalist imperialism hidden beneath the bland term *globalization*.

OUTSOURCING EMPATHY

If Michael Moore took his act outside the United States, his stunts might resemble those of "Andy and Mike," the Yes Men, dedicated to "changing the world one prank at a time." Chris Smith, Sarah Price, and Dan Ollman's film, *The Yes Men* (2004), follows along as Andy and Mike appear at conferences in various countries, masquerading as officials of the World Trade Organization. Their goal is "identity correction." "We want to show the hidden side of the WTO, which is doing lots of dark things. We steal their identity to make them more honest . . . to create a public spectacle, in order to reveal cultural problems."

Andy and Mike set up a parody Web site, identical to the real WTO site. When e-mail queries and invitations to speak at conferences arrive, Andy and Mike attend these functions as WTO officials, offering up outrageous proposals and stunts. But their satire often flies right by their audiences, who apparently think the WTO is just being more candid than usual. In Salzburg, as Andreas Bichelbauer, Andy proposes several ideas for boosting industrial productivity, such as abolishing the siesta in Latin countries and selling votes on the Internet to avoid wasting time and money on genuine elections. He shows an American vote-selling Web site in his PowerPoint presentation, "vote-auction.com." To Andy's chagrin, none of the delegates reacts with anger or surprise.

Appearing on CNBC's European business channel as Granwyth Hulatberi, Andy suggests that sound economics should combine the approaches of (laissez-faire conservative) Milton Friedman with (Yippie anarchist) Abbie Hoffman. The show's moderator does not blink. At a conference in Tampere, Finland, on the future of textiles, Andy, as Hank Hardy Unruh, offers delegates a brief history of labor problems beginning with the U.S. Civil War. Unruh explains that slavery would have died out eventually anyway without a war because it was not cost effective. "The cost of maintaining slaves in Tampere is expensive . . . but leave that slave back in Gabon and it's cheap." You can pay them less, you don't have to feed or house them, and you can employ their children. You don't even have to see them. Slavery's more evolved form is remote labor. Again, no one reacts, even when Andy rips off his cutaway business suit to reveal a gold "management leisure suit" with a giant inflatable phallus, equipped with an "employee visualization apparatus" to oversee distant workers, who are "fitted with implanted chips." The audience applauds politely. No one has any questions.

The Yes Men's only "success," in terms of provoking outrage, is their talk at the State University of New York at Plattsburgh, where they suggest a radical solution to world hunger. Since we only use 20% of food nutrients, we can recycle the waste. One hamburger can be eaten up to ten times. Mike tells the angry students that McDonald's, in partnership with the WTO, has been experimenting with this technology, using up to 20% of "postconsumer waste" in many of its hamburgers. This disgusts the students, especially because they are munching free McDonald's burgers the Yes Men handed out to them at the start of the lecture. Their PowerPoint illustrations leave "no doubts about what is being said: the WTO believes the poor should eat their own shit, or perhaps eat the shit of the rich, if an efficient pipeline can be established."

On their Web site (www.theyesmen.org), Andy and Mike conclude that the outrage of the students proves that their satirical lectures were not too "difficult." Their previous audiences were just too dense to get them. At a trade luncheon in Sydney, Australia, Andy, as Kinnithrung Sprat, declares that because of the widespread harm it is causing, the WTO has decided to "reconfigure itself" into an entirely different sort of group. The conservative audience greets this surprising news with pleasure. One of the accountants present calls the disbanding of the WTO a "terrific sign of hope." The news is gleefully reported to the Canadian parliament, only to be retracted in disappointment when it's discovered to be a hoax.

Though *The Yes Men* movie was already in release, Andy appeared on BBC World on December 3, 2004, the twentieth anniversary of the Bhopal disaster. He posed as Jude Finisterra, a spokesman for Dow Chemical, the parent corporation of Union Carbide, whose chemical spill in Bhopal, India, killed thousands and left 120,000 more incapacitated. Finisterra announced Dow's plan "to liquidate Union Carbide and use the resulting $12 billion to pay for medical care, clean up the site, and fund research into the hazards of other Dow products. After two hours of wide coverage, Dow issued a press release denying the statement, ensuring even greater coverage," reminding the world that Dow had refused to take responsibility for the accident or to make any amends. Occasionally the Yes Men's ability to expose their enemies exceeds their expectations, as when an exasperated George W. Bush reacted to their satirical Web site, GWBush.com, telling a press conference, "There ought to be limits to freedom." The Yes Men knew he and his cronies felt that way, but it was gratifying to hear him admit it out loud.

Parody can help raise consciousness about the true nature of the forces behind globalization. Political activists like the Big Noise Film Collective and the Guerrilla News Network (GNN) make films to reveal the consequences of globalization and to rally opposition to it. They seek to empower their audiences by making them part of a new community. As labor spokesman Tony Judd says in the film *This Is What Democracy Looks Like* (2000), made by Big Noise and the Seattle Independent Media Center, "The only way you can take on global capitalism is with a global movement of people." Big Noise and GNN aim to help create that movement with their art, their politics, and their lives, which they refuse to separate.

This new generation of filmmakers addresses their peers in a modern cinematic language that is redefining the frontiers of the documentary form. Music plays a role at least as important as visual images. The speed and rhythm of these edgy, nonlinear documentaries attract younger audiences who do not ordinarily see nonfiction films. Some older viewers may be less captivated, or even alienated by this "transformative" approach. But increasing visibility and industry recognition are bringing these artists up from the underground and closer to center stage of popular culture.

"We are not filmmakers producing and distributing our work," proclaims the Big Noise Web site. "We are rebels, crystallizating (*sic*) radical community and weaving a network of skin and images, of dreams and bone, of solidarity and connection against the isolation, alienation, and cynicism of capitalist decomposition." In 1996, Benjamin Eichert, Rick Rowley, and Stale Sandberg of Big Noise, "armed with credit cards and a couple of state-of-the-art digital video cameras," traveled to the state of Chiapas in southern Mexico to film the Zapatistas, "the first resistance movement of the twenty-first century." Eloquent Zapatista leaders, especially Subcomandante Marcos, enable *Zapatista* (1999) to relate the struggles of the Lacandon Mayan people to the destruction of indigenous cultures worldwide in the name of market forces and globalization.

The Zapatista National Liberation Army (EZLN) seized several cities in Chiapas on January 1, 1994, the day the North American Free Trade Agreement went into effect. NAFTA privatized water and land, overriding Article 27 of the 1917 Mexican Constitution, which granted public rights to land, water, forests, and mineral deposits and created the ejido system of cooperative farming. The Zapatistas know that indigenous people, dispossessed of the land that has sustained them for centuries, will cease to exist. The Mexican government response is swift and violent. Using U.S. helicopters, twelve thousand troops attack the Zapatistas, driving them into the jungle. But the Zapatistas are too popular. Though, as Marcos says, "They want to kill us," the army holds back.

Then, days after Mexico receives a massive $45.75 billion U.S. bailout in February 1995, the Zedillo government attacks again, with greater force. More than seventy thousand troops—half the Mexican Army—are stationed in Chiapas, Guerrero, and Oaxaca to suppress and disrupt the lives of potential Zapatista sympathizers. Military intimidation of the civilian population aims to erode popular support for the rebels. Marcos says that Mexico has been erased as a nation in the process of globalization. It is not the national government but international markets that decide which resources to exploit or which policies to enforce. The World Trade Organization makes the decisions and the U.S. Army enforces them. Mexico is buying weapons from the United States in ever-increasing quantities to carry out the will of the global corporations.

Zapatista relies on a variety of sources, from usual suspects like the ubiquitous Noam Chomsky and frequent progressive docko talking head Medea Benjamin of Global Exchange, to Mexican activists and even Chicano militant Zack de la Rocha of the band "Rage against the Machine," whose music provides some of the soundtrack. Male and female narrators—singer Michael Franti and actress Susan Sarandon—emphasize the urgency of the Zapatista movement and our connections to it. In powerful scenes, frightened but angry indigenous peasants confront heavily armed soldiers, asking why they are here, demanding that they leave.

These confrontations are reminiscent of Barbara Kopple's Harlan County picket lines. In some ways, Big Noise shows us that same struggle for human rights against corporate demands, but on a global scale now, more appropriate to the present moment. Marcos and others make the point that "Zapatismo is not an ideology, it is an intuition," uniting human beings worldwide whose rights are being infringed by profit-hungry corporations and who dare to ask, "What is it that has excluded us?"

A priest and several Zapatista leaders discuss the daily intimidation of the local people by the Army. We learn of atrocities, like the December 22, 1997, massacre by paramilitary forces of 45 people—including 36 women and children—in a church in the village of Acteal. In footage shot a month before the massacre, we see the terrified, ragged villagers, many of them children, some of whom will soon be murdered. It is chilling and heartbreaking, like the FBI video of the Branch Davidian children who are shortly destined to die in a fire the government caused and (poorly) covered up. The slaughter of innocents by their own authorities—in the United States, Mexico, or anywhere else—ranks among the greatest crimes of any era. Nor can we—as viewers, taxpayers, voters, and consumers—escape our own complicity.

Big Noise directors Jacqueline Soohen and Rick Rowley expand their argument and ratchet up the beat in *The Fourth World War* (2003), which looks and sounds like "Globalization 101" for the MTV generation. Here the Zapatistas are one of many elements in a planetary patchwork of oppression and resistance that pulses among Argentina, South Africa, Palestine, South

Korea, Italy, and Quebec, describing "a war without a battlefield, a war without end, a war that is everywhere."

In quick scenes and mini-doses, an impressionist collage of political realities bombards us, revealing the scope and nature of this genocidal conflict, which largely eludes media coverage. Eschewing historical, explanatory narration, Michael Franti and Suheir Hammad weave a poetry of politics and passion together with stunning graphics; battle images "shot on the frontlines of struggles spanning five continents"; and the driving rhythmic sounds of Manu Chao, the Asian Dub Foundation, Ozomatli, Muslimgauze, DJ Moosaka, and others. The effect is less intellectual than visceral. We see and feel the human costs of globalization, the poor and indigenous peoples crushed by the machinery of "development" and "economic progress."

As "an introduction to some of the people with whom we share the planet," *The Fourth World War* aims to establish the kinship of its young audiences with the larger world community opposed to, or victimized by, the corporate juggernaut. Big Noise wants to break down our mass-mediated isolation that renders "the rest of the world" invisible to our gaze. The film wants to open our eyes, though without providing the details of how disenfranchisement works, the kind of linear narrative found in Stephanie Black's *Life and Debt* (2001). Black's film explains precisely how policies of the International Monetary Fund destroyed the agricultural production and self-sufficiency of Jamaica, turning the island into an outpost of cheap labor for multinational corporations and low-end consumers of their products. *The Fourth World War* takes a more emotional approach. But its message is similar: we are all connected. United States trade and aid agreements come with strings attached that may turn into chains for underpaid workers or indigenous peoples whose customs conflict with international corporate desires. Audiences of these films wear and consume the products of this exploitation every day. Once we understand the system, we can see our own role in it. What then must we do?

FILM AS EMPOWERMENT

When the World Trade Organization met in Seattle in November 1999, Big Noise and the Seattle Independent Media Center hit upon a collective strategy to chronicle the massive protest that greeted them. "We had more than 100 cameras in the street—more cameras than any corporate press organization could mobilize," their Web site says. Tens of thousands of protestors converged on downtown Seattle, chanting "people before profits." The scale of protest stunned Seattle police and shut down the WTO meetings. Indian activist Vandana Shiva characterizes the WTO as "a stealth government," allowing corporations and agribusiness to prosper, though workers and farmers do not. Students, environmentalists, labor activists, and dissident officials of many countries united in Seattle to express their belief that, in Shiva's words, "Corporate rule is dictatorship."

Seattle's mayor declares an emergency, calls out the National Guard, and imposes a curfew. The police arrest hundreds and abuse hundreds more with nightsticks, pepper spray, and tear gas. But the demonstrators return to the streets each day to assert their civic rights. We cut from impassioned rallies to police bashing protestors. One activist says, "It radicalized some people when they saw their government was totally willing—in fact had a blueprint—for making war on their own people."

Jill Freidberg and Rick Rowley crafted this populist mosaic of "the first global citizens movement" into a cautionary tale of how world capital, when challenged, quickly bares its iron fist. Also instructive are snippets of local news coverage, spun to make the protestors appear as crazed vandals, with no discussion of the issues that sparked the demonstrations. On a much larger scale, though with many fewer cameras, Big Noise used a similar approach for *The Fourth World War*. So too did the makers of *Voices of Iraq*, who gave 150 video cameras to ordinary Iraqis, to elude the constrictive, misleading filters and imposed narratives of corporate mass media.

"Information is the ultimate weapon," declares *Ammo for the Info Warrior* (2002), a collection of nine "news videos"—of five to ten minutes each—produced by the Guerrilla News Network. GNN's news videos combine "high-impact images [and] commentary by media experts, scholars, and political leaders with music cuts by top recording artists like Peter Gabriel and the Beastie Boys." *Ammo*'s self-declared mission is to introduce "serious socio-political issues to a generation brought up on MTV and will serve as an ideal catalyst for discussion and debate, encouraging students to develop critical thinking."

In a story called "The War Conspiracy," GNN debriefs UC-Berkeley Professor Peter Dale Scott, whose book of that title, set for publication in 1970, was suppressed by the CIA. Scott says intelligence agencies have hijacked U.S. foreign policy and the United States has inherited the imperial role once played by the British and the French. As Scott talks, images move to the musical beat of the Nineteen Point Five Collective. Scott mentions oil company ties to intelligence operations and Vietnam and then—poof!—the story's done. "When the Smoke Clearz" is Taalam Acey's slam of hip-hop music industry corruption, set to the hip-hop beat of Dear Prez and "featuring some of Hip Hop's most memorable video clips." In "Countdown," Ralph Nader deconstructs the nightly TV news formula to Beastie Boys Ad-Rock, his voice and image altered as he utters a few sound bites: "If you're not turned on to politics, the lesson of history is, politics will turn on you." "The system is not working; it's time for a change."

Discussing his method, GNN co-founder and film producer Stephen Marshall says he aims "to merge the subliminal elements of the electronic music culture with the overt and traditionally barren transmission of socio-political data." For Marshall, a director of music videos and "a progressive trance DJ," "the primary focus is always on building synergistic media that is driven by a musical narrative. Because that is what the younger generation responds to. Nike knows this. Coca-Cola knows this." One GNN fan describes Marshall's technopolitical approach as "Trance meets Chomsky."

Some critics attacked GNN's *Aftermath* (2003) for featuring analysts who think 9/11 was "orchestrated by a covert U.S. intelligence cell, working through al Qaeda." But Marshall defends the film for presenting a wide range of views, not just conspiracies. GNN won a prize at Sundance for their news video "Crack the CIA"—also featured on *Ammo for the Info Warrior*—which Marshall calls "just a graphically enhanced, beat-driven rehash of the Contra scandal."

During the 2004 Republican National Convention in New York, Marshall shot his first feature film, *This Revolution* (2005), modeled on Haskell Wexler's *Medium Cool* (1969). New York police arrested Marshall and actress Rosario Dawson during production on a street near the RNC site, Madison Square Garden. The GNN Web site describes the film "as a low-budget, high-impact verite thriller for the political set." Like Wexler's film, *This Revolution* centers on a fictional TV network cameraman working a real political convention. Back from Iraq to cover the RNC, he meets Dawson's character, whose husband was killed in Iraq, and who is highly politicized against the Bush administration.

By delivering his "socio-political content in the most charismatic style possible," Marshall wants to "weaponize the media." He pronounces himself "seriously dedicated to the creation of transformative media—and by that I mean media which has, as its core goal, the (sub)conscious evolution of its audience." Marshall recognizes that social revolution begins with a change of consciousness. Each of us must transform ourselves before we can transform the world.

That is also the premise of the unclassifiable film *What the #?*! Do We Know* (2004). William Arntz, Betsy Chasse, and Mark Vincente assembled their movie from talking heads, talking mostly about quantum physics; a story about a photographer undergoing a spiritual crisis; and a fantasia of innovative animation representing neurons and synapses in the human brain. Is it a documentary? Not as we generally think of that term. It asks us to consider new ways of looking at our relationship to the world. What if, instead of being an insignificant part of a huge, complex universe, we are in fact the creator of that universe? We would then be empowered to change it.

Can we only "see" what we believe is possible, as Errol Morris suggests? Are we hypnotized by our environment and by media? Just considering such questions may stimulate viewers in ways most films never do. The talking heads in *What the Bleep Do We Know?* (as it's also called) challenge us to open new neural pathways and transcend our habitual patterns of thought and action. That's revolutionary indeed.

One amazing sequence displays a series of photos of water molecules taken under "different intent" by Japanese researcher Masaru Emoto. We see water molecules in a neutral condition, after being blessed by a Buddhist priest, after exposure to certain music, after being thanked or cursed at. The changes are startling. As one man says to the story protagonist, "If thoughts can do that to water, imagine what they can do to us."

The widely varied—sometimes bewildered—reactions to this film from professional critics indicate that some viewers will dismiss the movie as wacky and tangential, whereas for others the questions it poses may cut to the core of our existential dilemma. In the sense that spiritual/philosophical awakening can lead to political action—a kind of Mahayana Buddhist urge to democratize enlightenment—*What the Bleep* may act as a catalyst for the latent revolutionary tendencies in some people. As one famous spiritual philosopher used to say, "He that has ears to hear, let him hear."

Another film that can't really be called a documentary, but can't really be called anything else, concentrates on one fundamental question: How do we know whether we're awake or asleep? Richard Linklater's *Waking Life* (2001) features an appropriately hallucinogenic animation style as it takes us in and out of dreams, like Chuang Tzu dreaming he is a butterfly that dreams he is Chuang Tzu. "Was it all just a dream?" asked Michael Moore of the first Bush term. Or, as James Joyce put it, more than a hundred years ago, "History is a nightmare from which I am trying to awake."

Some of our greatest social and political difficulties derive from leaders who believe they have answers, when what we really need for the species to move forward are better questions. The tantalizing dance of ideas in *Waking Life*, to the beat of a sly tango, restores a tentative, luminous lightness to our notion of being that we too often weigh down with seriousness or dread. "They say that dreams are only real as long as they last," says one character in the film. "Couldn't you say the same thing about life?" Or what about the nonfiction films that ask us to invest in their visions of reality?

How do political documentaries relate to the world in which we live and work? To the extent that we believe in their visions, what does that belief demand of us? Can a film wake us up? If the way out is in, then the best documentaries are not escapist, but honest, even at the risk of causing pain.

"Film is not about darkness, it's about light," says film scholar Jeanine Basinger. "And the way light moulds things, shines on things, and reflects things is the beauty and power of film. . . . So when we come out of those rooms, leaving the light we have enjoyed on the screen, we want to find more light."

If films lead us to seek clarity, then perhaps they really do possess the power to open our eyes, literally and figuratively. The best political documentaries illuminate people and processes too often hidden from view, sometimes in plain sight, obscured by mediated images that act as camouflage. Facts can lend authenticity to fantasies, benign or malignant, or construct honest narratives. Our senses—our brains—cannot tell the difference. Without our own deeper resources, beyond mediated images, we are lost.

So-called transformative media may entice us to pursue social change, consume mass quantities, or fight a holy war. As modern politics flaunts the often fatal failures of human moral and intellectual progress, it is tempting to abandon one's consciousness to the promiscuous surfeit of images surrounding us, or to indulge in some other form of numbing obsessive-compulsive behavior. America was founded on escapism, after all. But makers of political documentaries ask us to turn toward reality, not away from it. Their faith is that once we bear witness, we may feel compelled to act.

NOTES

INTRODUCTION

xi "Consciously or not" A. O. Scott, "Helpmates & Heroes: Ordinary Women and Bold Men," *The New York Times*, 13 February 2005.

xii Eight of the top Box Office Mojo, www.boxofficemojo.com/genres/chart/?id=documentary.htm.

xiii "medium of progressivism" Louis Menand, "Nanook and Me: *Fahrenheit 9/11* and the Documentary Tradition," *The New Yorker*, 9 & 16 August 2004, 90–96.

xiii Several good histories For example, Erik Barnouw, *Documentary: A History of the Non-Fiction Film*, rev. ed., Oxford University, New York, 1983, and Richard M. Barsam, *Nonfiction Film: A Critical History*, rev. ed., Indiana University, Bloomington, 1992.

xv Within this framework I am grateful to David Tetzlaff for his suggestive typology of political documentaries.

xv "the creative treatment" John Grierson quoted in Barnouw, 313.

xv "meaningless" Barnouw, *Documentary: A History*, 313.

xv For *Nanook* Menand, "Nanook and Me," 90–92.

CHAPTER 1

1 "Anyone who believes" Edward R. Murrow quoted in A. M. Sperber, *Murrow: His Life and Times*, Freundlich Books, New York, 1986, 691.

3 "Top Value Television" Deirdre Boyle, *Subject to Change: Guerrilla Television Revisited*, Oxford University, New York, 1997, xiv.

3 "I'd rather be" Mike Wallace in Boyle, *Subject to Change,* 57.

4-5 "television's intrinsic" A. William Bluem, *Documentary in American Television,* Hastings House, New York, 1965, 99.

5 "The question now" Murrow quoted in Robert Slater, *This . . . Is CBS: A Chronicle of 60 Years,* Prentice Hall, Englewood Cliffs, NJ, 1988, 140.

5 "This is an old" Murrow, *See It Now,* 18 November 1951, on "The Best of See It Now," *The Edward R. Murrow Television Collection,* a VHS broadcast compilation. Ironically, Mike Wallace, an advocacy journalism opponent, hosts this Murrow retrospective.

6 "Murrow was a bit" Charles Kuralt interview, *The Dawn of the Eye: Inventing Television News 1946–1959,* Alan Mendelsohn, producer and director, CBC, BBC, History Channel.

7 the Air Force backed down Sperber, *Murrow,* 420.

7 "the line between" Murrow, *See It Now,* 9 March 1954, on "The McCarthy Years," *Murrow Collection.* Ironically, Walter Cronkite, Murrow's rival at CBS, hosts this paean to Murrow's courage and integrity.

8 "Wags began" Slater, *This . . . Is CBS,* 178.

8 "social conscience" *Time,* 30 September 1957, quoted in Sperber, 515.

8 Paley told Murrow Sperber, *Murrow,* 532.

8 "television in the main" Murrow in Slater, 190.

8 "the same intensive" Bluem, *Documentary,* 100.

9 "premature and even" Murrow in Sperber, 489–490, 645.

9 "the film was used" Barnouw, *Documentary: A History,*, 272.

10 "angry about Vietnam" Emile de Antonio in Alan Rosenthal, *The Documentary Conscience: A Casebook in Film Making,* University of California, Berkeley, 1980, 214.

11 "There is no film" Ibid., 211.

11 "a taut 97-minute" Douglas Kellner and Dan Streible, eds., *Emile de Antonio: A Reader,* University of Minnesota, Minneapolis, 2000, 17.

11 "the first full-length" De Antonio in Rosenthal, 208–209.

11 "the real *comèdie noire*" Susan Sontag quoted in Kellner and Streible, 18.

13 "Actually, it's a lot" James N. Mattis quoted in Esther Schrader, *Los Angeles Times,* "General Counseled After He Says, 'It's Fun to Shoot Some People,'" *The San Francisco Chronicle,* 4 February 2005, A3.

14 "By the end" William Rothman, "Looking Back and Turning Inward: American Documentary Films of the Seventies," in David A. Cook, *Lost Illusions: American Cinema in the Shadow of Watergate and Vietnam, 1970–1979,* v. 9, *History of the American Cinema,* Charles Scribner's Sons, New York, 2000, 422.

14 "the gospel of militarism" Barnouw, *Documentary: A History,* 282.

15 "propagandist manipulation" Spiro Agnew quoted in Slater, 262.

15   "the most un-American" Ibid.

15   *Interviews with My Lai Veterans* This short documentary is available as an extra on the DVD version of *The Savage Eye.*

17   "The best single" Richard Barsam, *Nonfiction Film: A Critical History*, rev. ed., Indiana University, Bloomington, 1992, 316.

19   "both heartless" De Antonio in Rosenthal, 217, 218.

19   "it was ironic" Peter Davis quoted in Pete Hammond, "Political Platforms Nothing New for Oscarcast," *Variety*, 21 November 2004.

19   "the strategic parallels" Anthony Lane, "Aftermaths," *The New Yorker*, 1 November 2004, 110–111.

CHAPTER 2

21   "Democracy is a great" James David Barber, "And Now, Mr. Lincoln, You Have 15 Seconds," *The New York Times Book Review*, 30 October, 1988, 36.

21   "showed that Lyndon" "War, Intelligence, Truth," *The New York Times*, 24 January 1982, quoted in Don Kowet, *A Matter of Honor*, Macmillan, New York, 1984, 163–164.

22   "Anatomy of a Smear" Kowet, *Matter of Honor*, 205.

22   "The issue here" William Westmoreland quoted in Kowet, *Matter of Honor*, 230–231.

22   "CBS is entitled" Hodding Carter quoted in Kowet, 263.

23   "preposterous. . . . What motive" Renata Adler, *Reckless Disregard*, Alfred A. Knopf, New York, 1986, 26–27.

23   "In 1984, the Federal" Brian Winston, *Lies, Damn Lies and Documentaries*, British Film Institute, London, 2000, 47.

23   "President Lyndon Johnson" B. J. Bullert, *Public Television: Politics & the Battle over Documentary Film*, Rutgers University, New Brunswick, NJ, 1997, 17.

24   "a series of documentaries" Ibid., 18.

24   For example, *Dark Circle* Ibid., 37–62.

24   "the only long-format" Ibid., 26.

24-25 "*Frontline* appears" Barbara Trent, with Shelton Waldrep, "Media in a Capitalist Culture," in Frederic Jameson and Masao Miyoshi, eds., *The Culture of Globalization*, Duke University, Durham, NC, 1988.

25   "become too much" Lynn Smith, "At PBS, a Fragile State of Balance," *The Los Angeles Times*, 14 February 2005.

25   "world of increased" Alberto Ibargüen quoted in John Tierney and Jacques Steinberg, "Conservatives and Rivals Press a Struggling PBS," *The New York Times*, 17 February, 2005.

25   "The truth is" Sheila Nevins, "A Conversation with Sheila Nevins," http://www.kodak.com/US/en/motion/forum/onFilm/nevinsQA.shtml.

26   Couturié began working Bernard Edelman, ed., *Dear America: Letters Home from Vietnam*, Pocket Books, New York, 1986.

26   "Then he " Roger Ebert, "Dear America: Letters Home From Vietnam," *The Chicago Sun-Times*, 16 September 1988.

27   "Dear Bill" Eleanor Wimbish quoted in Edelman, ed., *Dear America*, 299-300.

27   "Maybe the war" Richard Strandberg quoted in Ibid., 297.

27-28 "the moment when" Michelle Cottle, "Fallen Soldiers, Remembered in Their Own Words," *The New York Times*, 11 November 2004, B5.

28   "Sonneborn formed" Background information on *Regret to Inform* is on the film's Web site, www.regrettoinform.org/pages/background.shtml.

CHAPTER 3

41   "'We the people'" Kathy Schroeder in William Gazecki, *Waco: Rules of Engagement*, 1997.

42   "the deceptive practices" Barbara Trent quoted in Katherine Martin, *Women of Courage*, New World Library, New York, 1997.

42   "our films debunk" Barbara Trent, interview with Alec Baldwin, "Raw Footage," Independent Film Channel, 2 December 1996.

43   "The issue for me" Trent with Waldrep, "Media in a Capitalist Culture."

44   "intriguing . . . unsubstantiated" Hal Hinson, "Coverup: Behind the Iran-Contra Affair," *The Washington Post*, 4 February 1989.

46   "NBC ended" http://store.videoproject.com/now-102-v.html.

49   "some religious" Bill Clinton quoted in Dick J. Reavis, *The Ashes of Waco: An Investigation*, Simon & Schuster, New York, 1995, 267.

49   "I made" Clinton quoted in Lawrence L., Knutson, "Clinton: 'Terrible Mistake' on Waco, AP, 26 July 2000.

49   "using a toll-free" Joe Conason and Gene Lyons, "Temps for the Vast Right-Wing Conspiracy," *Salon*, 2 March 2000, http://dir.salon.com/news/feature/2000/03/02/case/index.html.

50   "It was not" Kenneth Starr quoted in Gina Holland, "Kenneth Starr Now a Lawyer and Dean," AP, 15 April 2004.

50   "investigative reporter" Murry Waas, "Newsreal: The Falwell Connection," *Salon*, 11 March 1998, http://wwww.salon.com/news/1998/03/cov_11news.html.

51   "The allegations" Ibid.

51   "The ACLU's got" Jerry Falwell on "The 700 Club," 13 September 2001, http://www.sacred-texts.com/ame/911/700clubhtm.

51   "The incumbent" James McEnteer, "The American Way: Find a Candidate to Vote Against," *The Los Angeles Times*, 27 September 2004, B11.

54   "commit their" Quoted in Peter Howell, "11'09"01 Trying to explain why," *The Toronto Star*, 11 September 2002.

54   "cheap shot" Jessica Chapel, "11'09"01." *Flakmagazine*, http://flakmag.com/film/110901.html.

55   "University of Ottawa" Michel Chossudovsky's Web site is www.global research.ca.

55   "what may be" James Bamford, *Body of Secrets*, Doubleday, New York, 2001, 82.

56   "The Bush Administration" David Barstow and Robin Stein, "Under Bush, a New Age of Prepackaged News," *The New York Times*, 13 March 2005.

57   "I'm guided by" Leonard Cohen, "First We Take Manhattan," http://www.serve.com/cpage/LCohen/lyrics/ImYourMan.html.

CHAPTER 4

63   "If you want" Barbara Kopple in David A. Goldsmith, *The Documentary Makers: Interviews with 15 of the Best in the Business*, RotoVision, London, 2003, 85.

63   "You commit a crime" A transcript of this episode is available at www.windowseat.org/homicide/scripts/512thedocumentary.html.

64   Based on a book www.tvtome.com/tevtome/servlet/ShowMainServLet/showid-110/Homicide_Life_on_the_Street/#stars.

66   "It was stupendous" Kopple in Goldsmith, *Documentary Makers*, 81.

67   "My daddy was a miner" Florence Reece, "Which Side Are You On?" http://www.geocities.com/Nashville/3448/whichsid.html.

67   "I definitely" Kopple in Goldsmith, 81.

67   "We were machine-gunned" Barbara Kopple in Peter Wintonick, director, *Cinema Verite: Defining the Moment*, National Film Board of Canada, 1999.

CHAPTER 5

79   "Who among us" Michael Moore, "Introduction," *The Official Fahrenheit 9/11 Reader*, Simon & Schuster, New York, 2004, xv.

82-83 "rude and rollicking" Vincent Canby, "Film Festival: A Twainlike Twist for Flint, Mich.," *The New York Times*, 27 September 1989.

83   "Motor Mouth" described in Roger Ebert, "Attacks on *Roger & Me* completely miss point of film," *The Chicago Sun-Times*, 11 February 1990.

83   "shallow and facetious" Pauline Kael, "Roger & Me" in *Movie Love: Complete Reviews 1988–1991*, Plume, New York, 1991, 242-245.

83   "I think he is" Ebert, "Attacks."

83 "Mr. Moore makes" Canby, "Film Festival."

84 "stay on top" Michael Moore interview, CNN, "People in the News," 2004, Moore TV tape. Moore appeared on many television programs in the summer of 2004, some of which are recorded (undated) on a "TV tape" compilation from June through August.

84 "Maybe I was" Michael Moore, "A Room with a View," *Mother Jones*, October 1986, 6.

84 "differences of political" Adam Hochschild, "A Family Fight Hits the Headlines," *Mother Jones*, December 1986, 6.

85 "everyone should be fired" Moore, CNN interview, 2004.

85 "Our intent was" Michael Moore and Kathleen Glynn, *Adventures in a TV Nation*, HarperCollins, New York , 1998, 1–2.

87 "a hybrid of two" Ginia Bellafante, "Pranks and Populism," *Time*, 25 July 1994.

88 "The phones rang" Ibid., 73.

88 "to report corporate" Ibid., 49.

89 "There is little here" Roger Ebert, "The Big One," *The Chicago Sun-Times*, 10 April 1998.

89 "a little troubling" James Berardinelli, "The Big One," http://movie-reviews .colossus.net/movies/b/big_one.html, 1998.

90 "loudmouthed, self-serving" Daniel Radosh, "Moore is Less," *Salon*, www.salon.com/june97/media/media970606.html, 6 June 1997.

90 Moore accused *Salon* Michael Moore, "Michael Moore Fires Back at *Salon*," *Salon*, www.salon.com/july97/moore970703.html. The Talbot and Radosh responses are appended to this article.

91 "By the morning" Michael Moore, "Re: *Stupid White Men . . . and Other Sorry Excuses for the State of the Nation!*," letter, 5 February 2002, www.michaelmoore.com.

94 "disturbing, infuriating" A. O. Scott, "Film Review: Seeking a Smoking Gun in U.S. Violence," *The New York Times*, 11 October 2003.

94 "cheap shots" Andrew Sarris, "Latest 'Message' Movies: Anti-American, but Entertaining," *New York Observer*, 9 December 2002.

94 "inconclusive, fragmentary" Ned Depew, "Bowling for Columbine," www.surferz.net/~ned/reviews/BfC.html.

97 "Okay, let's say" Michael Moore, "*Fahrenheit 9/11*—The Screenplay," *The Official Fahrenheit 9/11 Reader*, Simon & Schuster, New York, 2004, 36. This book contains the shooting script, Moore's evidence for charges he made in the film, reactions from the audience and reviewers, editorial cartoons, and photos of the crowds attending the movie.

98 "largest grossing" Ibid., xiii.

98   "occasionally effective" Stephanie Zacharek, *"Fahrenheit 9/11:* Nay!,*"* *Salon*, 23 June, 2004, www.salon.cpm/ent/movies/review/2004/06/23/ 911_nay/print.html.

99   "an enormous film" Andrew O'Hehir, *"Fahrenheit 9/11:* Yea!,*" Salon*, 23 June 2004.

99   "Moore's most" David Denby, "George & Me: Michael Moore's viciously funny attack on the Bush administration," *The New Yorker*, 28 June 2004.

99   "In 20 years" David Edelstein, "Proper Propaganda: Michael Moore's *Fahrenheit 9/11* is Unfair and Outrageous. You Got a Problem with That?" *Slate*, 24 June 2004.

99   "weakest" Kirk Honeycutt, "Fahrenheit 9/11," *The Hollywood Reporter*, 18 May 2004.

99   "best" Mick LaSalle, "Persuasive and Passionate. *Fahrenheit 9/11* Is Both. It's also Michael Moore's Best Film," *The San Francisco Chronicle*, 24 June 2004. The film reviews cited and many more can be found on the Internet Movie Database, a valuable resource for film research, www.imdb.com.

99   "presents a vision" David Tetzlaff, remarks at a panel discussion of *Fahrenheit 9/11*, Film & History Conference, Dallas, Texas, 13 November 2004.

CHAPTER 6

101   "Unfortunately, we believe" Errol Morris, interview, *American Amnesia*, 24 February 2004, www.errolmorris.com/html/blog/conversation_amnesia0204 .html.

101   "I think the human" Robert McNamara in *The Fog of War*. The film transcript is on Morris's Web site at www.errolmorris.com/film/ fow_transcript.html.

101   "I developed this" Errol Morris quoted in David A. Goldsmith, *The Documentary Makers: Interviews with 15 of the Best in the Business*, RotoVision, London, 2003, 102.

103   "We shall not cease" T.S. Eliot quoted in Robert S. McNamara, *In Retrospect:* The Tragedy and Lessons of Vietnam, with Brian Van De Mark, Random House, New York, 1995, xviii.

103   "the main reason" Errol Morris, remarks at a presentation of the Graduate School of Journalism, University of California, Berkeley, 4 February 2004.

105   *Salon*'s Charles Taylor Charles Taylor, "The Fog of War," *Salon*, 19 December 2003.

105   "metaphysics of mass murder" Mark Singer, "Predilections," *The New Yorker*, 2 February 1989, www.errolmorris.com/content/profile/singer _predilections.html. Morris biographical data and quotes, except where noted, are from Singer's compendious, fascinating profile.

106   "instead of being" Morris in Goldsmith, *Documentary Makers: Interviews*, 98.

106   "I like the irrelevant" Morris in Singer, "Predilections."

106   "comedy, pathos, irony" Roger Ebert, "Gates of Heaven," *The Chicago Sun-Times*, 9 November 1997.

108   "even the 'semi-normal'" John Nesbit, "Some Whacky Floridians (or It Wasn't Just the Chads)," *CultureDose.net*, 4 January 2002, www.toxicuniverse .com/review.php?rid=10001372.

109   "I've been told" Morris in Goldsmith, 105.

109   "Stephen Hawking is arguably" Morris in *The Making of A Brief History of Time*, British Broadcasting Corporation, 1993.

111   "Then I got interested" Morris in Singer, "Predilections."

111   "Oh a mole-rat expert" This is a variation on the "Fifty-Third Calypso" of *The Books of Bokonon*, in Kurt Vonnegut, *Cat's Cradle*, Delacorte, New York 1963, 2.

The original reads:

Oh, a sleeping drunkard
Up in Central Park
And a lion-hunter
In the jungle dark,
And a Chinese dentist,
And a British queen—
All fit together
In the same machine.
Nice, nice, very nice;
Nice, nice, very nice;
Nice, nice, very nice—
So many different people
In the same device.

112   "I became involved" Fred Leuchter in *Mr. Death: The Rise and Fall of Fred A. Leuchter, Jr.* Transcript at www.errolmorris.com/film/mrd_transcript .html.

112   "And you cross-connect" Morris in Ben Chappel, "As Time Closes In: A Conversation with Errol Morris," *Gothamist*, 27 October 2004.

113   "Morris, who followed" Mark Singer, "The Friendly Executioner," *The New Yorker*, 1 February 1999.

113   "What is the film" Fred Leuchter in Singer, "Executioner." Also Morris quotes.

114   "I'm often annoyed" Morris in Tom Ryan, "Errol Morris Interview," *Senses of Cinema*, August 2001, www.sensesofcinema.com/contents/01/ 16/morris.html.

114 "consisted of vignettes" Philp Gourevitch, "Swingtime: Former Bush voters advertise their disaffection," *The New Yorker*, 23 August 2004, 34.

114 "MoveOn sent out" Ibid., 36.

115 "All of life" Errol Morris, "Not Every Picture Tells a Story," *The New York Times*, 20 November 2004.

CHAPTER 7

119 "Democracy is not" Robert Greenwald, "The Director's Introduction," July 2004, www.truthuncovered.com/greenwaldletter.html.

119 "If DVDs really were" Mark Rahner, "Spouting Off: Political DVDs," *The Seattle Times*, 5 October 2004.

119 "I never considered" Greenwald, "Director's Introduction."

120 "organized to produce" www.publicinterestpictures.org/about.htm.

123 the Election Protection program expanded Election Protection 2004, "Shattering the Myth: An Initial Snapshot of Voter Disenfranchisement in 2004," www.pfaw.org/pfaw/dfiles/file_477.pdf.

124 "I got a knot" Greenwald, "Director's Introduction."

125 "mandatory" "Movie Guide," *The Christian Science Monitor*, 20 August 2004, www.csmonitor.com/2004/0820/p14S02-almo.html.

125 "smashingly effective" Owen Gleiberman, "Uncovered: The War on Iraq," *Entertainment Weekly*, 26 August 2004, www.ew.com/ew/article/review/movie/html.

125 "a crisp historical" Jack Matthews, "Docu Calls WMDs a Big Neo-Con Job," *The New York Daily News*, 20 August 2004.

126 "this film captures" Andrew O'Hehir, "*Soldier's Pay*," *Salon*, 21 October 2004, www.salon.com/ent/feature//2004/10/21/soldiers_pay/html.

126 "While working" Robert Greenwald, interview, Patrick Philips, "Robert Greenwald: 'Fox News Is an Example of What Happens When We Have Extreme Media Control,'" *I Want Media*, 12 July 2004, www.iwantmedia.com/people/people39.html.

128 "The on-air Fox" A. O. Scott, "Spin Zones, Flag Waving and Shouting to Catch a Fox," *The New York Times*, 20 July 2004.

128 "no effort at fairness" Howard Kurtz, "Tilting at the Right, Leaning to the Left," *The Washington Post*, 11 July 2004.

129 "rambling screed" Dave Kehr, "Film Review: Big Media as a Force That Bends the Truth," *The New York Times*, 23 July 2004.

130 "We created *Unconstitutional*" Robert Greenwald, www.publicinterestpictures.org/unconstitutional/index.htm.

133 "These communities represent" Ibid.

133   "puts faces and bodies" Dan Devine, *"Unconstitutional: The War on Our Civil Liberties*: Shedding Light," *PopMatters*, 24 November 2004, www.popmatters .com/film/reviews/u/unconstitutional-war-on-civil.shtml.

CHAPTER 8

135   "Politics is ultimately" Karl Rove in *Last Man Standing*.

139   Alexander decided Paul Alexander, interview with Jonathon Marlow, "'Men Who Actually Served': Paul Alexander," *GreenCine*, 16 September 2004.

140   "unfit to serve" Joe Conason, "Smear Boat Veterans for Bush," Salon.com, 4 May 2004.

141   "Any Questions?" All the anti-Kerry ads are available for viewing on www.swiftvets.com.

142   Butler's film rehearses The Swift Vets charges are examined in "Republican-Funded Group Attacks Kerry's War Record," 22 August 2004, http:// www.factcheck.org/article231.html.

143   The Sinclair Broadcasting Jim Rutenbery, "Broadcast Group to Pre-Empt Programs for Anti-Kerry Film, *The New York Times*, 11 October 2004.

143   Controversy surrounding Frank Ahrens and Howard Kurtz, *Washington Post*, "TV Company Changes Plan, Won't Run Entire Kerry film," *San Francisco Chronicle*, 20 October 2004, A12.

144   *Stolen Honor*'s rhetorical "Dana Stevens, "Uncivil War: *Stolen Honor* Rewrites the History of the Vietnam War, *Slate*, 20 October 2004, http:// slate.msn.com/if/2108458.

144   "unintentional and considerably" Frank Rich, "Now on DVD: The Passion of the Bush," *The New York Times*, 3 October 2004.

145   "informative and inspiring" Mark Moring, "George W. Bush: Faith in the White House," *Christianity Today*, 24 August 2004, www.christianityto-day.com/movies/reviews/georgewbush.html.

146   "the nation's most influential" David D. Kirkpatrick, "Evangelical Leader Threatens to Use His Political Muscle against Some Democrats," *The New York Times*, 1 January 2005.

146   "mythic solace" Leo Braudy quoted in Neal Koch, "With Election Waning, It's Film Business as Usual," *The New York Times*, 28 October 2004.

146   "The Gibson conflation" Frank Rich, "2004: The Year of 'The Passion,'" *The New York Times*, 19 December 2004.

146   "a sinister exercise" Christopher Hitchens, "Unfairenheit 9/11: The Lies of Michael Moore," *Slate*, 21 June 2004.

147   "disingenuous filmmaker" Michael Moore, "The Ebert and McCain
      Show," *USA Today,* 1 September 2004.

147   "Should a 400 lb. man" www.mooreexposed.com.

148   "a thorough examination" Jason Clarke, www.moorelies.com/book/
      about/. Other prominent anti-Moore sites include moorewatch.com and
      bowlingfortruth.com.

150   "disenfranchisement of countless" U.S. Commission on Civil Rights, "Voting
      Irregularities in Florida during the 2000 election: Chapter Nine, Findings
      and Recommendations," June 2001, www.usccr.gov/.

150   Mansoor Ijaz Disinfopedia, Center for Media and Democracy,
      www.disinfo.org/wiki.phtml?title=Mansoor_Ijaz. For why Ijaz had a
      motive to disparage the Clinton administration, see Manohla Dargis, "Film
      Review: Lowering the Subtlety of Political Discourse," *The New York
      Times,* 22 October 2004.

150   Michael Ledeen William O. Beeman, "Who Is Michael Ledeen?" *Pacific
      News Service,* 8 May 2003, www.alternet.org/story/15860.

151   "tyrannized by his method" Albert Maysles quoted in Robert Koehler,
      "Michael Moore Hates America," *Variety,* 11 October 2004.

151   "He's trying to suck" Brian Orndorf, "Michael Moore Hates America,"
      FilmFodder, 24 October 2004, www.filmfodder.com/movies/reviews/
      michael_moore_hates_america/20041025.htm.

151   "that much of" Errol Morris quoted in Nancy Ramsey, "Politically
      Inclined Filmmakers Say There Is Life after the Election," *The New York
      Times* 27 December 2004.

152   "In other words" Robert Jensen, "Stupid White Movie: What Michael
      Moore Misses about the Empire," *CounterPunch,* 5 July 2004, www
      .counterpunch.org/jensen07052004.html.

152   "about the Iraq war" Michael Moore in Ramsey, "Politically Inclined
      Filmmakers."

CHAPTER 9

155   "We have" Jon Else quoted in Irene Lacher, "Documentary Criticized for
      Re-Enacted Scenes," *The New York Times,* 29 March 2005.

155   "Things change" Bill Nichols, *Blurred Boundaries: Questions of Meaning in
      Contemporary Culture,* Indiana University, Bloomington, 1994, 93.

155   "in the form" Ibid., ix.

156   "explicitly allowed" Lacher, "Documentary Criticized."

156   Chris Kentis Carla Meyer, "Arrogant Vacationing Couple Takes Deep
      Dive into Frightening Tropical Waters," *The San Francisco Chronicle,*
      6 August 2004, E1.

156   Elliot Greenebaum David Grand, "Indecent Exposure?" *The New York Times,* 27 February 2005.

158   "Armstrong Williams" Associated Press, "Education Secretary Criticizes Williams Payments," *USA Today,* 15 April 2005.

158   "'video news releases'" Anne E. Kornblut, "Administration Is Warned about Its 'News' Videos," *The New York Times*, 19 February 2005.

158   E! Entertainment Television Lola Ogunnaike, "A Fake Michael Jackson's Big Break: A Fake Trial," *The New York Times,* 1 March 2005.

162   "no doubts about" www.theyesmen.org/hijinks/plattsburgh/index.shtml.

163   "to liquidate" http://en.wikipedia.org/wiki/The_Yes_Men. More details about the Bhopal incident and a transcript of "Jude Finisterra's" BBC interview at www.democracynow.org/article.pl?sid=04/12/06/1453248.

164   "We are not" www.bignoisefilms.com/about.htm.

167   "Information is" www.mediaed.org/videos/CommercialismPoliticsAnd Media/AmmoForTheInfoWarrior.

168   "to merge the subliminal" Stephen Marshall, interview with Geert Lovink, "GNN's Digital Documentaries," *Nettime,* 9 December 2003, http://amsterdam.nettime.org/Lists-Archives/nettime-l-0312/msg00018.html

168   The GNN Web site www.gnn.tv/videos/video.php?id=29.

168   "socio-political content" Marshall, "Digital Documentaries."

170   "Film is not" Jeanine Bassinger quoted in David Low, "Projecting the Future," *Wesleyan,* winter, 2005, 16.

INDEX

Page numbers followed by an *n* indicate a reference to a footnote.

ABOUT THE AUTHOR

JAMES McENTEER is an independent scholar, journalist, and author of *Deep in the Heart: The Texas Tendency in American Politics* (2004) and *Fighting Words: Independent Journalists in Texas* (1992). He is a former Fellow of the Joan Shorenstein Center for the Press, Politics, and Public Policy at the John F. Kennedy School of Government, Harvard University.